SMASHING

UX DESIGN: FOUNDATIONS FOR DESIGNING ONLINE USER EXPERIENCES

Jesmond Allen

James Chudley

WILEY

A John Wiley and Sons, Ltd, Publication

This edition first published 2012

© 2012 John Wiley & Sons, Ltd

Registered office

John Wiley & Sons Ltd, The Atrium, Southern Gate, Chichester, West Sussex, PO19 8SQ, United Kingdom

For details of our global editorial offices, for customer services and for information about how to apply for permission to reuse the copyright material in this book please see our website at www.wiley.com.

Reprinted January 2013, January 2014

978-0-470-66685-2

A catalogue record for this book is available from the British Library.

Set in 10/12 Minion Pro Regular by Indianapolis Composition Services

Printed in the UK by Bell and Bain.

For Robbie, Caitlin, and Edie
– Jesmond Allen

For Lou, Matilda, and Jack
- James Chudley

PUBLISHER'S ACKNOWLEDGMENTS

Some of the people who helped bring this book to market include the following:

Editorial and Production
VP Consumer and Technology Publishing Director: Michelle Leete
Associate Director–Book Content Management: Martin Tribe
Associate Publisher: Chris Webb
Publishing Assistant: Ellie Scott
Development Editor: Kezia Endsley
Copy Editor: Kezia Endsley
Technical Editor: Ben Bywater
Editorial Manager: Jodi Jensen
Senior Project Editor: Sara Shlaer
Editorial Assistant: Leslie Saxman

Marketing
Senior Marketing Manager: Louise Breinholt
Marketing Executive: Kate Parrett

Composition Services
Compositor: Indianapolis Composition Services
Proofreaders: Melissa Cossell, Susan Hobbs
Indexer: Potomac Indexing, LLC
Photography: James Chudley
Illustrations: Jesmond Allen and James Chudley

ABOUT THE AUTHORS

James and Jesmond are User Experience Directors at cxpartners, a UK-based user experience consultancy.

James Chudley has been working in UX for 14 years for UX consultancies, full-service digital agencies, within academia and client side in the public sector. He has grown and managed UX teams, managed digital products, and provided UX research and design consultancy to some of the web's biggest brands.

In his role as UX Director at cxpartners, James runs large user-centered design projects for clients such as Expedia, Aardman, Hotels.com, Lovefilm, Vodafone, Kelkoo, Moneysupermarket.com, and Channel 4.

James is actively involved in the UX community. He writes for *Smashing Magazine* and sits on their UX experts panel. He regularly speaks at local and international UX events and co-founded UXBristol in 2011.

Jesmond Allen is a skilled user experience consultant. She has many years experience designing user interfaces and information architectures for web, mobile, and computer applications. Jesmond has a BA in Fine Art and an MSc in Computer Science and has worked in the Internet industry since 1996. She has a passion for good design and wants "usable" to also mean "beautiful."

Jesmond has worked with clients such as TUI Travel, Nokia, Kelkoo, Microsoft, and UKTV to create compelling, usable interfaces. Jesmond led the Charles Tyrwhitt project that won Redesign Of The Year at the 2011 National eCommerce Awards in London.

AUTHORS' ACKNOWLEDGMENTS

This book couldn't have been written without the support of our wonderful colleagues at cxpartners. In particular the owners—Richard Caddick and Giles Colborne—encouraged us and provided unfailing support. And to everyone else at cxpartners, a big "thank you" for letting us pick your brains and take photos of you in various UX poses—Amy McGuinness, Anna Thompson, Chloe Furlong, Chris Berridge, Chui Chui Tan, Fiz Yazdi, Mandy Milton, Neil Schwarz, Nik Lazell, Rob Matthews, Steve Cable, James Rosenberg, Jay Spanton, Joe Leech, Karina Cockell, Tamlyn Driver, Verity Whitmore, and Walt Buchan.

Thank you to all our clients for making our work so interesting, and for providing the experience that underpins this book. Thanks in particular to Jennie Blythe and Luke Kingsnorth at Charles Tyrwhitt and to Stephen Molloy and Paul Burrows at iExplore for being fantastic and allowing us to write about our work for them. Thanks to David Jarvis at Specialist Holiday Group for helping us to understand what life is like as a client and also for his motivational tweets as we wrote this.

Thanks also to all the companies and individuals who granted us permission to use their work in our figures and illustrations.

We want to extend a huge thank you to the wonderful team at Wiley who have supported us through the process of writing this book. In particular we would like to thank Chris Webb, Sara Shlaer, Kezia Endsley, and Ellie Scott, for their advice, guidance, and support.

Thank you to Ben Bywater for casting a UX eye across everything and for providing suggestions and improvements along the way.

Thank you to the people we spoke to at the beginning of the project that helped us work out the right book to write, as well as those who provided feedback along the way. In particular Michael McKelvaney, Kit Allen, and Mark Skinner.

A personal thanks from Jesmond: Thank you Robbie for encouraging me to do this, and for all the practical support along the way. Thank you Caitlin and Edie for being wonderful, and for understanding that I had to spend a lot of time writing. I promise to be around at weekends from now on. Thank you Mum and Dad for all the support over the years.

A personal thanks from James: Lou, your love and support has been incredible. The timing of this was awful but we made it work and I will be forever grateful for your patience and understanding. Matilda and Jack you are everything a daddy could wish for, you make me so proud. Thank you Mum and Dad for all your love, support, and encouragement over the years; you are an inspiration! Thank you Anna and Peter for all your tireless help looking after Matilda and Jack; we are so grateful for everything you have done for us. Thank you Mum, Dad, Laura, and Simon for all your support, encouragement and friendship. I am blessed to have such a wonderful family and I love you all.

CONTENTS

INTRODUCTION

Welcome to *Smashing UX Design*.

This book is a user experience (UX) reference manual: a handy guide to different UX tools and techniques to read from cover-to-cover, or to dip into as the need arises. It is designed to be both a helpful and pragmatic handbook to help digital design practitioners add valuable user insights to their real world projects.

This book has been co-authored by James Chudley and Jesmond Allen. We are both User Experience Directors at cxpartners, a user experience consultancy based in Bristol, UK. Between us, we have more than 30 years experience of designing digital products for clients such as Orange, Vodafone, TUI Travel, Aardman, Nokia, Expedia, Hotels.com, and the BBC. Over that time, we have seen our job titles vary from "web designer," "usability engineer," "information architect," "user-centered design consultant," and beyond.

We've used illustrations, examples, top tips, and detailed how-tos to share with you the knowledge we've built up working on user experience projects both within UX consultancies, design agencies, and large public and private sector organizations.

WHAT IS THIS BOOK ABOUT?

This book is aimed at UX practitioners as well as digital designers and developers who may not have everyday access to a UX specialist. We hope that it will be an invaluable reference for anyone involved in taking digital products from conception to deployment and beyond.

We work for a UX consultancy, hence lots of use of the words "client" and "project." However, the tools and techniques are just as relevant for use by in house teams.

The UX research and design tools and techniques we outline in this book are applicable to the web and other platforms such as applications, mobile apps, and emerging devices and platforms.

We've documented the processes we go through every day at work and we've shared lots of the secrets that we've learned along the way. Of course, the way we do UX isn't the only way to do UX, and we love to learn new things. The unifying factor is the desire to put the user at the heart of any design work we undertake.

PART I

In Part I, we examine UX processes and projects. We provide an overview of the principles of user-centered design and look at how to weave UX into the fabric of your digital projects. We illustrate this with real client case studies and practical examples that you can apply to your own work. We provide insights into planning the best project to suit the time and budget available.

PART II

Part II of the book covers UX research and evaluation tools and techniques. This section outlines methods for understanding users, documenting their needs, and evaluating whether those needs are being met. It is a pragmatic look at key research techniques, and aims to provide options suitable for all budgets.

PART III

Part III of the book looks at UX design tools and techniques. Here's where we look in detail at how to weave your understanding of user needs into successful design solutions. For each tool and technique we explain why they are important, when to do them, and how to do them, and we share examples of the results you get from using them.

Many of these individual tools and techniques have had entire books written about them. We have covered them in digestible levels of detail and to have referenced our favorite resources for if you want to find out more.

PART IV

In Part IV, we share our knowledge on best practice when designing various typical UX components that are likely to need designing in your projects. We cover a range of components from home pages, navigation, and search, to designing for internationalization and behavioral change.

UX is one of the fastest evolving and highest profile growth areas within digital design. There is a global shortage of good UX designers and ever increasing demand from employers who are desperate to snap up new talent. There's a huge amount of satisfaction to be gained from spending time with people to understand their problems and designing that understanding into products that delight.

This book can be used to learn more about UX, to help you move into a career in UX or to help you in your existing role as a UX professional. We hope it helps you to learn more about the people you design for and to design successful products that people will love.

Good luck with your own UX projects and let us know how things go via Twitter or at www.smashinguxdesign.com.

James (@chudders) and Jesmond (@jesmond)

UX PROCESSES AND PROJECTS

CHAPTER

1

UNDERSTANDING THE USER-CENTERED DESIGN PROCESS

WHAT IS "USER-CENTERED DESIGN" (UCD) and why does it matter? What has UCD got to do with a book about smashing UX? UCD matters because great digital experiences are born from considering the end user of your product at every stage of the conception and design process. Who will use this product? Why will they use this product? How will they use this product? If you can answer these questions, you are well on your way to a great UX.

This book discusses digital user experience design in the form of websites and apps, but user-centered design can be applied to any design discipline. Here's Wikipedia's definition of UCD:

> *User-centered design... is a design philosophy and a process in which the needs, wants, and limitations of end users of a product are given extensive attention at each stage of the design*

process. User-centered design can be characterized as a multi-stage problem-solving process that not only requires designers to analyze and foresee how users are likely to use a product, but also to test the validity of their assumptions with regards to user behavior in real world tests with actual users. [Wikipedia, "User-centered Design" article, 12 July 2011]

Designers practice UCD because it helps them make better decisions. By thinking about the end user of a website or app at every stage of the design process, the designs are more robust. By testing the designs with real users, the designs improve and are validated. UCD helps you to design the right thing, and to design the thing right.

THE VIRTUOUS CIRCLE

At the heart of UCD is the idea of consulting the end user of the product as often as possible. This sounds like a big task, but there are lots of techniques to help you do just that without taking up all your time and energy. There is what can only be described as a virtuous circle of user research to design to research and design again. This is an iterative process—the design changes over time to reflect the knowledge gained from research. Each successive iteration is better than the last. Figure 1-1 shows an iterative UCD process.

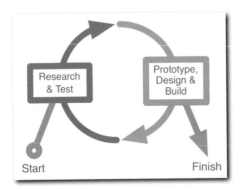

Figure 1-1: The virtuous circle, an iterative user-centered design process

RESEARCH

The beginning of a project is the time to really get to know the users you will be designing for. To start a project, user research might include evaluating existing products to find usability issues or to understand competitor products. This is a great time to talk to your users about their needs and how they organize their offline approach to your subject.

DESIGN

The next step is to feed all this information into your initial designs—it will provide you with lots of inspiration and help with the decision making process. Techniques such as task models, customer experience maps, personas, information architecture, sketching, and wireframes help you to weave your user insight into compelling prototypes and designs. Whether that prototype is a low-fidelity sketch or a clickable mockup, the reason for generating it is to test the idea—with peers, with your client, and with users.

AND RESEARCH AGAIN...

Once you have a candidate design, you need to test it to evaluate its worth. Usability testing is invaluable here. Can your potential users find what they're looking for? Complete any transactions? Does your product appeal to them? Sometimes the outcome of a usability test is as simple as changing the wording on a button. Other times, a drastic re-think is needed. But if you've tested early in your design cycle (and it's perfectly possible to test paper-based sketches or early wireframes), you'll have saved yourself a lot of redesign, rebuild and heartache.

This research, design, and test cycle can be repeated as needed. For example, where budget allows, you might revise wireframes based on the results of usability testing. These revised wireframes then form the basis for visual design and development work. A further round of usability testing on a functional product can validate further and inform tweaks to the UI before launch. You can launch your product knowing that the design has been validated with real people.

Figure 1-2 shows the UCD process for a typical web design and build project.

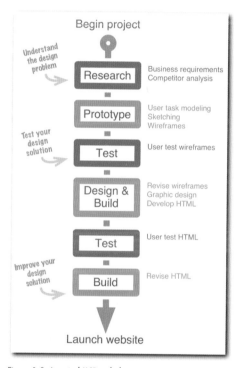

Figure 1-2: A typical UCD web design project

UX AND DEVELOPMENT PROCESSES

In organizations with large teams of developers, there is a need to organize developers' activities to maximize the quality and speed of their output. These development processes fall broadly into two categories: Waterfall and Agile.

In order to produce designs that development teams can utilize, it is helpful for UXers to understand the development process they will be using. As external UX consultants, we do not always have the opportunity to work with development teams on a daily basis as they create a functional product from our designs, although we always strive to make ourselves available to developers as they work. Internal UX staff will likely have a much closer relationship with their development teams.

WATERFALL DEVELOPMENT

In Waterfall development, activities flow from one stage to the next: from requirements to design to implementation to validation. Design is done up-front, and there is an emphasis on one stage being documented and signed off before the next stage proceeds. This fits in well with UX activities happening before development starts. UX deliverables, such as wireframe decks, can form part of the specification of the product.

AGILE DEVELOPMENT

Agile is a newer development methodology that was conceived as a response to the perceived failings of Waterfall development. These failings include the fact that poorly gathered or shifting requirements can mean that development time is wasted. Development realities often require changes when there is no available UX guidance. Proponents of Agile software development argue that initial design time should be sacrificed in the interests of developing a working product that can be tested, built on, and changed as necessary.

Many in-house UX practitioners now find themselves working alongside developers using Agile development processes.

UX, Product Management, and Development

There is certainly a potential for conflict between a traditional UCD process (which fits extremely well with Waterfall development) and Agile development. Some developers may see UX activities as troublesome *big design up front*. However, UX activities contribute to requirements gathering and backlog prioritization activities. These activities typically take place long before development sprints begin. Competitor analysis, usability testing on high-level wireframes, contextual analysis, task models, and personas all help here. UX practitioners consider who will use a product, why they will do so, and which features are required. These types of activities are typically required in order to get the go-ahead from the organization to build the product. They are also activities that may be "owned" by different roles within the organization, for example by product managers. In order to produce robust products, it is important that UX research and design activities take place throughout the design and build cycle, whether it is product managers, UXers, or developers who perform the activities.

Top Tips for Great UX in Agile Teams

UX teams can and do produce great work alongside Agile developers. Here are a few pointers as to how to do that. Figure 1-3 shows example UX activities within a Scrum development process.

Phase	UX Activities
Pre-development	Business requirements Competitor analysis Contextual analysis Task models Personas High level wireframes
Sprint 0	Detailed wireframes for sprint 1
Sprint 1	UX support for current sprint Detailed wireframes for next Sprint Preparation for user testing
Sprint 2	UX support for current sprint Detailed wireframes for next Sprint User test work to date and latest wireframes
Sprint 3	UX support for current sprint Detailed wireframes for next sprint Preparation for user testing
Repeat until development complete	UX support for current sprint Detailed wireframes for next sprint User test work to date and latest wireframes
	UX support for current sprint Detailed wireframes for next sprint Preparation for user testing
Final sprint	UX support for current sprint User test work to date

Figure 1-3: UX activities within Agile Scrum development

Be Prepared

Be well prepared for the beginning of development work. Model the problem up-front: understand the business requirements, user requirements, and the competition before the developers become involved

Make Friends

Make friends with the whole team, including product managers, product owners, and developers. UX activities can support all of these roles. For example, the results of usability testing can be broken down for incremental delivery and used to help prioritize the backlog or can be used to validate an idea and get buy-in from the wider business.

Join In

Be a member of the Agile team. Don't just hand your designs over and disappear. Be there when the decisions are made.

Parallel Work Streams

Use parallel work streams alongside the developers:

- Prepare high-level wireframes before development begins.
- Work on detailed interactions during the sprint before they'll be developed.

Test Regularly

Test regularly, for example every two sprints. Even if you don't know what you'll be testing when you set the tests up, something will have come up by the time you get there. Use light-touch, guerilla testing techniques. Test what's just been built, or designs for what's about to be built. Invite the whole team to attend.

Everyone's a UXer

Share the rationale and vision and get everyone on the team to do the UX work. Increasing the collective UX IQ of the team will lead to shared responsibility and better decision making.

CASE STUDIES: UCD IN PRACTICE

The goal of the case studies sections is to bring the UCD process to life by talking about some projects we've worked on recently and the processes we went through for them to be successful.

LIGHT-TOUCH UX PROJECT TO IMPROVE AN EXISTING WEBSITE

A recent website project called for a light touch. The client was concerned that its recently developed website was not converting as well as they expected. They had a limited budget and an extremely restrictive content management system (CMS).

The goal for the project was to improve the number of site visitors who contacted the company to make an appointment. This involved finding local company branch, and filling in a form to get a quote and book the appointment.

In the absence of budget for usability testing, we conducted an expert review. We stepped through the website, imagining we were customers wishing to book an appointment. Did we have enough information at every stage of the process? Could we understand how to fill in the forms? Did the website make it clear what was happening at every stage? This was an eye-opening process, as there were plenty of places where it was extremely unclear what had been selected and what the user needed to do next.

Having identified a number of key usability issues, we drew *quick win* improvements onto the existing website projected onto a whiteboard. This was a simple way of collaborating on design decisions. Photographs of these sketches were used as an inexpensive way of acquiring approval from the site's stakeholders. Once approval was attained, our graphic designer made the changes straight into Photoshop.

Figure 1-4: Projecting a website onto a whiteboard to explore
quick win improvements

The design improvements were made to the site. Once the revised site was live, we conducted a usability test and found users to be having little difficulty using the site. Additionally, statistics from the revised site showed improved conversion rates. Figure 1-5 shows the UCD process we used for this project.

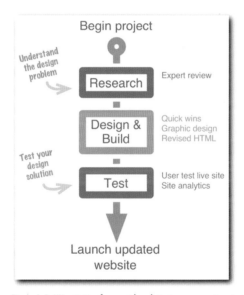

Figure 1-5: UX activities for a quick website improvement project

UCD PROJECT TO REDESIGN AN EXISTING WEBSITE FROM THE GROUND UP

Britain's leading online supplier of quality menswear, Charles Tyrwhitt, approached us with a view to completely overhauling their existing website. Charles Tyrwhitt started as a mail order company, and continues to be, but with a large online presence in Germany, the US, and in the UK. They have the largest competitor market share in the UK, and ship worldwide.

Prior to the redesign work, Charles Tyrwhitt's website was still market-leading in terms of conversion rates, and customer retention was high, due in part to a commitment to excellent customer service. The website was, however, beginning to feel slightly dated and inflexible. The information architecture was convoluted as new product categories had been added over time, without a change to the navigational structure. Product sizing options could be made clearer, and the checkout was more complicated than it really needed to be.

Our mission was to update the site to be robust, flexible, international, elegant, and easy to use.

Figure 1-6 shows their homepage prior to the redesign.

Why UCD?

> "Our previous website was a result of 10 years' cumulative good ideas that converted well and had a loyal user base, but that held the legacy of this ad hoc development in its dated and sometimes confused look and feel. We selected a user-centered design agency to conduct the work as we felt confident that our existing customers would be valued as highly as we value them, while the usability issues would be managed in the right way to lift conversion. Conversion has lifted by 27% year-on-year (July to July 2011) and our Net Promoter Score is up by eight points." Jennie Blythe, Web Merchandising and Sales Manager, ctshirts. co.uk

Requirements Gathering

We embarked on a user-centered site redesign, working closely with Charles Tyrwhitt's in-house web team. To begin the process, we ran a month of requirements gathering activities. We conducted usability testing on the Charles Tyrwhitt and competitor websites. This was to understand how users went about buying men's apparel in general and shirts of the type that get worn with a tie in particular. (These shirts have sizes more complicated than small, medium, and large.) We also went to the Charles Tyrwhitt telephone call center, listened in to customer calls, and interviewed call center staff. This activity provided fantastic insight into typical contacts between customers and the business. It was first-hand evidence that Charles Tyrwhitt customers expect and get first-rate service and that the website needed to reflect this relation-ship. This insight was backed up by store visits. We spent time observing customers in Charles Tyrwhitt's London stores (see Figure 1-7). We watched as men browsed the shirts, looked for their size, compared shirts, and hunted for matching ties. We listened to customers' queries to the sales assistants and their responses. We understood how Charles Tyrwhitt staff listen to the customer in order to be able to meet their needs in terms of both product and service.

Figure 1-6: Charles Tyrwhitt homepage, prior to redesign

Charles Tyrwhitt store product display

Formal shirts are grouped by fit and quality/price
- Classic or slim fit
- Standard / non-iron / 140 /etc
- Columns represent a single color or pattern
- Two shirts of each size are in each
  pigeonhole: 1 single cuff & 1 double cuff

Ties are dramatically fanned out and grouped by color
- Customers observed placing their chosen
  shirt over the tie fan to find the best match

Figure 1-7: Annotated photographs from a visit to a Charles Tyrwhitt store

We conducted stakeholder interviews with the Charles Tyrwhitt team. These were designed to understand what the business wanted the revised site to do for them. We came away with a thorough understanding of their products, so we could help to sell them in ways that fitted with existing business thinking.

Sketching

There followed an intense period of ideas generation. We had lots of thoughts on how to improve online shirt sales and needed to capture them. The trick here is to get everybody's ideas recorded so that there's an abundance to choose from. We went through several activities to document these ideas. We spent a lot of time as a team huddled round whiteboards sketching ideas (see Chapter 16 for more on sketching). We surrounded ourselves with printouts of competitor sites. We conducted an ideation workshop with the Charles Tyrwhitt team (see Chapter 11 to find out about ideation workshops). This was a fun day that revolved around some key pages for the new website. Primarily, we deconstructed the existing shirt product page and put it back together based on our knowledge of user and business priorities.

Information Architecture and Wireframing

The ideation workshop resulted in agreement on direction for the stage to come—wireframing key site templates. We began with a sitemap to establish the site information architecture. High-level navigation and required templates flowed from this. (For more on these activities, see Chapter 15 on information architecture and Chapter 17 on wireframes.)

We began wireframing with five key templates: the homepage (see Figure 1-8), a category page (we started with "men's formal shirts" as this was a key category for the business), the shirt product page, a product listing page, and the shopping basket. These five pages allowed us to experiment with the shape of the entire website while also concentrating on the specifics. Wireframing was a great way of communicating detailed designs with the Charles Tyrwhitt team and getting quick and accurate feedback. The Charles Tyrwhitt team was honest and exacting in its feedback at all times. This can sometimes be frustrating as a designer. You have to work to a deadline and you love your latest design, but the client isn't convinced. However, it's precisely these tensions that deliver the most robust and well thought out designs in the end.

We user tested a deck of key wireframes with existing and potential Charles Tyrwhitt customers (see Chapter 5 for more on usability testing). This testing ensured that we were on the right track. Users understood the terminology, interacted easily with the navigation and sizing controls, and found they had all the information they required in order to make a purchase decision.

The wireframing activities for this project lasted three months. Basing our work on those five key templates, we delivered a final deck containing 25 templates plus associated flows and states. Each of those wireframes had been thoroughly examined by the Charles Tyrwhitt team and been back and forth several times before achieving signoff.

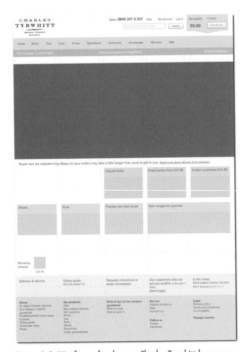

Figure 1-8: Wireframe for the new Charles Tyrwhitt homepage

SOURCE: Reproduced with permission of Charles Tyrwhitt © 2011 Charles Tyrwhitt LLP

Graphic Design

There are already plenty of excellent books on the subject of graphic design, so we're not going to go into detail here. However, handing over wireframes to graphic designers is always an interesting process. Will they understand the thinking? Will they want to make radical changes? Will they feel empowered enough to do more than simply "color in" the wireframes? We had made sure that our graphic designer had viewed the wireframe usability testing so he had a great feel for our design rationale. He spent a lot of time working with the Charles Tyrwhitt team to understand the essence of their brand and the online presence the new site should project.

User test participants will be vocal when things are not as expected. However, good design often goes unacknowledged in testing. Consider a design that meets participants' needs and expresses their understanding of the brand. This design will feel right, and it will flow beautifully. Test participants will simply get on with using it, feeling no need to comment.

When we ran usability tests on the graphic design concepts, they tested really well. How do I know this? Existing Charles Tyrwhitt customers barely commented on the graphics. They just dived in and assumed that the flat JPEGs we were showing them belonged to Charles Tyrwhitt. It meant that the new design fitted seamlessly with their understanding of the brand. Gold-dust in redesign terms. Clearly this can be tricky for a graphic designer to watch: "My beautiful design! Why are they not praising it highly?" The new design for the Charles Tyrwhitt homepage was radically different from the old version, but users accepted it because it was classy, British, and had distilled the brand personality.

Build and Launch

Again, this book is not about HTML, so you're just going to look at the interaction between UX and build activities here.

The key to a successful handover from UX practitioners to coders is a shared understanding of the desired outcomes for the project. We ensured that our front-end developer observed the usability testing on the graphic design, so he had an in-depth knowledge of the site we were asking him to build, the rationale behind the design decisions, and a good understanding of the way users wanted to interact with the site.

We user tested the front-end build prior to handing the HTML over for integration with existing back-end systems. This allowed us to fine-tune interactions such as rollover states, drop-down menus, and error messaging prior to launching the site.

As a UX team, we made ourselves available to the Charles Tyrwhitt back-end development team and our front-end developer throughout the build and integration process. If they had a question about the exact way something should be implemented, we answered it. If they told us that technical constraints meant a particular interaction was impossible, we redesigned it.

We're immensely proud of the Charles Tyrwhitt site that is now live (www.ctshirts.co.uk, see Figure 1-9). It is of course a living website and changes over time. The Charles Tyrwhitt team is actively involved in multi-variant testing to maximize their conversion rates and it has been fascinating to hear about the outcomes. A wireframe is a blueprint for a potential website. When that website is launched it has the capability to learn and grow and the Charles Tyrwhitt team is achieving that.

Figure 1-9: The redesigned Charles Tyrwhitt homepage

SOURCE: Reproduced with permission of Charles Tyrwhitt © 2012 Charles Tyrwhitt LLP

The user-centered design process we went through for the Charles Tyrwhitt project (see Figure 1-10) has resulted in a live website that meets the needs of the business and its customers.

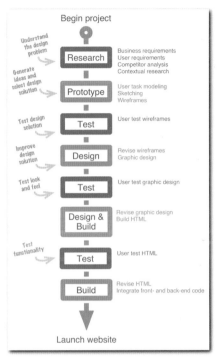

Figure 1-10: UX activities for the Charles Tyrwhitt redesign project

SOURCE: Reproduced with permission of Charles Tyrwhitt
© 2012 Charles Tyrwhitt LLP

PROJECT TO DESIGN THE MOBILE VERSION OF A NEW TRAVEL WEBSITE

iExplore is a portal website developed by the holiday company TUI Travel Plc to bring all their adventure holidays under one roof. The goal was to encourage users who would not generally choose an adventure holiday to do so.

Having been through a user-centered design process to produce wireframes and graphic designs for the new site (see Figure 1-11), iExplore asked us to produce wireframes for a mobile version of the site. We knew the desktop site inside and out, but now needed to consider how mobile user's needs might differ. The budget for this project was limited, so we need to get creative with our activities in order to give iExplore the best design in the time available.

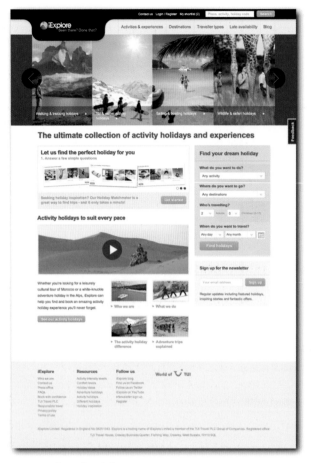

Figure 1-11: The iExplore desktop site

SOURCE: Reproduced with permission of iExplore © 2012 iExplore Ltd.

Competitor Review

We reviewed competitor's mobile offerings to determine best practice. We investigated key mobile use cases. It was thought unlikely that users will be making high-value transactions via their mobile phones, but they are very likely to be researching upcoming holidays in their downtime (for example on the daily commute on the train). During holiday research, users are very likely to want to save candidate holidays for later or to share with their partners.

Ideation Workshop

We ran a two-day ideation workshop with the iExplore team. This was to determine business requirements and to co-design key templates. Starting the design progress like this meant that design decisions could be made quickly, without a lengthy feedback loop with the client. iExplore chose to invest their time early in the project in order to allow us to produce rapid designs later.

The iExplore desktop site was designed to be highly experiential—to help users imagine themselves on an amazing adventure holiday. Mobile offerings tend to be highly stripped-back, to prioritize key information over rich content. This tension was discussed at the workshop and we worked on ideas that struck a balance between the two.

The key workshop activity was sketching (for more on this, see Chapter 16). Workshop attendees drew their ideas for the mobile site. We then discussed these ideas and voted on what to include and exclude. The workshop output was a deck of sketches with notes detailing which features should be included in the final designs.

The workshop was successful because the attendees were a small group of iExplore's decision-makers. They were able to make choices without consulting with their bosses and were happy to commit their time to the workshop.

Wireframes

There were less than two days allocated to wireframing within the project. As we had gained client buy-in to design decisions in the ideation workshop, this was an achievable deadline. The wireframes were shared with the client at the halfway point, to ensure we were on the right track.

Figure 1-12 shows a wireframe from the iExplore mobile project.

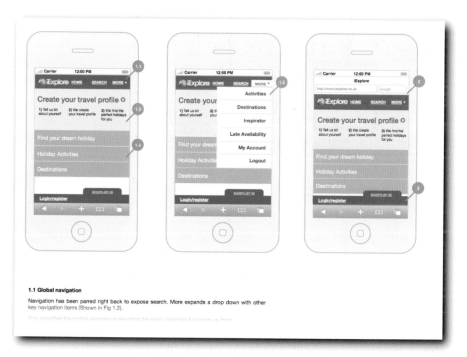

Figure 1-12: iExplore mobile homepage wireframe

SOURCE: Reproduced with permission of iExplore © 2012 iExplore Ltd.

Guerilla Usability Testing

Once we had completed wireframes the client was happy with, we conducted a guerilla usability test to validate the designs. A *guerilla* test is one that uses a light touch and minimal resources to elicit user insights. Typically, this means recruiting passers-by for short (10–20 minute) tests. For iExplore testing, we asked permission from our local airport to canvass landside passengers, asking them to spare a few minutes to participate in the test. Beyond being about to get on an airplane, the only recruitment criterion was that the participant must have a smartphone. We offered a small cash incentive to participate.

During our day at the airport, we showed six participants our designs. We used a prototyping app to make the wireframes into a clickable user journey that could be viewed on an iPhone.

The testing was extremely successful in that it largely validated our designs. We learned a few key lessons around the need to be explicit with controls for mobile use. For example, the original designs did not include a home link as it was felt users would click the company logo. However, this was found to not be the case and a home link was added to the wireframes.

The final deliverable for this project was the wireframe deck amended to incorporate feedback from usability testing. At the time of writing, the iExplore team is still working on implementing the mobile site. Figure 1-13 shows the user-centered design process for the iExplore mobile project.

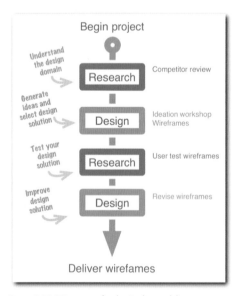

Figure 1-13: UX activities for the iExplore mobile project

SOURCE: Reproduced with permission of iExplore © 2012 iExplore Ltd.

RESOURCES

The Agile Manifesto: http://agilemanifesto.org/

Information Architecture for the World Wide Web (2nd Edition) by Louis Rosenfeld and Peter Morville

Web ReDesign: Workflow that Works by Kelly Goto and Emily Cotler

A Project Guide to UX Design: For User Experience Designers in the Field or in the Making by Carolyn Chandler and Russ Unger

Undercover User Experience Design by Cennydd Bowles and James Box

Lean UX: Getting Out of the Deliverables Business by Jeff Gothelf
uxdesign.smashingmagazine.com/2011/03/07/
lean-ux-getting-out-of-the-deliverables-business

Don't Make Me Think! A Common Sense Approach to Web Usability (2005) by Steve Krug

2

PLANNING UX PROJECTS

PLANNING UX PROJECTS is a balancing act between getting the right amount of user input within the constraints of your project. The trick is to work out the best use of your time. How can you get the most UX goodness for your client's budget? This book describes your armory of UX tools. This chapter explains how to choose the right mix of tools for the task at hand.

GETTING STARTED WITH UX PLANNING

The planning phase is all about understanding what you have been asked to do and working out the best combination of activities that will give you the outcome you need, within the time, budgetary, and resource constraints of the project. It is your job as a UX professional to deliver the best user experience within the time and budget available.

The planning of projects may take place when you are writing a proposal to do work that is yet to start as well as at the beginning of a "live" project. When planning work for proposal purposes, you can be faced with issues such as lack of information around budgets as well as limited access to clients to ask questions.

In many ways the planning of UX projects can become a design challenge in its own right. You have an outcome that you need to get to and it's up to you which approach you take to get you there. You need to be confident that the tools and techniques you choose will be the right ones to get you the insight you need within the constraints of the project.

The budget for the piece of work is always the key piece of information that can be really useful to help with planning, but often this is not always available. This information is useful if you charge by an daily rate, because it then determines the time you will have on a project, which in itself will determine the approach you take.

The beauty of UX projects is that there is always something you can do to add value regardless of the budget. A low budget may result in a more light touch, "guerilla" approach, whereas a larger budget may allow you to do more extensive user research. If you can, always try to get an idea of budget as it will save both you and your client time by avoiding re-cutting proposals.

Your client may not want to share their budget (as they may think you will spend it all for them) so have a few different options to present if they cannot share this information to suit different potential budgets.

The key principle for all UX projects is that you must ensure that you involve users in the design process in some way. Challenge yourself to see how you can work within the constraints of the project to involve users as much as possible. User involvement will not only improve the output of the project but will also help to inform decision making which can often delay projects.

UX projects typically consist of three main phases, a research phase, a design phase and a further research phase, designed to test and validate the designs.

- The research phase is where you immerse yourself in the project to get the background you'll need to make design decisions later in the project. During this phase you will try to learn as much about your client's business, objectives, users, and competitors as possible.
- The design phase is where you work out how what you are designing will work and how it will fit together. This phase will define its scope, its features and functionality, and how it behaves.

■ The validation phase is where you identify whether what you came up with in the design phase actually works with its intended audience. This phase is typically followed by further rounds of design and testing to solve the problems you inevitably find when you test with users.

We find that using a research, design, and validation framework helps to structure your projects. We often start working out the approach we would ideally like to take and then calculate how long we would need to do that work and then adjust the methods, tools, and techniques to fit the constraints of the project. Figure 2-1 shows an early sketch of a project taking shape.

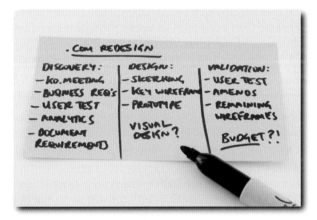

Figure 2-1: It is useful to sketch out your proposed approach within the UX project framework

Project constraints include factors such as budget, time available, delivery deadlines, resource availability, information availability, related projects, access to tools, and legal documentation. Regardless of the constraints you must be able to focus on the objectives of the project and how you can deliver the best user experience that meets those objectives. Often this is the true (and hidden) skill of a great UX professional.

Once you have defined the approach you want to take, is much easier to talk to a client about flexing project constraints such as increasing the scope of the project or change your original plan. All clients have to start with some sort of ballpark budget and approach and, if you can justify why you might need more time and budget, you will clearly be more likely to get it!

Later in this chapter, you'll see a matrix of UX tools and techniques that you can use on your UX projects. These are all fully explained within their corresponding chapters within this book. We also share some case studies of real projects. These examine the clients' objectives and highlight the approach we took to the project. These are designed to provide you with a template approach, which you can compare and contrast with your own project challenges and proposed approach to tackle them.

SELLING USER-CENTERED DESIGN TO YOUR CLIENTS

Despite the huge growth in the awareness of the importance of user experience over the last 10 years, you may still have to sell the benefits of this approach to your clients and colleagues. Here are some of the many benefits that we have seen from adopting a user-centered design (UCD) approach:

- **Better products**—A process that deliberately involves end users as well as one that understands the commercial objectives will always result in a product that works better for its intended purpose.
- **Cheaper to fix problems**—By involving users within the design process, you learn what doesn't work when it's most cost effective to fix it. An amendment to a wireframe or prototype is many times cheaper than a technical fix once a product is launched.
- **Less risk**—A UCD approach helps to ensure that design issues are discovered and fixed in the design phase and not once products have been launched. A digital product may never truly ever be "finished," but a UCD approach will result in products with a lower risk of failure.
- **Deliver to deadline and avoid scope creep**—By identifying more of the dynamics at play and addressing these challenges earlier in the process, there will be a better chance of avoiding scope creep and delivering to meet your deadline.
- **Research brings insights**—A UCD approach provides in-depth analysis and research that uncovers opportunities to differentiate products to gain competitive advantages. A UCD approach provides a solid and robust research-led approach to design. Design decisions after all should be based on evidence and not opinions.
- **Products that are easy to use make more money**—Often this is the primary commercial reason behind adopting a UCD approach. The reality of many UCD projects is that despite being "user-centered," the focus is really on designing something that primarily achieves a commercial objective. The UCD process provides the rigor that ensures the commercial objectives are met while still providing the best user experience—so everyone wins.
- **User led projects can get products to market more quickly**—Projects that take a pure UCD approach let the customers decide which route to follow. This can circumvent time-consuming client-side decision-making processes and politics. When you reach a point of conflicting views that stalls a project, the involvement of users can be a great way to help to make decisions and get the project moving again.
- **Ease of use is a common customer requirement**—In our user research, we often hear customers using terms such as "usability" and even "user experience" when describing what qualities they seek from products. This is often a result of products being advertised as being easy to use and as such it's a selling point that customers are seeking products that they buy.

WHAT DOES A USER EXPERIENCE PROJECT LOOK LIKE?

Planning a UX project is to some extent an art in itself. Working out how to do the best work in the time and budget available is a learned skill. There is no right answer: the optimal project will differ between clients.

The important thing when planning a user experience project is to put the user front and center of your activities. Conduct user research, design, test, and iterate. It's impossible to describe what you do as UX if you don't include users in your workflow. Equally, if you don't understand your client and their business, you will not be able to produce designs that meet their needs.

So how do you plan a successful UX project? For a design project, you need to include activities to answer each of the following questions:

- What are the business requirements?
- What are the user requirements?
- What is the best design solution that meets both the business and user requirements?

WHAT ARE THE BUSINESS REQUIREMENTS?

Why is the project going ahead? What would make your client feel that the project is a success?

Often, the process of eliciting business requirements can lead to a definition of a project vision that can be referred to throughout the design process in order to aid decision-making.

Make sure you understand the reasoning behind the project's existence by considering one or more of the following.

Project Brief

Is there a formal project brief? If so, read it and ensure you understand it by asking questions if necessary. A good brief will clarify the reasons for the project and outline expected outcomes. Sometimes a brief will expose conflicting requirements, and it always helps to know about these early!

Every project needs a brief of some sort. How can you design something if you don't know what it's for? If there isn't a brief, ask for one. Or start asking questions that allow you to write your own.

A useful brief will generally contain information on these subjects:

- **Description of the project**—What is the project to do? The must-haves and must-nots.
- **Business goals, objectives, and expected outcomes**—What the organization expects to gain from the project. For an online shop this might be to increase conversion rates, but other organizations may have less concrete goals such as improving understanding or feedback ratings.
- **Target audience**—Who does the organization want to be using their new product? The depth of this audience information can differ wildly, from everybody to detailed demographic and behavioral breakdowns.

- **Brand guidelines**—Any requirements to convey existing brand personality, such as tone of voice, logos, use of imagery, and so on.
- **Key stakeholders**—Who is your point of contact? Who must you show your findings to? Who must approve your designs?
- **Expected timings**—When must the project be completed by? Are there any deadlines you should know about?
- **Technological constraints**—Are there any technologies the project must use? For example, content management systems or merchandising software. What are the strengths and weaknesses of the technology?
- **Related activities**—Are there any other projects that intersect with this one? For example, we often find that clients run re-branding exercises alongside our UX work. Another example is implementing new technical solutions, such as changing a back-end system or search supplier. It is useful to know at the outset when the results of other projects will be available to incorporate into your project, and to flag if this causes difficulties.

Kick-Off Meetings

Schedule a kick-off meeting to get the project started. This is your chance to make sure you've fully understood the brief. If there was no formal brief, make sure you use the kick-off meeting to understand answers to the questions outlined previously.

Another key reason for scheduling a kick-off meeting is to meet the stakeholders. Your client may not be located near you, and you may work remotely much of the time. It is much easier to conduct a design review over the phone if you have previously met the people you are talking to. An opportunity to get to know your clients and understand what they want from the project will set the project off on the right foot, even if you will all be working in the same place.

A kick-off meeting is the perfect time to discuss a project plan. Which activities will you be doing when? Can everyone make the required dates for delivery and feedback?

Stakeholder Interviews

Stakeholder interviews are a structured way for you to gain insights into the reasoning behind your project, as well as its expected outcomes. You schedule time to talk to key individuals within your client's organization in order to gain a deeper understanding of the business requirements. Chapter 3 goes into detail about stakeholder interviews.

Requirements Workshops

A requirements workshop is a collaborative method for fleshing out your project brief. You gather key stakeholders together, discuss the brief, and conduct exercises designed to give you a deeper understanding of the project. A successful requirements workshop leads to a shared understanding of the problems your project aims to solve. It has the added benefit of building a sense of teamwork with your client. Chapter 4 describes requirements workshops further.

WHAT ARE THE USER REQUIREMENTS?

For great user experiences, understand your users' needs before you design for them. Use a selection of the following techniques to understand user requirements. Try to ensure you use at least one technique that involves real users (such as usability testing or contextual research), rather than just those that involve extrapolating user needs from other research.

Usability Testing

Observe real users interacting with existing and competitor products to understand more about their needs. Use usability testing to identify problems with a product you are about to tweak, or to inform task models and customer experience maps for a new product or drastic redesign. See Chapter 5 for more on usability testing.

Competitor Benchmarking

Competitor benchmarking allows you to understand the features that are present in competitor products. This is often a good way of understanding users' expectations and needs. Chapter 6 looks at competitor benchmarking in depth.

Contextual Research

Contextual research involves going out and about and observing users in the real world. Contextual research is particularly valuable when multiple channels are involved (offline, online, and more). This type of research is also important if the end user is likely to be in an unusual or stressed context when interacting with your product, such as in an emergency situation or perhaps with poor Internet access. Common techniques include store visits, call center listening and research with users in their own environment. Chapter 7 covers how to conduct contextual research.

Analytics

Analysis of server statistics from any existing product can paint a vibrant picture of what your users are doing now. It can point you to areas of high drop out where you may want to concentrate any redesign efforts. However, analytics cannot tell you why users are behaving as they are—usability testing is best for this. Chapter 8 looks at analytics in more detail.

Surveys

You can ask a large number of users a set of questions with a survey. This can be a great way of finding out about demographics. Surveys can reach a broad audience, and are best for eliciting facts rather than a deep understanding of user behaviors. Chapter 9 looks at surveys.

Expert Reviews

An expert review is an evaluation of an existing product based on a set of usability guidelines, the target users, and their tasks. It is a low-cost method for understanding an existing product's key usability issues. There's more on expert reviews in Chapter 10.

Task Models

A task model is a description of the activities users perform in order to reach their goals. They help you understand how your product can fit into users' lives. Task models are typically generated after a round of usability testing alongside additional user research. See Chapter 12 for more on task models.

Customer Experience Maps

A customer experience map is a visualization of how users go about completing a task mapped against the way a digital product actually allows them to do it. As a designer, it is useful to map the entire the customer experience to see where user needs are not being met. Customer experience maps are typically generated from usability testing and additional user research. See Chapter 13 for more on customer experience maps.

Personas

Persona profiles are a representation of a digital product's users. A persona is a short, vivid description of a fictional character that represents a group of the product's users. Personas bring the product's users to life, in an easily understood, sharable format. They help production teams to prioritize user needs and core tasks. There's more on personas in Chapter 14.

WHAT IS THE BEST DESIGN SOLUTION?

What is the best design solution that meets both the business and user requirements? Choose a selection of techniques that allow you to design, build, test, and iterate your product.

Ideation Workshops

Ideation workshops are a collaborative design method. They help you and your client decide which design solutions are suitable for the project. For more on ideation workshops see Chapter 11.

User Journeys

The aim of producing user journeys is to ensure that users' tasks are streamlined and easy to accomplish. User journeys are useful when designing the flow of your product. How can you structure your product to ensure key journeys are smooth? See Chapter 12 for a detailed look at user journeys.

Information Architecture

The information architecture (IA) of a digital product defines the product's underlying structures. Structures include content, consistent naming, grouping, and navigation. Typical IA deliverables are content plans, process flows, and site maps. For more on IA, see Chapter 15.

Sketching, Wireframes, and Prototypes

Sketching, wireframes, and prototypes are ways of generating and iterating design ideas before they go into production. Use them to quickly and easily get designs reviewed, tested, and refined. There's more on sketching in Chapter 16, wireframes in Chapter 17, and prototyping in Chapter 18.

Usability Testing

Testing with real users is the best way of finding out if your designs work. Conducting a user test will reveal insights you could never have guessed, and suggest improvements that will make your product stand out. Usability testing is easy and need not be expensive, especially if you use light-touch "guerilla" approaches. Find out more about usability testing in Chapter 5.

HOW MUCH TIME AND BUDGET SHOULD YOU MAKE AVAILABLE FOR UX?

This is a common question that we are often asked, particularly by clients or designers who are relatively new to UX. It often comes from a full-service agency mindset where client budgets are fought over by representatives of each main discipline such as UX, visual design, and dev.

This "departmental" mindset can be detrimental, as UX can become something that is dialed up or down whereas in reality it should be a component of both the visual design and dev work as opposed to being considered as a separate work stream or cost centre.

A different way of considering this question is to think of UX as a project philosophy as opposed to a set of tools, methods, and deliverables. If your client has bought into the principles of UX then in effect their project becomes a "UX" project so all of their time and budget is dedicated to it.

When considering client budgets, you'll get a feel, with experience, for what is the right amount of time to apportion to the different phases of the project. It isn't as simple as offering a rule of thumb such as "dedicate 20% of project budgets to UX" because each project will have its own unique priorities, challenges, and objectives that will require different levels of UX input.

The matrices shown later in this chapter will give you an idea of which different tools and techniques you can use to suit different types of projects with differing budgets. In reality there is always some form of user research you can do even on the smallest budget projects.

CHOOSING UX TOOLS AND TECHNIQUES

Table 2-1 shows all the tools and techniques described in this book. Use it as a cheat sheet to help you decide which activities best suit your project.

Table 2-1   UX Tools and Techniques

UX Activity	Good For	Bad For	Find Out More
Stakeholder Interviews Talk to key individuals within your client's organization to understand business requirements.	Clients with lots of people who have something to say about their new project. When you need information about the goals for your project.	Making design decisions. Projects that are very short on time.	Chapter 3
Requirements Workshops Gather key stakeholders together to discuss the brief and conduct exercises to give you a deeper understanding of the project.	Complex design challenges. Complex clients. Disparate teams.	Projects with very tight deadlines and small budgets.	Chapter 4
Guerilla Usability Testing Very informal user involvement when little or no budget exists for usability testing.	Involving users when budgets prevent larger scale user research. Gaining a quick user opinion to help to progress designs.	Recruiting participants to a specific brief. Difficult for clients to observe.	Chapter 5
Lab Usability Testing Involving end users in the design process to understand their needs, find out how they do things, and see if they can use your products in a controlled environment.	Involving clients in user research as they can observe tests in real time. The controlled environment allows you to test what you want with the right people.	Projects with very tight deadlines and small budgets. An artificial environment may influence user behavior on some projects.	Chapter 5
Remote Usability Testing Conducting user research in a different location than where your user is situated.	When you need to test geographically dispersed groups of people. When people can't travel to a lab. When time is tight, as you can run tests in parallel.	Involving clients is difficult. You can lose a sense of empathy with people when you're not meeting them face to face.	Chapter 5
Competitor Benchmarking Evaluating competitor products to determine their strengths and weaknesses and opportunities to innovate with your own product.	Projects where lots of competitors exist. Clients who work in unfamiliar sectors: a great way to immerse yourself in a new world.	Some projects may not allow the time to do this activity. In sectors you are familiar with, this becomes less important.	Chapter 6
Contextual Research Conducting research in the environment that users are naturally within.	Gaining the most representative insight into how people actually behave in their own environment, and the methods they use to overcome the problems they face.	Projects with very tight deadlines and small budgets.	Chapter 7

UX Activity	Good For	Bad For	Find Out More
Analytics Evaluating quantitative data to understand what people are doing when using a product or service.	Identifying interesting user behavior to focus research activities to find out why.	Projects with very tight deadlines and small budgets. Clients who have no analytics data! Analytics do not uncover the reasons behind user actions.	Chapter 8
Surveys Collecting information from a dispersed set of people by asking them to respond to a predetermined set of questions.	Collecting information from dispersed sets of people in a relatively short period of time. Collecting qualitative and quantitative information.	Can present issues with data accuracy. Analysis of qualitative data is notoriously time consuming.	Chapter 9
Expert Reviews Evaluate an existing product based on a set of usability guidelines, the target users, and their tasks.	Gathering a quick understanding of a product's key usability issues.	Acquiring a deep understanding of real user issues.	Chapter 10
Ideation Workshops A collaborative design method to help you and your client decide on design solutions.	Generating a shared vision for the UX design work. Getting early input from different disciplines such as visual designers and developers.	Clients who don't want to be involved in the design work—they want you to go away do the "magic."	Chapter 11
Task Models Descriptions of the activities users perform in order to reach their goals.	Ensuring your product matches user expectations. Providing insight into buying processes and thus helping you design transactional sites that support user needs.	Projects with very tight deadlines and small budgets.	Chapter 12
Customer Experience Maps A visualization of a process that users follow before, during, and after using a product or service.	Visualizing the entire customer journey and highlighting the specific areas where a product or service meets and fails to meet user needs.	Projects with very tight deadlines and small budgets that don't allow you to gather the research you'll need for this approach.	Chapter 13

continued

Table 2-1   continued

UX Activity	Good For	Bad For	Find Out More
Personas Short, vivid descriptions of fictional characters who represent a product's users.	When production teams need an easy way to understand user needs and core tasks. As a collaborative exercise to get production teams to think about their users.	When you can do no research with real users to generate personas from. When the personas are generated externally with no opportunity to integrate them with the teams who will go on to use them	Chapter 14
User Journeys Identify how users flow through your product. Design the structure of your product to ensure users can flow through it efficiently.	When it's important to keep steps to complete a task to a minimum. To ensure key tasks are easy to accomplish.	Single step tasks.	Chapter 12
Information Architecture The process of organizing information to make its retrieval as simple as possible.	An essential component of any project, as it provides an information structure and means of navigating that has been designed to reflect the specific user and business needs of a product or service.	Some small projects such as designing e-mails and campaign landing pages will require significantly less IA work than large-scale redesign projects for information-rich and complex products and services.	Chapter 15
Sketching Hand-drawn design ideas.	Quickly generate and gather feedback on lots of design ideas. Decide which ideas to pursue in higher fidelity.	When clients expect higher fidelity work from you as a designer. When clients can't see beyond the unfinished nature of a sketch.	Chapter 16
Wireframes Static diagrams that represent the framework of a product, exploring content, navigation, and interactions.	Explore design and interaction ideas before they move into graphic design and development. Agree on the direction with the clients. Test ideas with users. Refine ideas based on feedback and test results.	Highly interactive products that need to be used in order to be understood.	Chapter 17
Prototypes Mocking up ideas quickly in an interactive form that brings them to life to elicit feedback.	Producing something so that members of a project can have a shared understanding and approval of the direction it is taking. Creating a candidate design for user testing.	Projects with very tight deadlines and small budgets. Complicated prototypes can be time consuming to amend.	Chapter 18

PLANNING UX: CASE STUDIES

The tools and techniques you select are determined by the design challenge you have been given, as well as the time and budget available. Clearly, a different approach is required for designing a campaign micro-site from scratch, compared with making large-scale usability improvements to an existing shopping website.

DOING UX ON A SHOE-STRING BUDGET

When a client or organization is unfamiliar with usability and user-centered design, it can often be difficult to get the budget you want to involve users regularly during the design process.

The joy of UX is that there are so many tools and techniques that you can use to suit the specific constraints of your project so you can still involve users in some way.

Recently we were asked to provide some UX consultancy on a new website. Our client wanted an expert opinion on how usable it was and how it could be improved.

Our client had spent a large amount of their budget on designing and building the site, and had then been told by their boss that they should do some user testing before it went live. The budget was so tight that we had a day in total to do the work.

We decided that the best approach was to run an internal workshop and invite a bunch of our consultants along to critique the site as we looked at each of the designs. This identified loads of issues in a short period of time.

We also managed some guerilla user testing. A few of us went to local cafes and asked members of the public to show us how they would use the website to complete some simple tasks. We offered to buy them coffee and cakes in return. Within a few hours we had some great user insights to add to our expert review.

All of the issues were documented as a simple bulleted list in an e-mail, which we followed up with a quick call to discuss the biggest problems that we had identified.

This demonstrates how you can always do something, no matter how restrictive the project constraints. Any user testing will result in improvements to the product or service that you are designing.

Project Outline

Constraints: tiny budget!

Activity	Timing
Internal workshop	0.25 days
Guerilla testing	0.5 days
Summarize findings and feedback to client	0.25 days

A USER-CENTERED REDESIGN PROJECT

We are lucky in that many clients come to us and ask specifically for user-centered design projects that include specific UX activities such as user research or that deliver specific outputs such as customer journey maps or persona profiles.

We were asked by a client to design an online quoting tool. Our client was fully versed in the benefits of involving users throughout the process and requested that we ran regular user testing and UX seminars within the business to educate her colleagues.

The project began with a large user research exercise that involved benchmarking competitor services. This gave us a unique insight into what the competition were doing, how well they were doing it, and also what the specific user requirements were from such a tool.

In parallel to the user research we conducted a wide range of stakeholder interviews as well as a series of workshops with some internal business analysts who had been collecting detailed functional requirements.

We presented our findings from the user research exercise to the business. The key part of this presentation involved discussion around some ideas we had had for some features we thought they should offer which would give them a significant competitive advantage.

This identifies how user research can be far more than just involving users. Often you will see opportunities for features, content, and functionality that will meet some quite unexpected user needs. Once met, these can often result in significant increases in product performance as well as huge financial returns for the service provider.

Following the research phase we developed some early prototypes of the different elements of the quoting process. This involved breaking the required set of data into logical chunks and working out how a user would move between them. Once worked up into rough wireframes we shared this with the project team, amended it following their feedback, and then tested it with users to improve it further before entering the wireframe production phase of the project.

Once a set of complete wireframes was produced these were tested again to further refine them. During the process we met with designers and developers to share our vision for how we should work to ensure that when it was built it retained the features that we deliberately added to meet specific user needs.

Later in the project we were involved as a point of sign-off for the final designs that were produced by a third-party agency. Users were also involved at this stage, as we wanted to ensure that the execution of the quoting form was suitable for the target audience. This was also critical once some front-end elements were available to test, as it was important that interactive elements such as error-handling worked as well as possible.

Finally, we were asked to conduct a review of the live site six months after launch. This was to evaluate how well the form was working and also to evaluate how users were responding to the new product features that we had helped to identify.

Project Outline

Constraints: Huge complexity, high-profile project but good budget, and excellent client buy-in for a UX approach.

Activity	Timing
Kick-off meeting	1 day
Desk research and document review	2 days
User research	10 days
Stakeholder interviews	3 days
Presentation of findings to board	1 day
Stakeholder interviews	3 days
Prototype development	10 days
Validation testing	5 days
Wireframes, stakeholder reviews, and amends	10 days
Validation testing	3 days
Wireframe amends	2 days
Handover to design and development	0.5 day
Sign-off workshops	2 days
Post live usability review	10 days

A NEW WEBSITE NOT CONVERTING AS EXPECTED

Recently, we were approached by an organization that had just launched a shiny new website. Unfortunately, they had not seen an improvement in conversion when compared to the old website. This was surprising, given that the old website was difficult to use and the new one appeared to offer significant improvements.

The client wanted to keep their budget to a minimum, both for investigating the problem and for fixing it.

We came to the conclusion that the most cost-effective use of our time would be to run an analytics workshop. This involved key client team members—the boss, plus a developer and a visual designer.

We used a day of our time to prepare for the workshop—understanding the server statistics and key user journeys.

Two UX consultants attended the workshop—to fuel debate and ensure that there was a depth and breadth of knowledge present. We printed out the screens for the key user journeys onto large paper and put them on the wall in order. This gave everyone present a shared, unambiguous understanding of the task at hand.

We began the day by documenting the drop-out rate at each particular stage in the user journey—using sticky notes right onto the screen printouts. This gave us a clear indication of which screens to concentrate on for the rest of the day.

We stepped through the screens that showed a worryingly high drop-off rate and discussed what was happening from the user's point of view. For example, "this is the first time they've seen the full price for their order," "they were expecting to see a summary here, not a different product," or "this confirmation is reassuring." We documented these comments, again with sticky notes on the printouts.

For each screen where we identified a possible negative user reaction, we discussed possible remedies. It was particularly useful to have a developer present, as they were able to comment on the development resource required for suggested improvements. Collectively, we agreed what should be changed, for example changing the order of a list of products for the user to choose from. Where possible, we drew these changes directly onto the screen printouts.

"Quick-wins" are changes to a digital product that are fast and simple for the development team to implement.

The workshop outcome was a list of *quick-wins*: tweaks to the website that would be fast and simple for the development team to implement. These quick-wins aimed to improve the overall UX and hence conversion. Improvements that required a large amount of development rework were documented, but not classified as quick-wins. Everything was documented by taking photographs of the whiteboard and printouts as we worked. This obviated the need for write-up time.

The simple act of collectively stepping through a user journey with the site's users in mind produced a detailed list of improvements. Essentially, this was a hybrid of server analytics (see Chapter 8) and an expert review (see Chapter 10). Running these activities as a workshop ensured that the client participated in uncovering the findings and designing the solutions. Thus, they were able to go away and work with the outcomes, utilizing their deep understanding of the underlying rationale.

Project Outline

Constraints: very small budget for research, design, and development

Activity	Timing
Server analytics and workshop preparation	1 day
Analytics workshop	1 day

NEW PRODUCT LAUNCH

A new product launch calls for a deep understanding of user needs and hence some up-front user research. For a recent project with a modest budget, we were asked to design a wholly new website for an organization. The website itself would not be transactional, but needed to convey complex technical information to the general public.

The key here was to uncover what lay people typically understood of the technical information. What terminology did they use? What process did they go through when researching the field? How could a website support that research?

So we planned a project that spent time at the beginning on understanding user's tasks. First, we ran stakeholder interviews to build a picture of the organization and its needs from the new website. This particular organization had a large number of vociferous stakeholders and we were able to make them all feel heard. We ran user testing and developed a task model. We ensured that we verified the task model with the client, before we began wireframing work. In contrast to lots of our projects, the wireframing aspect of this project was relatively light. Once we had a strong understanding of the user needs, the UX design work was relatively simple. During the design process, we ran a wireframing workshop with the client's subject matter specialists. This ensured we had a common understanding of the user needs, the design solutions required to meet them and, importantly, that the proposed designs were technically accurate. It is often the job of a UX specialist to come into an organization and understand the organization's world in order to translate it into something the layperson can understand.

Finally, it was important to be sure that our interpretation of the user needs and underlying data into wireframes was successful. We ran user testing to validate our wireframes. The user testing was successful in that users were able to easily complete their tasks. As always with user testing, we learned several lessons that allowed us the tweak the designs to fine-tune them further.

Project Outline

Constraints: complex information to portray, lots of interested parties

Activity	Timing
Kick-off meeting	1 day
Stakeholder interviews	1 day
User testing to gather requirements	Half a day test prep Half a day recruitment screener 2 weeks recruitment 1 day testing
Task model development	3 days
Information architecture	2 days
Wireframe workshop	1 day
Wireframes (eight templates)	5 days
Wireframe user testing	1 day wireframe deck prep 2 weeks recruitment 1 day testing
Wireframe amends	1 day

TIPS FOR WORKING WITH...

One of the joys of being UX consultants is getting to work with lots of different disciplines on a daily basis. We get to hear different perspectives, and our designs are critiqued from lots of different angles. Each new view tests our approach and helps us to strengthen the design.

The key to a successful multi-disciplinary design and development project is to include as many different skills as possible early on in the project. There's more on how to work well with clients in Chapter 30.

PRODUCT MANAGERS

In many organizations, a product manager may well have commissioned your work. They could be your main point of contact for your project.

So, what is a product manager? They are responsible for one or more products within a business, such as a specific piece of software, or perhaps a set of related features on a large website. They gather requirements for their product and gain strategic sign-off. They own the product within the business: planning and execution throughout the lifecycle from design and development to deployment, new releases, and perhaps withdrawal. They are the company expert on the product and its competition in the marketplace.

Product managers can come from very different backgrounds. Some are UX and design focused whereas others are business orientated and others again are much more technical.

Here are some tips on working smoothly with product managers:

- Make sure you understand the brief, meet any deadlines, and keep in touch with status reports. Product managers are very busy. They have a lot of plates to spin and need to know that things are going to plan.
- Make sure you ask questions early. Your product manager may have to consult other team members to answer your questions and this could be difficult on short notice.
- Share your work with them as often as possible. Involve them in user research. If they share your understanding of their users, they can go away and build on your work.
- Ask what your work will be used for. Is it to gain sign-off, prove to the wider business that their product is successful, gather user requirements, or inform a product's redesign? This will inform the scope and tone of your work.

PROJECT MANAGERS

It is the project manager's job to keep a project on time and on budget. They often coordinate disparate teams working to different processes and timeframes. They need to see clear signs of progress being made. Any change in UX scope will impact other teams' budget and timelines, so you need to keep your project manager up to date.

Here are some tips on working with project managers:

- At the beginning of the project, explain what you will be delivering and when. Be flexible and try to fit in with their required timings.
- Be honest. If you don't know how long something will take, let your project manager know. If you don't tell them, it may be set in stone in the project plan.
- Work with your project manager to involve different team members in your work, so that the overall UX vision is shared from conception to deployment.
- Explain when you need feedback. Project managers can be useful in getting key stakeholders together to critique your work in time for you to meet your deadlines.
- Meet agreed deadlines. It sounds obvious, but doesn't always happen.
- Communicate any problems as soon as they occur. The sooner you let your project manager know that you'll be unable to meet a deadline, the easier it is for them to alert others and find a workaround.

VISUAL DESIGNERS

Visual designers have to work very closely with many UX outputs. The visual designs can determine whether a user experience succeeds or fails, so it makes sense to work closely with the visual design team throughout the lifecycle of your project. If the visual designers are in-house, they will be experts on the brand you need to embody in your product.

It is the visual designer's job to bring the final look and feel to a product. This will encompass subtle layers of brand identity and emotion on top of IA and wireframe work. This will be achieved by creating a visual language of styles (including typography, colors, layout schemes, spacing, imagery, and texture) that work together to communicate the appropriate tone and emotion to bring the user experience to life.

Here are our tips for working with visual designers:

- Involve visual designers from the start of the project. Invite them to participate in the requirements gathering and ideation process.
- Share your work with the visual designer as often as possible. Elicit their feedback and aim to act on it. Ask if there's anything you can include in your deliverables that will help with their tasks.
- Involve visual designers in user research. They will get a feel for priority and design rationale, which will help with visual design. If they share your understanding of users, they can build on your work long after you have stopped contributing to the project.
- The visual designer brings invaluable expertise to a product's overall user experience. Make sure they don't feel that all they can do is "color in" the wireframes. When visual designers are not involved in the UX process, they can feel constrained rather than empowered by UX deliverables, leading to dull, lifeless designs, or designs that ignore your UX goodness.

Figure 2-2 shows visual design work in progress.

Figure 2-2: Visual design work in progress

SOURCE: Reproduced with permission of cxpartners
© 2012 cxpartners Ltd.

DEVELOPERS

Developers have to work very closely with many UX outputs, so it makes sense to work closely with them throughout the project. It is the developer's job to build UX and visual designs into a fully functional product.

- Involve developers early on in the project. This will help you to understand technical constraints, build relationships, and gain their support.
- Share designs often and early, and elicit feedback. They will be able to advise on the capabilities of the technologies to be used for the project (for example, can you use the

latest HTML widget, or is it not yet widely supported?). They will be able to advise on programmatically tricky interactions before stakeholders become wedded to them.

- Ask if there's anything you can include in your deliverables that will help with their tasks.

- Invite developers to user testing. During requirements gathering, so they understand the reasoning behind the work in the first place. During validation testing, so they understand design rationale and priorities. If developers share your understanding of user needs, they can build on your work when you are no longer there.

- Speak the developer's language and understand their constraints. Be prepared to work with them to overcome problems in a pragmatic fashion—don't stamp your feet and say "but it only works my way."

- If you're out of house, be available to talk through your designs after you've delivered them. It will build good will (think about the next project!). A simple five-minute conversation with a developer struggling with a tricky interaction can mean the difference between a great UX and a broken one. Something that you know to be important to usability may not be obvious to others, and you can't specify everything. They may have found that they cannot exactly implement your recommendations—help them find a user-friendly workaround.

- If you're in-house, make sure you're available to the developers as they work. Find out from them the best way for you to do this. This may involve sitting with them throughout the development process, or attending daily or weekly meetings.

Figure 2-3 shows coding in progress.

Figure 2-3: Development work in progress

UX EXPERTS

UX experts in large organizations often hire external UX expertise for a number of reasons. It may be that they do not have enough staff to cover a particular project. They may want a fresh approach to a new project. They may wish to outsource specific tasks such as user testing or customer experience mapping. They can be extremely fruitful and stimulating clients. They can also sometimes be tricky clients, as they will have a really clear picture of how they expect the work to be done, and may not see the need to express it precisely.

Here are our tips for working with UX experts:

- Find out exactly what they want and how it fits into their program of work. If possible, ask for examples of previous work that they like. Where required, use their templates and house style.
- Don't be afraid to challenge their ideas during discussions. They've hired you because they value your opinion. However, don't forget they are the client—your deliverables need to match their expectations.
- Share your work with the UX team as often as possible. Elicit their feedback and act on it.
- Don't tread on their toes. If you are engaged for a specific task, stick to it. For example, if you are running user testing, you may be tempted to add recommendations for fixing usability problems to your report. Make sure you're sure this is what they want before you do it: in-house UX experts may well be better placed to decide on appropriate usability fixes and would prefer you to concentrate on the detail of the problem.
- Remember you can learn a lot from their experience—be open to new ideas. Their practices just might be better than yours.

SEO EXPERTS

Search engine optimization experts are an integral part of web design projects. As with other experts, the key is to involve them early so that incorporating their feedback into your work is straightforward.

- Ask about any natural search analytics they have. Natural search will give you information on the vocabulary users are using to get to any existing site.
- Ask for information on any planned paid search activity—knowing what traffic the marketing department is hoping to drive to your new site may help you to prioritize your design work.
- Involve SEO experts early in your process. That way, you will have time to negotiate mutually acceptable solutions and include their recommendations in your design work. In particular, they will be interested in your information architecture and sitemap. They will be able to comment on the terminology, site hierarchy, and likely content.

CONTENT SPECIALISTS

Content specialists write and commission the copy and other media users will come to your digital product to view. A brilliant user interface is pointless if it does not relay content that is of interest to users. Involving content specialists in the research and design process will allow them to begin their work at an early stage.

- Ask to see any content plans and inventories that may already exist.
- Collaborate with content specialists to draw up content requirements.

- Involve content specialists as early as possible—remember that it will take time to generate the required content, so you want to be sure that everyone has a shared understanding of what that content should be.

- Invite content specialists to user testing so they can see for themselves user reactions to their work.

RESOURCES

A Project Guide to UX Design: For User Experience Designers in the Field or in the Making (2009) by Russ Unger and Carolyn Chandler

Undercover User Experience Design (2011) by Cennydd Bowles and James Box

Alan Colville's slides on A Shared Vision—the coordinating force behind great UX: www.slideshare.net/alancolville/a-shared-vision-the-coordinating-force-behind-great-ux

Jesmond Allen on working with product managers on the cxpartners blog: www.cxpartners.co.uk/cxblog/what_does_a_product_manager_do_a_brief_primer_for_uxers/

UX RESEARCH AND EVALUATION TOOLS AND TECHNIQUES

3

PLANNING AND CONDUCTING EFFECTIVE STAKEHOLDER INTERVIEWS

STAKEHOLDER INTERVIEWS ARE a fantastic way of finding out what your client wants from the work you are embarking on. They are designed to open a conversation between yourself and important members of your client's team—the stakeholders. They are an opportunity for you as a designer to ask lots of questions up-front and really understand your client's business and what they want from the work you're doing for them.

WHY ARE STAKEHOLDER INTERVIEWS IMPORTANT?

Stakeholder interviews are an important tool in the UX professional's armory. They are a structured way for you to gain insights into the reasoning behind the project you are working on. How will success be measured? What do they really want from the project? Are there any intersecting projects? Are there any internal conflicts you should know about?

Another use for stakeholder interviews is to gain buy-in from senior stakeholders—they feel that they've had their say and will be more comfortable with your involvement. You'll also find out about the background to your project, which may give you important insights into how to proceed with the design. Stakeholder interviews are a good opportunity to look out for potential conflicts between business goals and user requirements or even between key stakeholders.

These are key business requirements for your project. As a user-centered designer, it can be easy to get wrapped up in user requirements and assume that your client has told you everything you need to know about their business requirements. However, a deeper understanding of your client's needs will lead to a more robust design solution for them. After all, the most user-friendly online shop is one where the merchandise is free, but clearly that shop would not be meeting any sound business requirements.

WHEN TO CONDUCT STAKEHOLDER INTERVIEWS

Stakeholder interviews are great for clients with lots of people who have something to say about their new project. They are intended to elicit information about the organization and background of the project. They are also good when you need information about the goals for your project and the client hasn't been explicit about them up front.

The stakeholder interviews described here are useful for adding an understanding of the wider business to your requirements-gathering process. They differ from requirements workshops (Chapter 4) in that they concentrate more on the background of your project, and do not involve making any functionality or design decisions.

WHAT ARE STAKEHOLDERS?

Stakeholders are the people who can affect your project. They are also the people within an organization who are affected by your project. For example, if you are redesigning a content management system (CMS), some stakeholders will be involved directly with commissioning your project. Others will have approved the financial commitment but will not have day-to-day involvement. Others still will be end users of the CMS. Their requirements from the project will differ and the sooner you know this, the better.

WHO SHOULD YOU TALK TO?

The key to successful stakeholder interviews is in talking to the right people. Your primary client contact (likely the project owner) should know whom to begin with. Clearly, every organization is different, so there are no hard and fast rules as to who to speak to. It may be you cannot get access to director-level stakeholders. However, here's a list of the types of stakeholders you should ask to interview:

- The project owner, who is usually your day-to-day project contact.
- The project sponsor, who is often the project owner's boss. The person who advocates the project at the financial decision-making level.
- Representatives of the team who will be involved in the production of your project. Depending on the project, this may include front- and back-end coders, graphic designers, content specialists, and others.
- Someone to represent customer services, preferably a very experienced operative or manager.
- An expert in the product your project will be selling. Ask her to explain the product range to you, along with any long-term plans for the range.
- Company directors. The Chief Financial Officer will understand the financial reasoning behind the project. The Chief Technical Officer will be able to tell you about any important technical innovations or constraints. The Chief Executive Officer is interesting to talk to about the company vision and longer-term goals.
- Someone to represent the company's marketing strategy. He may have specific targets that have not been articulated by the project commissioning team.
- Representatives of stakeholders who will be affected by the project. For example, a salesperson or someone else who must act upon reports generated by the new system, or someone who must input data into a redesigned CMS.

Figure 3-1 shows a checklist of people you may want to conduct stakeholder interviews with. If you cannot get access to senior-level stakeholders, ask the project owner who else in the organization would be able to provide similar information.

Consider the example project to redesign a company's content management system. Imagine that the company sells bouquets of flowers by post and via a countrywide network of franchisees. Talking to the project team would provide a good initial brief for the system. Talking to franchisees may reveal that they are not particularly computer literate and are in a busy shop environment where the computer is far from their primary focus. A business requirement that could be drawn from this is that franchisees' interactions with the new system must be easy to leave and come back to, perhaps with an option to print daily tasks.

Interviewing a product specialist will deepen your understanding of what your project must sell. For example, you may learn that only one particular variety of bouquets is suitable for delivery to a hospital bedside. This may lead to a business requirement to categorize products according to their suitability for different uses. You may also learn that they plan to double the number of products they offer in the next two years. This implies that your navigation and search systems need to be flexible enough to expand to include these new products.

Talking to a customer services manager may reveal that there are a lot of calls to the call center asking if a bouquet has been delivered. Thus another business requirement may be that the system generates a notification to the purchaser that their flowers have been delivered.

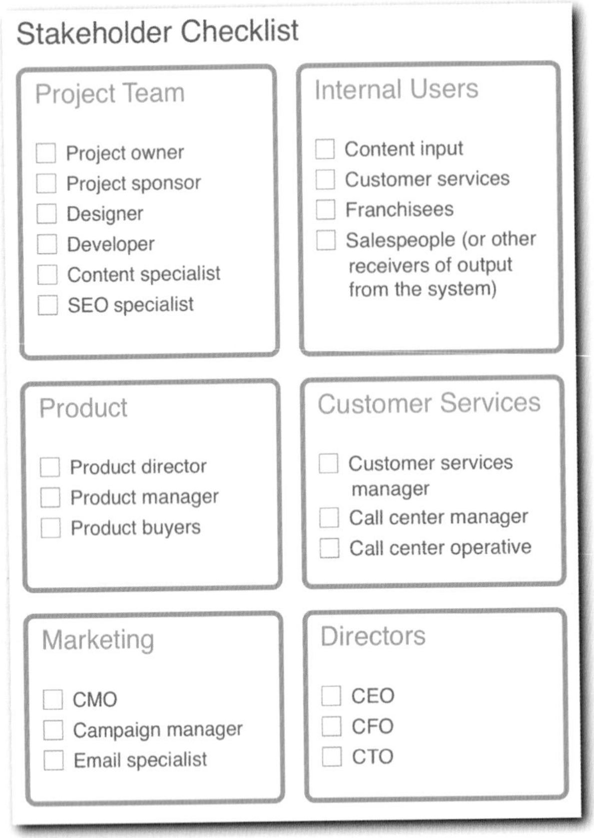

Stakeholder Checklist

Project Team

- [ ] Project owner
- [ ] Project sponsor
- [ ] Designer
- [ ] Developer
- [ ] Content specialist
- [ ] SEO specialist

Internal Users

- [ ] Content input
- [ ] Customer services
- [ ] Franchisees
- [ ] Salespeople (or other receivers of output from the system)

Product

- [ ] Product director
- [ ] Product manager
- [ ] Product buyers

Customer Services

- [ ] Customer services manager
- [ ] Call center manager
- [ ] Call center operative

Marketing

- [ ] CMO
- [ ] Campaign manager
- [ ] Email specialist

Directors

- [ ] CEO
- [ ] CFO
- [ ] CTO

Figure 3-1: Checklist of stakeholders to ask to interview

Talking to someone from marketing may reveal that they'd like to capture bouquet recipients' birthdays so that they can send reminder e-mails. Clearly, there may be a conflict between user needs and business needs over this, but it is extremely useful to capture the requirement. The CEO may tell you that the business plans to expand internationally within the next three years. Thus, there may be another business requirement to produce an internationalizable system (for more on internationalization, see Chapter 32).

HOW TO CONDUCT STAKEHOLDER INTERVIEWS

Stakeholder interviews require a bit of planning and preparation to get right. Here's how we go about it.

PLANNING STAKEHOLDER INTERVIEWS

Plan a day to visit your client's offices to conduct your stakeholder interviews. Often these days need to be scheduled around the senior stakeholders, as they are likely to have the fullest diaries.

It may not be possible to meet everyone you'd like to talk to face to face. Alternative options include:

- Conducting the interview over the phone
- Asking the project owner to conduct the interview and share the results with you
- Asking the stakeholder to complete a written questionnaire

It is a good idea to share your questions with the stakeholders beforehand. This will allow them to prepare their answers and come up with useful examples.

When planning your interviews, allow a half hour to an hour for each interview. If possible, run through your questions with a friend or colleague to ensure they are unambiguous and are in a logical order.

CONDUCTING STAKEHOLDER INTERVIEWS

Spend a little time explaining to your interviewee who you are and why you want to speak to them. Most people are flattered to be asked for their input so will be happy to be there. Tell them how long you expect the interview to last and stick to any time constraints. Of course, if you strike gold in your interview and need more time, you can always arrange this. Figure 3-2 shows a stakeholder interview in progress.

Figure 3-2: Conducting a stakeholder interview

You need to record the answers your interviewee provides. The method you choose will come down to personal taste and the environment you conduct the interviews in. We often type the answers straight into a prepared questionnaire, be that in note-taking software, Word, or a spreadsheet. If you prefer to hand write notes, a printout of your questions for each interviewee, with space to write in the answers, is useful. Alternatively, you may want to record the audio of your interview, either via your computer or a Dictaphone, and transcribe it later. Clearly, this has a time implication in that you must listen to the interviews again in order to take notes.

It is a good idea to prepare *prompts* for interviewees—illustrations or observations that may help set the scene for the stakeholder, or help them to formulate an answer. For example, when asking about success criteria for a project, you could mention reducing calls to the call center, improving conversion rate, or improved customer satisfaction scores. If someone is struggling to provide examples of competitor websites they like or dislike, having some examples ready for them to comment on may remind them.

Here are some example questions you could ask in a stakeholder interview. You certainly don't need to use all of them—pick out the ones that are right for your client and project. It may be that you develop some core questions to ask all your stakeholders and additional questions to ask a particular group, such as senior stakeholders like the CEO or CTO.

We've used the redesign of an existing website as an example project here, but you could substitute *app, mobile site,* or other digital product or a design from the ground up and the questions would be just as relevant.

Example Stakeholder Interview Questions

Introduction

As part of our requirements gathering activities for the new website we are interviewing key stakeholders.

The aim of these interviews is to elicit your views on:

  The existing website

  Where the website should be in the future

  Any key aims and goals you have for the website

We will interview you in person, but do please review the questions before we arrive, and bring with you [printouts /URLs] of any examples you'd like to share.

Questionnaire

About you:

  Name

  Job Title

  What's your role in this project?

Your company and products:

Tell me about your customers.

Tell me about your products.

Which products sell best? Which products sell less well? Which products do you most want users to buy? Are there any plans to change the product range?

How does your company compare to your competitors? (For example, are you more or less upscale? Bigger or smaller? Cheaper or more expensive?) Why should a customer come to you instead of to a competitor?

What is the vision for the company for the next five years?

The current website:

How do you interact with the website? How do you interact with the web team?

What works well?

What could work better?

How do you feel about the existing website?

Is there anything you particularly like about it?

Is there anything you particularly dislike about it?

Which competitor websites do you particularly like?

What exactly is it that you like about them?

Are there any competitor websites do you particularly dislike?

What exactly is it that you dislike about them?

Who are your current website's users?

Are they the same people you want to use the website in future?

How loyal are they? Do they use competitor sites?

Thinking about this project to redesign the website:

Why is this project happening? What's the new website for?

What will make this project successful for you?

How will you be measuring this project's success?

What is the experience you want customers to have from the website?

Are there any burning issues that we must address with this design?

What is the most important thing we should do?

Is the organization working on any other projects that may impact this one? (For example, a branding exercise, change in back-end technologies, or purchase of third-party content)

ANALYZING AND REPORTING YOUR FINDINGS

You need to distil the results of your interviews into something that's useful to you and useful to your client. Did any themes emerge? Did any conflicts emerge? (Common conflicts are between business goals and user goals—the marketing team may want to harvest bouquet recipients' birthdays, but how many users will be happy to supply them? There may also be conflicts between different business goals. Call center operatives won't want the new website to threaten their jobs by reducing calls to customer services. Someone who is keen to increase sales may well be extremely reluctant to require that extra date of birth field to be completed before the sale goes through.)

To begin the analysis process it is useful to see all the answers to a specific question next to each other. This will help identify themes and outliers.

REFLECT YOUR CLIENTS' ANSWERS BACK TO THEM

We find that a good way of reporting findings back is to prepare slides identifying key themes that emerged under the headings used in the questionnaire: Company and Products, Current Website, and the Project.

Figure 3-3 shows a slide from a report on stakeholder interviews. In this instance, we spoke to 14 people over two days and the full report ran to 20 pages. Note that stakeholders' thoughts on the current website have been brought together. Where appropriate, specific quotes have been used to illustrate the point.

Figure 3-3: Slide reporting on the results of stakeholder interviews

The goal here is to reflect your client's answers back to them and ask if you've understood them correctly. Ideally, you will present your findings back to the project owner and anyone else who must sign off your work. Hopefully, this is far fewer people than you conducted stakeholder interviews with.

GENERATE A SHARED UNDERSTANDING

List the various success criteria and find out which are the most important. List any new requirements and find out which must be met and which can be discounted. Include screen-shots of competitor products with your stakeholders' comments alongside. Agree common themes, discuss potential conflicts, and come away from the meeting with a strong, shared understanding of what the project needs to do.

RESOURCES

Human-Computer Interaction by Alan Dix, Janet Finlay, Gregory Abowd, and Russell Beale (an academic textbook that contains an interesting piece on classifying stakeholders)

A Project Guide to UX Design by Ross Unger and Carolyn Chandler (2009)

http://www.uxmatters.com/mt/archives/2007/09/conducting-successful-interviews-with-project-stakeholders.php

Undercover User Experience Design by Cennydd Bowles and James Box

4

ORGANIZING AND RUNNING A SUCCESSFUL REQUIREMENTS WORKSHOP

WHAT SHOULD YOUR UX project to do for your client? What is their vision for the project? How can you help them reach their goals? Conducting a requirements workshop with your client will bring these questions alive. A successful requirements workshop leads to a shared understanding of the problems your project aims to solve.

WHY ARE REQUIREMENTS WORKSHOPS IMPORTANT?

Before embarking on any project, you will have received a project brief. Even if this is as informal as a chat with your client, you will have learned something about what they want from the project. Now you need to flesh out that brief and record any requirements and constraints.

Some clients may have written you a full brief supported by a hefty requirements specification. Others will have taken a much less formal approach. Not everyone's good at articulating exactly what is required from a project, even if they have written a long spec. Requirements workshops are designed to pick apart and explore the brief and to add to it if necessary.

You should leave a requirements workshop with a good understanding of the UX work to come. You will also have established a sense of teamwork with your client.

WHEN TO RUN A REQUIREMENTS WORKSHOP

Requirements workshops should be considered as part of your requirements gathering armory: they help you build a picture of the business and user needs for your project. There are no hard and fast rules for which requirements gathering methods to use for a specific project—you need to choose the method or methods that work for you, your client, and the time and budget available.

Plenty of other research methods for eliciting requirements are covered elsewhere in this book: stakeholder interviews (Chapter 3), usability testing (Chapter 5), competitor benchmarking (Chapter 6), contextual research (Chapter 7), analytics (Chapter 8), and surveys (Chapter 9). It may be that you run a combined requirements and ideation workshop (Chapter 11).

Stakeholder interviews and requirements workshops have similar purposes, but are not exactly the same. Stakeholder interviews are designed to obtain a picture of the high-level aims and objectives from senior players. Requirements workshops focus on hands-on decision-making, likely with a small project team. You'll often spend a day at a client's offices, perhaps conducting stakeholder interviews with senior figures in the morning and running a requirements workshop with the project team in the afternoon. Figure 4-1 shows a requirements workshop in full swing.

Choose to run a requirements workshop if you have a large, complex project where different stakeholders and different requirements may conflict. If you are running a selection of different requirements gathering activities, conducting a requirements workshop to feed back your findings works well.

Figure 4-1: Running a requirements workshop

HOW TO RUN A REQUIREMENTS WORKSHOP

It takes a bit of planning to run a successful requirements workshop. You need to consider when to run it, who to invite, and which workshop activities will be most useful.

PLANNING A REQUIREMENTS WORKSHOP

Think about what you know about your project and what you need to know in order to proceed. Who are your users and what are their requirements? What are your client's objectives (and have you understood them fully)? Are there any constraints? What is the vision for the project? When planning a requirements workshop, you need to identify any gaps in your knowledge and plan activities to address those gaps.

Workshop Activities

Consider what you need to learn from your workshop and plan activities accordingly. Figure 4-2 lists possible activities for a requirements workshop. Choose the information you most need to know and plan to elicit it. How much time do you have available? Allow enough time for each activity and prioritize the activities that will garner the most information. Don't feel you need to conduct all the activities on the menu—pick a few that will meet your needs.

If possible, alternate activities where participants will sit and listen with those where they get to discuss and participate. It will maintain high energy levels in the room.

Figure 4-2 provides a menu of workshop activities to choose from.

You Need To...	Workshop Activities
Set a shared vision for the project and get a feel for your client's desired outcomes	Elevator pitch exercise Competitor likes and dislikes User journey exercise Template prioritization exercise
Understand the thinking behind a hefty requirements spec	Elevator pitch exercise Work to date review
Understand the users of your project	Customer and brand briefing Work to date review Analytics review
Understand user requirements	Analytics review User journey exercise Existing product walkthrough Competitor likes and dislikes
Understand the strengths and weaknesses of any existing product	Analytics review Existing product walkthrough Competitor likes and dislikes Work to date review
Feed back the results of your work to date	Work to date review
Understand any research your client has conducted	Work to date review
Develop a clear brief	Elevator pitch exercise User journey exercise Template prioritization exercise Technical briefing
Understand any products your project will be selling or promoting	Merchandise briefing Customer and brand briefing
Understand technical constraints and opportunities	Technical briefing Involve technical specialists in the whole workshop
Understand your client's brand	Customer and brand briefing

Figure 4-2: Menu of workshop activities for different project needs

Customer and Brand Briefing

Ask your client to provide a briefing on their customers—the users of your product. They may need to bring in one of their marketing experts to do this. Ask them to provide you with demographic and lifestyle information such as age, gender, income, purchasing habits, and so on. This will help you build a picture of whom you are designing for. Being briefed by your client's expert on their customers will allow you to ask questions and test your assumptions. If you plan to create personas (Chapter 14) or conduct usability testing (Chapter 5), this information is a valuable building block.

A digital product should embody the brand values of the organization it represents. If you understand the brand values, you can begin to design the product.

Ask for the briefing to also address your client's brand values. You want to understand the tone of voice your product needs to take and types of imagery it needs to use. How does their brand differ from that of their competitors? What brand values should you be taking into account when making design decisions?

Allow about half an hour for this activity. Make sure that the person who provides the briefing knows how much time they have.

Analytics Review

Your client may have an existing website (or other live product) and collect statistics, for example with Google Analytics. If so, ask their analytics expert to talk through any key findings. Are there any pages with unusually high dropout? Or any that are working particularly well? Google Analytics can't tell you why users behave the way they do, but it can give you some good ideas as to where to look for interesting stories.

Allow about half an hour for this activity. Make sure that the person who provides the briefing knows how much time they have.

User Journey Exercise

This exercise focuses attention on the pages or screens you want your users to visit when they interact with your product.

If you were designing an online shoe shop, the primary user journey would be to purchase a pair of shoes. Another journey might be to add items to a wish list and return later to purchase them. Additional journeys might consider the differences between first time users and those who have visited before.

To conduct a user journey exercise, first agree on the primary user journey. In the case of the shoe website, it will be "a new user buys a pair of shoes." Now, think about the pages a user must visit to complete their task. Discuss the pages with the workshop participants. Write the name of each page on an individual file card or sticky note and stick it to the whiteboard.

Order the cards on the whiteboard to represent the optimum user journey. As you discuss the journey, you may find you need to rearrange the order of the cards. If necessary, draw arrows between the cards to show direction or other annotation.

In the shoe shop example, a user may visit the home page, a category page (such as ladies' high heels), a product page, the shopping cart page, delivery and payment pages, and a confirmation page.

Key functionality can be added to the individual page cards. This may be a note to say that it is possible to refine search results (such as to view only red ladies' high heels) or choose the size of a shoe on a product page. Figure 4-3 shows the results of a user journey exercise.

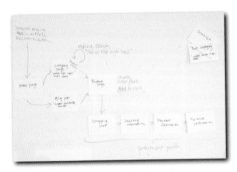

Figure 4-3: User journey for an online shoe shop

This exercise allows you to prioritize templates and understand the journeys that your project should streamline. Don't forget to photograph the results of your discussions for later reference.

The amount of time to allow depends on the number of journeys you need to consider. You will likely be able to cover a couple of simple journeys in half an hour. However, if you need to consider different journeys for several user groups, allow more time.

Competitor Likes and Dislikes

Ask everyone to bring printed screenshots of competitors that they like or dislike to the workshop. Three or four examples for each participant is a good number—not too many to be daunting, but enough to provide plenty of discussion points. Don't forget to include yourself in the exercise.

On the day, ask everyone to share their choices and rationale. Which competitor do they particularly like and why? Which do they hate? Pin the printouts to a wall or whiteboard where everyone can see them. It is sensible to record the key like or dislike on sticky notes attached to the printouts.

When everyone has shared their thoughts, discuss the chosen competitors as a whole. Do any themes emerge? It can often make sense to group the printouts at this point. Perhaps simply under likes and dislikes, but sometimes other interesting patterns emerge. For example, many of the likes may include large product imagery or an informal writing style. Themes can be noted with sticky notes—consider using one color for positive comments and another for negative.

This exercise is a great way of getting a feel for what your client wants from your project. What does a successful product look like to them? What must you not do? A group discussion will dive a lot deeper into the rationale behind your client's choices than a simple list of likes and dislikes would. Don't forget to photograph the results of your discussions, or take them away with you, for later reference.

Allow around 15 minutes per workshop participant for this exercise.

Existing Product Walkthrough

If you are embarking on a redesign project, ask your client to talk you through it. Hook up a computer to a projector and step through key user journeys. Find out what they like about it, what they don't like about it, and why it is being redesigned.

The time this will take depends on the size and complexity of the product, but half an hour should be enough for you to get a good product overview.

Work to Date Review

Have you already completed user research or other requirements gathering activities such as stakeholder interviews, store visits, or competitor reviews? Take some time to present your findings to your client. Don't forget to look at positive as well as negative findings. Elicit their feedback—have you drawn accurate conclusions?

Has your client had any research done prior to you becoming involved? They may have commissioned usability testing or a survey. Ask them to present these findings to the workshop. Now is your chance to ask questions and ensure that there is a shared understanding of the validity of the conclusions. Ask for a copy of the research to take away with you.

You know how long it will take you to review your work to date. However, try to limit this exercise to an hour or so—you want everyone to maintain their concentration. If necessary, present report highlights and share the full version later.

Merchandise Briefing

If your project involves selling or promoting products, you need to have a good understanding of those products. Ask a representative of your client's buying or product team to brief you on their merchandise. What is the product range? Why should users choose one product over another? Why should users choose their product over a competitor's? Which products would the business prefer their customers chose? Are there any plans to expand the product range in the near future?

This will help flesh out requirements such as the number of products any navigation system must accommodate, and how many it will need to accommodate in a year's time. Also, if there is any persuasion required to help customers select the business's preferred product. What are key descriptors for the product page? How can the project help the business differentiate itself from the competition?

Ask for a presentation of up to half an hour on merchandise. If they can bring samples along with them, all the better.

Technical Briefing

Are you providing UX input to a project to which others are providing the technical expertise? You need to understand if there are any design constraints caused by the technical implementation.

Ask a member of your client's technical team (or any outside agency providing technical expertise) to brief the workshop on the technologies to be used and any design implications. These implications will include both constraints and opportunities.

Ask for a short 15 to 30 minute briefing.

Elevator Pitch Exercise

Use this exercise to develop an *elevator pitch* for your project. The discussions required to complete the exercise should uncover some great information about what your client wants from your project. The finished elevator pitch will provide an excellent reference point for design decisions later.

The exercise centers on filling in the blanks in the following sentence:

> *For [primary user group] who [has a key need], [product name] is a [description of product] that is [brand quality]. Unlike [primary competitor], the product is [unique selling point].*

For the online shoe shop example, you could end up with something like:

> *For ladies who wear fashionable shoes who are short on time, ShoeUX.com is an online shoe store that is up to the minute. Unlike RubbishShoes.com, ShoeUX.com stocks 1000s of shoes to choose from.*

To derive this sentence, you need to discuss the product's user groups and their needs, the product's reasons for existence, and its differences from the competition. We like to run this discussion by writing lists on flipcharts or whiteboards. Start with user groups. Write a list of everyone the client expects to use the product. For the shoe shop example, it may be women aged 18–35, men aged 18–35, and mothers buying for their children aged 8–14, all interested in high fashion. Your client wants to sell mainly to women buying for themselves, so this is your primary user group; the first gap in your sentence is filled.

When you have agreed on your primary user group, move on to list their needs. The shoe buyers may live away from cities with boutique shops, they may work full time and struggle to find the time to shop, or they may find the range of shoes available to them locally is limited or not cutting-edge. In the previous example, the workshop participants have agreed that the main issue for their customers is lack of time to shop. Figure 4-4 shows an elevator pitch exercise in progress.

Figure 4-4: Elevator pitch exercise for an online shoe shop

Continue in this way until you have enough information to complete the sentence: describe your product, its key brand qualities, competitors, and unique selling point. Brand qualities can be a little tricky, but here you're looking for words like traditional, modern, trustworthy, fun, friendly, authoritative, quirky, and other adjectives.

The conversations you have in order to complete the sentence are often as valuable as the completed sentence itself. We often write the lists before revealing that we have a sentence to finish. Discuss and write the lists, and then reveal the sentence and agree on the primary item on each list in order to complete the sentence. Allow at least an hour for this exercise—you have several lists to write and plenty to discuss.

These exercises are designed to produce interesting discussions. Often the key insights come from the conversation itself, rather than the output of the exercise.

Are you working on a project where you design and build an entire app or website? If not, you may be delivering a specific number of page templates from which the entire product will be extrapolated. If so, you need to agree with your client exactly which templates to produce.

List on the whiteboard or flipchart any screens you know your project will need. This exercise works well in conjunction with the user journey exercise—run the user journey exercise to identify key screens and prioritize them in your templates list. For example, the user journey exercise may help identify the need for a "wish list" template.

Once you are happy with your list, number them in order of priority. For an online shop, there will be several pages that the site simply cannot exist without. After that, priority may be determined by a number of factors, including release phases, length of development time, as well as user requirements. For the shoe shop, you might write a list something like this:

1. Homepage
2. Product page
3. Shopping cart
4. Shipping details
5. Payment details
6. Purchase confirmation page
7. Category page (for example, women's high heels)
8. Wish list page
9. Account area
10. Customer services
11. About us page
12. Search results
13. How to fit shoes page
Etc.

The first six templates are so numbered because they represent the primary user journey: to purchase a pair of shoes. After that, the category page may be considered a vital tool in finding the right pair of shoes. A search tool could be less important because users are more likely to browse via the category page than search. This exercise often identifies pages that can use the same template. In this example, a category page and a search result may in fact be very similar, and both the about us page and the how to fit shoes page can likely both utilize a generic "content" template.

How many templates have you agreed to work on? If you have more templates on your template list than you have agreed to design, this exercise is very useful for understanding your client's priorities. Draw a line under the last template you will work on. Is everyone happy that the project will work without the templates below the line? Are you designing a product that will get built in phases? This exercise will help your client to plan logical phases and to brief developers as to the functionality required for each release. Figure 4-5 shows a template prioritization exercise.

Figure 4-5: Template prioritization exercise for an online shoe shop

Allow 30 minutes to one hour for this exercise. You will need less time if you have already run the user journey exercise.

Who to Invite

To keep your requirements workshop manageable yet useful, you need to invite the key decision makers within your client's team. You need to be sure that the information you glean is correct and complete. But you need the discussion to stay focused, so keeping the number of attendees to a minimum is sensible. Consider inviting:

- The project owner (likely your project contact)
- The project sponsor (the person with financial responsibility for the project, often the project owner's boss)
- A representative from the technical team
- A representative from the graphic design team
- A representative from the internal UX team
- The project manager

Before the Workshop

Discuss with the project owner who to invite and agree a date.

Plan your workshop activities and write an agenda, including timings. Highlight any "homework" activities that attendees must complete before the workshop. Don't forget to schedule lunch and coffee breaks. These workshops can be intense and everyone needs a breather. Figure 4-6 shows an example requirements workshop agenda.

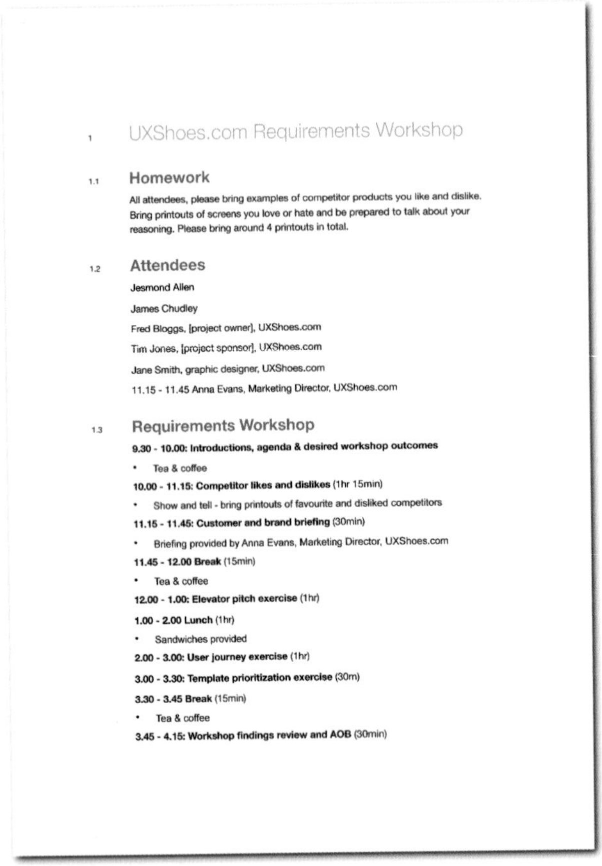

1 UXShoes.com Requirements Workshop

1.1 **Homework**

All attendees, please bring examples of competitor products you like and dislike. Bring printouts of screens you love or hate and be prepared to talk about your reasoning. Please bring around 4 printouts in total.

1.2 **Attendees**

Jesmond Allen

James Chudley

Fred Bloggs, [project owner], UXShoes.com

Tim Jones, [project sponsor], UXShoes.com

Jane Smith, graphic designer, UXShoes.com

11.15 - 11.45 Anna Evans, Marketing Director, UXShoes.com

1.3 **Requirements Workshop**

9.30 - 10.00: Introductions, agenda & desired workshop outcomes

- Tea & coffee

10.00 - 11.15: Competitor likes and dislikes (1hr 15min)

- Show and tell - bring printouts of favourite and disliked competitors

11.15 - 11.45: Customer and brand briefing (30min)

- Briefing provided by Anna Evans, Marketing Director, UXShoes.com

11.45 - 12.00 Break (15min)

- Tea & coffee

12.00 - 1.00: Elevator pitch exercise (1hr)

1.00 - 2.00 Lunch (1hr)

- Sandwiches provided

2.00 - 3.00: User journey exercise (1hr)

3.00 - 3.30: Template prioritization exercise (30m)

3.30 - 3.45 Break (15min)

- Tea & coffee

3.45 - 4.15: Workshop findings review and AOB (30min)

Figure 4-6: Requirements workshop agenda

If you are running the workshop at your client's offices, ask for a room big enough for all the attendees to move about in—you want everyone to have a chance to grab a marker pen and contribute. If possible, secure a room with a whiteboard, flipchart, and projector. If any of these things are unavailable, it's better to know in advance and come prepared.

Take the kit you'll need with you:

- The agenda (so you can stick to it!)
- Your homework and any other printouts
- Blu-Tack putty (for sticking up homework and completed flipchart sheets)
- Whiteboard pens in different colors

- Flipchart stand, paper, and pens (especially if there's no whiteboard in the meeting room—it's vital that you have somewhere to write and draw throughout the workshop)
- Sticky notes (different colors if possible—such as pink for negative comments, green for good, and yellow for neutral)
- Camera to record whiteboard contents before erasing (we use the cameras on our phones—they're plenty good enough for this purpose)
- If you use a Mac, take a monitor dongle to connect your laptop to the projector

RUNNING THE WORKSHOP

Start the workshop with introductions and a quick run-through of the agenda and aims of the workshop.

As the workshop progresses, try to stick to the schedule—you can always park lively areas of discussion and make a note to come back later.

As the workshop facilitator, it's your job to stimulate and lead discussion, not to just stand and talk. Kick the discussions off, stand at the whiteboard and write, but make sure you're writing what others are saying.

If possible, write up any key decisions somewhere you can keep them visible to all throughout the workshop. Filled flipchart sheets stuck to the walls work well for this, or a second whiteboard. This way, you can refer back to earlier discussions throughout the day. If you have to clear a whiteboard to make space for more workshopping, photograph it before you wipe it.

Wrap up the workshop by reviewing your decisions—reiterate the findings from the day's activities, the key points that were written up. Do the notes that were made early in the day still stand? Did any patterns emerge? You should now have a good sense of where the project must go next, and hopefully a strong sense of teamwork with your fellow workshop participants.

AFTER THE WORKSHOP

After a successful workshop, you and your client should have a shared understanding of requirements for your project. Depending on the activities you conducted, you'll have various useful insights and lists: prioritized templates, user journeys, an elevator pitch, and more. You may also have notes from one or more briefings.

If your workshop included briefings, for example on customers, brand, or analytics, ask for copies of any materials you were shown. If you showed any work to date, share digital copies with the client.

If possible, spend some of the next day writing up your notes and the contents of the flipchart paper and photos of whiteboards. You don't need to write up every word, but distilling the essence of the workshop is a useful exercise. It may be that you come away from the workshop and write up a list of specific requirements, or it may be that it is enough to have absorbed the day's activities. Share your notes with your client, along with any whiteboard photos—it's good to have a record of the workshop to refer back to as you progress with the project. Ask your client to comment on your notes—this will verify that your understanding of the workshop outcomes is the same as theirs.

RESOURCES

Alan Colville's "A Shared Vision" slides:
http://www.slideshare.net/alancolville/a-shared-vision-the-coordinating-force-behind-great-ux

Harvard Business Review blog, *A Logo is Not a Brand* by Dan Pallotta:
http://blogs.hbr.org/pallotta/2011/06/a-logo-is-not-a-brand.html

A Project Guide to UX Design: For User Experience Designers in the Field or in the Making (2009) by Russ Unger and Carolyn Chandler

Game Storming: A Playbook for Innovators, Rulebreakers, and Changemakers (2010) by Dave Gray, Sunni Brown, and James Macanufo

5

PLANNING, CONDUCTING, AND ANALYZING A USABILITY TEST

USABILITY TESTING SIMPLY involves asking people to use something and observing what problems arise from using it. It can be used to test all manner of things, from websites, mobile apps, and software to consumer products, services, and business processes.

Despite its name it's nothing to do with testing "users" themselves. It's all about testing things with people who might use them with an objective of improving them and learning more about how they are used.

Usability testing can sometimes get confused with market research. Market research is all about gathering opinions, whereas usability testing is about observing actual behavior in some sort of controlled environment and learning from it.

WHEN TO PERFORM A USABILITY TEST

Usability testing can be conducted at any time in the User Centered Design (UCD) process but most beneficial usability testing happens as early as possible. This is because the cost of fixing any issues is typically lower in the early stages when little if any budget has been spent on design or development.

Ideally, usability testing happens more than once during a project. Usability testing may be used to benchmark an existing site initially and then again later in the process to validate a new design approach. Other projects may do numerous small-scale tests to rapidly iterate a product.

Remember, you should always try to involve users in some way, whatever the constraints of your budget or deadlines.

A key principle of user experience design is that you should always try to involve users in some way whatever the constraints of your budget or deadlines. You will be amazed how much you will learn from even one quick test with someone in your office.

When you test will often reflect on why you are testing in the first place. You might also be choosing to test with users early in the project because you have one of the following problems to solve.

HOW CAN YOU BENCHMARK THIS EXISTING DESIGN/ MOBILE APP/ PAPER FORM?

Usability testing is a great way of benchmarking something because it will uncover a long list of problems that you can solve within your project. It also serves to validate the issues that your client may feel are the problems that might, in reality, be superseded by bigger issues that you uncover by testing.

Benchmarking happens early in a project because it allows the project team to get a sense of what they are dealing with. It allows them to answer questions such as the following:

- How broken is this?
- Where are the majority of the issues?
- Have we planned the project correctly given the extent of the issues?
- Is the focus of the project brief still correct given what we now know?

Figure 5-1 shows a mobile app being tested early in the design process.

HOW DO YOU GATHER THE USER'S REQUIREMENTS?

User requirements are hard to identify. Business requirements by comparison are relatively easy, as you often have access to everyone you need and they generally know what they want.

Users are harder to pin down. Who are they for a start? Where do they hang out? How do you know what to ask them when you find them? Will they be able to articulate their "requirements" in a way that helps you?

Figure 5-1: Mobile apps, as with any other digital product, will benefit from early usability testing

Usability testing is a great way of identifying requirements. If you are redesigning a new hotel-booking site and ask someone to show you how they would go about booking a room they will demonstrate their requirements to you. At the end of just a few sessions it will start to become clear what the website must allow the users to do.

WHY ISN'T THIS WORKING AS WELL AS IT SHOULD?

Often a client or colleague will come to you as a user experience person with a problem that they want you to investigate. As a web professional it is likely that you will have an idea of what is wrong but a great way to investigate further is to run some usability tests to see what problems become apparent.

A typical focus on e-commerce sites for optimization is around the checkout process. In a commercial environment a small change to improve the user experience can reap huge financial rewards and is as such a prime area for user research. Usability testing allows you to try to understand why your client is seeing drop off in certain parts of the process and will identify the steps that users don't understand which lead to incomplete transactions.

Because you, your colleagues, and your clients are so close to the product you can often struggle to understand how users are failing to complete seemingly simple tasks. Usability testing provides an ideal method to remind you how "real" people will perceive your product and can often recalibrate your projects team's understanding of their users.

HOW GOOD IS THE COMPETITION?

Often with a new project you may find yourself working in an unfamiliar industry or with organizations you may have never heard of. A great way of immersing yourself into this strange new world is to run some user tests with users who are familiar with the market.

This approach works so well because you can ask users to explain what things mean as well as see how well, or how badly, the competitor's sites perform. It is often tricky to ask a client what you think might be a stupid question but your users will not care and will probably enjoy sharing their knowledge.

Usability testing of competitor sites will uncover what they do well and what they do badly. When this is combined with a benchmark test of an existing client website, you can quickly understand the domain your client is operating within and where you can make suggestions that will offer significant competitor advantage to your clients.

YOU'VE REACHED A STALEMATE IN YOUR PROJECT; NO ONE CAN DECIDE WHAT TO DO NEXT!

Design projects can become highly political, particularly when an agency doesn't agree with a client's decision or when there is disagreement within an organization or between departments. In this situation one of the best things you can do is to run a usability test.

This works well because it not only diffuses a potentially harmful conflict but it represents a practical solution for moving the project forward. In effect, the decision-making is passed to the users. The conversations following the testing change from "I think we should do x" to a more useful, "Do you remember the problems that feature x created; we really should prioritize fixing that."

The output of every usability test is usually a long to-do list, such as the one shown in Figure 5-2. A prioritized to-do list gives a derailed project back its direction and focus. It's also really useful when the client asks you a tricky question to be able to answer "That's a really interesting question, we should include that in the testing and find out."

YOUR CLIENT HAS ASKED FOR SOMETHING "INNOVATIVE" THAT WILL WIN AWARDS

Often agencies are under pressure to innovate and to show clients something new. They may be focusing on winning pitches or awards. People may feel they need to really push the boundaries of web design to stand out from their competitors.

As someone who is responsible for the user experience of a product this can be a difficult situation, particularly if you work within an agency. It's no easy feat to design something that is truly innovative and impresses you clients, yet remains easy to use. As the UX person, you may be viewed as the killer or innovation if you keep questioning how usable all the seemingly crazy ideas will be in reality.

Often with a particularly different creative concept, a client may be worried about investing in something that is so different from the norm. You can use this anxiety to help ensure that you get support to hold some usability tests. These tests will keep the more "innovative" ideas in check and ensure the end result remains useful and usable.

Prioritized 'to do' list

	Issue area	Severity
Users are given no sense of progress within the checkout	User expectation	●●●●●
The form doesn't make it clear where & when errors have been made.	Form validation	●●●●●
Users were given reassurance that the checkout was secure.	Messaging	●●●●○
There is a lack of help during the checkout process.	Help & support	●●●●○
Users wanted to be able to split deliveries between different addresses.	Delivery	●●●●○
Verified by Visa caused some people to give up.	Payment methods	●●●●○
Gift wrapping is confusing and comes at the wrong point in the process.	Upsell	●●●●○

Figure 5-2: Prioritize your recommendations to convey to the readers what you feel are the priority issues that need to be addressed first

As user-centered design becomes a more and more widely adopted design approach, the issue of usability stifling creativity and innovation will become less of an issue. However, you are still likely to come across it. I have even seen usability test results withheld by project stakeholders when they don't support their ideas. It's a jungle out there! Make sure that you can get stakeholders to view tests so they can see the issues first hand.

The outcome of any usability testing in these circumstances can clearly become highly political. Often you may need to make recommendations that you know will lead to amends that there is no budget to pay for. You also need to be careful that you rate the severity of the issues appropriately and that you recommend appropriate remedies to problems. All you can do is give an honest report of what you saw and make the recommendations you feel that will make the biggest improvements.

YOU'VE HAD AN IDEA BUT YOU'RE NOT SURE THAT IT WILL WORK

During a design project there will always be certain aspects that you feel unsure about how they will work with users. They are often the result of a random requirement from a client or an "innovative" idea that may have come from a member of the project team.

Usability testing presents a perfect solution to determining a direction of travel. If conducted early enough it can allow project teams to either kill a feature or an idea dead or to pursue it. This approach represents appropriate due diligence on the part of the designer as at every possible stage you've tested your designs.

In summary, the examples given here illustrate how usability testing can be useful at many different points within the design process for all manner of different reasons, some political, some tactical, and some just plain sneaky in order to keep you design projects on track.

WHY IS USABILITY TESTING IMPORTANT?

Usability testing is fundamentally important because by doing it and acting upon what you learn, you will improve whatever it is you are designing. The most important aspect of usability testing is that by doing it you are involving users in the design process. By testing, you will be able to watch something you have worked on be used. This in itself can be immensely rewarding and educational.

Another important aspect of usability testing is that it allows project stakeholders to see the product being used. This serves to open their eyes to its strengths and weaknesses as well as generating usage stories that the project team can refer back to when making design decisions. You will find you no longer need to justify changing something if it has failed in testing when team members have also witnessed it first hand.

One of the most wonderful aspects of usability testing is getting a chance to talk to people and to understand how they see the world. I believe that user experience people are fascinated by people and by testing with others, they get a chance to be reminded what real users are really like.

> Tip: It's all too easy when surrounded by experts in typical design environments to assume that everyone is as savvy as you. You will be too close to your product and you will know it too well. Watching someone completely fail to be able to use a design can be a humbling experience and one that acts as a reality check for many designers.

Sometimes it can be hard to convey to project stakeholders what problems people will have with the designs they are proposing. I love getting designers and developers to watch testing because this means they will see if for themselves.

My favorite experience involved a graphic design colleague who was watching his designs being tested. He watched in amazement as users failed to understand some icons he had designed. Before the tests had finished he had ran off to his desk to rectify the problems. I didn't have to explain the issues; he saw them for himself and from the day evangelized usability testing, having previously been somewhat under enthusiastic!

One benefit of usability testing that is seldom discussed is how it can be used to identify areas for product innovation and competitive advantage. I remember testing an insurance quoting tool with financial advisers. They described to me how the tool could be improved if it showed the profit they would make from the quotes. They told us how they had been crying out for this and how none of the competition was offering it. It is these genuine insights that can give you such a buzz because you know how big an impact they will have on the final product.

Usability testing can be a good way of getting a wayward project back on track, as it will generate a long list of things that need to be addressed. In this way it can be used to evaluate products at any stage of the lifecycle, both new and old. As long as findings are prioritized it can offer a way of identifying where improvement work should be focused, thus making the most effective use of available budget.

HOW TO CONDUCT A USABILITY TEST

A typical usability test breaks down into four phases—planning, doing, analyzing, and reporting.

This checklist starts at the point when you have had approval to undertake the usability testing and is designed primarily to be used for face-to-face "observed" testing however much of it is still relevant for other methods such as remote testing.

PLANNING YOUR USABILITY TEST

A well-planned usability test will help to ensure that you have recruited the right people, set the right objectives, and used the correct methodology to match your budget and timescales.

If you fail to plan properly, it is likely that something will go wrong that will jeopardize both the quality of your results and your client's confidence in using you again.

What Are the Objectives of the Research?

You will need to establish clear objectives for the usability testing to allow you to prepare the necessary material to test, to write a good test plan, and to help with the structure of your report. It's okay for your objectives to be high level—such as "can users find out the weather forecast for their vacations"—just make sure you have something, because your objectives become the foundations around which the test is built and reported upon. Figure 5-3 shows that outcomes and objectives should be the focus of any project kick-off meeting.

The best way to get good objectives is to hold a kick-off meeting with the project team and ask the stakeholders to clarify what they want to find out about. Make sure you understand them clearly and that they are realistic, as they will form the basis of your test plan.

Figure 5-3: Kick-off meetings should focus on gathering overall project objectives

A suitable agenda for a kick-off meeting could look like the following:

1. Introductions
2. Roles and responsibilities
3. Objectives of the usability testing
4. Scope of tests and test materials

   What will be tested?

   When will test material be ready?

5. Recruitment

   Who do you need to recruit for the testing?

   What will the incentive be for participating?

   What are the different user groups and how many will be represented in testing (recruiting both representatives from business and leisure users of travel websites)?

   Are there any existing documents that will assist the recruiters (customer lists and marketing segmentation documents)?

   Are recruits to be recruited from client lists or from recruiters databases?

   Are there any special considerations you need to consider for recruitment? Anyone that you need to make sure you don't recruit?

6. Test logistics

   Where will the tests take place?

   Will stakeholders be able to observe tests? If so, how many will come? Will they need food?

   Do the tests require specialist equipment such as eye trackers?

   Will participants require any login details to access any test materials?

7. Reporting and analysis

Agree on delivery date and format of report as well as date and location of presentation if applicable.

8. Next steps

Agree on dates for delivery of typical documents, such as recruitment brief, project plans, and other project management documentation, test plans, and presentation reports.

Test Material

The exact nature of the test material can vary from sketches (such as those shown in Figure 5-4) and printouts to clickable wireframes and fully functioning websites. You will need to agree with project stakeholders exactly what is required for the testing and ensure that it is signed off before it goes into testing.

Figure 5-4: Rough sketches are some of the first design outputs that become available to test

Test Plan

A test plan, such as the one shown in Figure 5-5, documents the objectives and structure of the test. It is written once the objectives and test materials have been established. It is important, as it clarifies the scope of what is to be tested and is used by the facilitator during the tests to make sure everything is covered.

You should make sure that your client has seen and signed off the test plan. This gives them confidence that you will be asking the right questions and also gives you the peace of mind that you haven't missed anything.

Test Plan

(60 minutes)

General topics to note

- Any general usability issues – roadblocks to efficiency/effectiveness/satisfaction
- Focus on usability issues that could impact upon conversion

Pre test

(10 minutes)

Previous experiences:

- Talk me through a recent online shopping experience.
- What were you trying to buy and were you successful?
- Which websites did you use?
- How did you go about choosing what to buy?
- Did you have any problems? Did the website make it easy to buy from?
- What should the website have offered to improve your experience?

We will endeavour to get each participant to play out a familiar scenario that is as similar as possible to their own real experiences in order that they engage with the process as meaningfully as possible.

Switch user over to clients homepage

http://prototype.webshopper.com

Figure 5-5: A well written test plan is absolutely essential to a successful usability test

Recruitment of Users

If your test participants are not representative of your client's users then redo your recruitment again until they are. It only takes one experience of a client walking out of a report presentation because the recruitment wasn't right to make this sink in (and we were only on slide 3)!

There are all manner of ways to recruit people, from professional recruiters (which can be expensive) to more guerilla techniques such as recruiting from social networks or adverts in the paper. Whatever method you choose, expect it to take 10 times the amount of work you expected. If your budget allows, find a professional to do it for you.

The best way to ensure you get good recruits is to write a recruitment brief (as shown in Figure 5-6) that details exactly how many people you want from each user type, the time, date/s, and location of testing, the incentive, and any people to screen out such as web designers and people who have recently taken part in a similar session.

Ask your client to sign off on your recruitment brief and then send it to your recruiter, who will create a screener. The screener is used to "screen" potential recruits when they are qualified over the phone. We would recommend that you get your client to sign off on the screener too, to make sure everyone has seen all of the recruitment documents.

However many people you test, always assume some won't show up. You should always recruit extra people (budget for one extra per day) and pay them to be available all day should someone not show up.

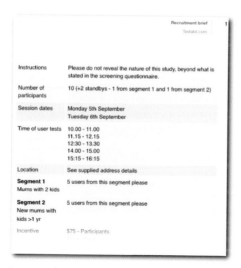

Figure 5-6: The recruitment brief contains all the information a recruiter needs to get the right users for testing

Incentives

The amount you offer to pay depends on whom you are testing with and how long you need them. If you need doctors and lawyers or anyone to whom time is money expect to pay larger incentives. Your recruiter can help you to judge what will is appropriate to offer people if you get stuck.

Make sure that you check with your accountant about the tax implications of handing out incentives to users. You may need to ask users to sign a disclaimer that states that they will take responsibility for paying tax on that incentive.

Often your client may want to offer vouchers for their products as incentives, which can present a very cost-effective way of providing incentives. Whatever you decide, don't forget that your incentives need to be suitable in order to encourage people to participate.

Test Location Logistics

It is essential that you are familiar with the location within which you are testing. Check how test participants will be dealt with when they arrive, where clients/stakeholders will sit, and what kit is required for your testing.

If you are using a venue for the first time, always visit it in advance of your testing and make sure it has what you need. The day of the test with a room full of clients is no time to find out the equipment is subpar.

If you plan for everything to go wrong, you will be prepared when something inevitably does!

Do a Test Run

Always do a test run of your usability test a week before your proper tests. The test run gives you a chance to get familiar with the test plan and get a clear idea of whether you can fit everything into the allotted time. It is tempting to try to cram lots into testing and you need to make sure the scope remains achievable within the allocated time.

CONDUCTING A USABILITY TEST

The environment within which you are testing will generally determine what kit you'll need to set up. If you are in a formal lab you will need to organize feeds of the user's monitor and video and audio feeds of the room to be available in the observation room.

A more "guerilla" (outside of the lab) approach will mean you'll need less kit. Software like Silverback (http://silverbackapp.com/) and Morae (http://www.techsmith.com/morae.html) allow you to turn a laptop into a mobile usability-testing lab, which allows you to test pretty much anywhere. Before you use these tools make sure you have loads of disc space to save videos to as they output large files.

Facilitation Team

Taking notes while you're facilitating a usability testing session can be very tricky as you're essentially trying to do two things at once. An easier alternative is to ask someone to take the notes for you. You should ensure that this person is fully briefed and writes notes in a format that is conducive to report writing. You may, for example, decide on a way of coding the notes so that it is easy to pull out different categories of observations such as user errors, tasks start and end times, system errors, and great ideas to fix problems!

The team can include people who welcome users and get them signed in as well as people who keep the flow of drinks and food arriving in the observation room.

Conducting a Test

A typical test will involve a test facilitator asking a user to attempt to complete a series of tasks and encouraging that person to describe what they are doing as they do it. This is known as the "think aloud" protocol, as users are essentially thinking aloud while they get on with their task. Another protocol you may hear is the "retrospective think aloud" protocol, where users are asked to tell you about something they did after they did it. We generally use the think aloud protocol as it makes it easy to pick up on things as and when they happen. You also don't rely on people's memory to recollect why they did things.

Figure 5-7 shows a facilitator doing their job identifying the user's expectations and understanding of a product so that the product team can understand more about how people expect it to behave.

Figure 5-7: Test facilitation often involves juggling taking notes, keeping to time and making sure you get feedback on all of the key areas of your digital product

A well-facilitated session results in usability issues becoming apparent from the user using the product in the most realistic way possible. Good facilitators are good with people and are able to put them at ease within strange environments such as usability labs. Good facilitators are also able to keep a session on track to ensure the important elements are covered.

One way of planning a test session is to think of it in terms of a hierarchy of needs. First make sure the users are comfortable so offer them a drink and let them adjust the keyboard and mouse. Then put them at ease by discussing what the session will involve and reassure them that they are not being tested and that there are no right or wrong answers. Then finally explain the context of the session and explain in detail what they will be doing. Thinking of it in this way helps you to both remember what to say and also to keep the sessions consistent between users.

To allow the session to change based on particular user behavior, we often run Skype between the observation and testing room to allow observers to send questions over and get more involved with the test. This is an excellent way of ensuring specific client questions are addressed at the most relevant point within the usability testing session.

Duration of Tests

The duration of the session will depend on how formal the testing is and the amount of material you want to test. Regardless of this, you should not be running test sessions that exceed 60 minutes, as everyone involved becomes tired and the value of the sessions quickly diminishes.

Test Observers

As a rule it's a good idea to locate observers away from the room where testing is taking place as can be seen in Figure 5-8. A separate room that takes a video feed as opposed to one that is located next door with a two-way mirror has two advantages. Using a two-way mirror means the observation room needs to be dark and sitting in a dark room for a day sends people to sleep! Secondly, observers generally like to discuss what is happening (often very loudly), which can disrupt the testing session itself.

You should encourage as many project stakeholders as possible to watch test sessions. The benefit of them seeing people fail to use their products first-hand far exceeds any report or anecdote that recalls the same situation.

You should always ensure that a few copies of the test plan and lists of recruited users are available in the observation room so that observers can follow the sessions.

Figure 5-8: Separating observers from the live sessions results in a better experience for everyone

How Many Users Are Enough?

The constraints of your project, such as budget and timescales, will generally dictate how many users you test with more than any rules of thumb. Remember that user testing is predominantly used as a form of qualitative research, so you needn't worry about statistical significance.

If you can get six users to spend an hour each, you will generally generate more issues than most projects have the budget to address. If your user base has many different user types you may wish to get a few of each, which may push the numbers up.

Jakob Nielsen has some great advice on how many users to test with. He advises that you will expose the majority of your issues from testing with five users at a time but critically you should then be running multiple tests. So if you have a budget for 10 users, test with 5 and fix the issues, then test with the remaining 5. This is much more beneficial than testing with 10 first off, because it gives you an extra iteration of improvements to the design.

Be prepared for senior managers to comment on the validity of your recommendations on the basis of having tested it only with five users. If you are conducting explorative research, small numbers are absolutely fine for identifying the major design problems.

Although you can't infer from the tests that a certain percentage of end users will have a particular problem, you can say this target customer had this problem, and this is the reason why, and if you don't fix it, you can expect others to have the same issue. It can be a judgment call as to how likely a problem might be a one-off issue. Factors like the number of users in the test who had the same problem, the level of severity, and the confidence of the facilitator that the scenario was realistic and uncompromised all contribute to the severity rating of the issue.

However, if you are asked to prove or measure something, more quantitative methods like multivariate testing (MVT) or large-scale remote testing are probably more appropriate to offer the confidence levels that may be needed to make large-scale changes.

Recording Test Sessions

If possible you should record your usability tests. You'll forget what people said after a number of sessions and a recording gives you the option of showing video clips to stakeholders who could not attend the sessions. Video clips can be extremely effective to get senior stakeholder buy-in mainly because they are quick and easy to view.

The downsides to recording include the size of the recording files and the time it takes to go back through recordings to pull out key clips. If you need to supply clips be sure to secure the extra time this will take in the plan. You should timestamp interesting usability testing events in your usability-testing notes so it's easier to go back and find those events should you wish to make clips of them.

No Shows

It is inevitable that one or more of your users will not turn up for whatever reason. Your recruiter will often inform you that someone cannot attend as they will usually call round them in the morning to remind them of the sessions. Ensure that your spare person stays within a five-minute walk away from the testing so they can be drafted in at short notice.

Involving Observers in Taking Notes

You can involve observers by asking them to record usability issues they spot on sticky notes (as shown in Figure 5-9), which can be discussed in a workshop following the sessions or just stuck on a wall to be used to write the report. This approach can work well if you don't have the luxury of a note taker or if you just want to involve observers more in the process.

This may seem an attractive idea because you are essentially getting the observers to help you to record issues, but remember they are not necessarily seeing the sessions through impartial eyes and may not record issues in the same way as a UX focused note taker would.

This approach has worked very well for us in the past when we have been commissioned to test products on a very small budget, which didn't allow a longer analysis and reporting phase. We simply got all observers to record issues and then facilitated a quick prioritization workshop after the testing which gave the client an ordered to do list to focus on.

Figure 5-9: You can involve test observers by asking them to record usability issues on sticky notes

ANALYZING AND REPORTING YOUR FINDINGS

A good usability report provides project stakeholders with what they need. Ensure that you understand what their often-tacit needs are. Often, people on a team need an external objective opinion in order to do something they already know needs doing; presentations and standalone documents might be appropriate. Or perhaps the team needs to build on the findings and reach consensus about the next step, in which case a light debrief and a stakeholder workshop with documented outcomes might be needed. Or perhaps the client is working in an Agile environment and would rather you were on hand for a series of small consultations over the coming weeks as issues emerge in sprint. Often, you may only need to provide a summary e-mail or a telephone debrief instead of a full report.

Assuming a report is required, good usability reports need to be usable in the own right. A report should offer the reader the same experience and opinion of the issues as an observer of the testing itself.

So what is the best way of going through your notes to spot issues worth reporting? Everyone has their own favorite techniques but a good way is to write individual issues on sticky notes and put them on a wall. These may each represent a user quote, a problem, a recommendation, or an idea. Once you have gone through all of your notes, group the sticky notes into clusters that represent topics, functionality, or categories as shown in Figure 5-10. These will then form the structure of your report. Work through them one by one to make sure they all are represented in the final report.

A report should start with listing the objectives of the study and then should present an executive summary. When writing an executive summary, imagine that it's all that anyone will read because it that is often the case. Once you've described whom you tested with and how the testing was done, move straight into outlining the issues that you found.

The structure of the report will often follow either the structure of the test plan or will group issues into issue categories such as homepage, navigation, and trust. Which structure you choose will generally be your call depending on the nature of the project.

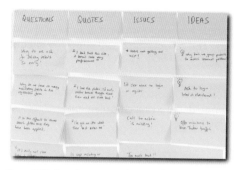

Figure 5-10: Record issues on sticky notes then cluster them into groups

A report should be written so that it makes it easy for someone to do something constructive with it. You should provide annotated screenshots for all points that you raise to make it easy for readers to see what you are referring to. You should include user quotes alongside pictures of their faces to bring the users and their issues to life.

For each issue you should describe what it is, rate how severe it is (in terms of impact on usability), and suggest how it can be fixed as shown in Figure 5-11. Some clients may not want recommendations, so check before to write your report.

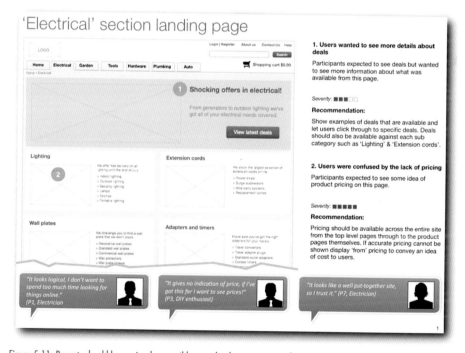

Figure 5-11: Reports should be as visual as possible to make them easy to read

To make your report as actionable as possible, provide an appendix that lists all of the issues in order of severity. You client can then put these into their own spreadsheet and add practical factors such as "cost to fix," "fit with roadmap," and so on, which will allow the client to reprioritize them in the context of their business.

You should always allow time to issue a draft to your project team. There will inevitably be amends required and you may need to add more detail to specific elements.

Presentations

We generally write reports in a presentation format in Keynote or PowerPoint, which means we don't need to create a presentation version if a client needs one, as can be seen in Figure 5-12. This format also forces you to create a more visual and succinct report that if you were using a word processing tool. Clarify what your client needs in terms of the final report in the kick-off meeting to ensure you have allocated sufficient time.

Figure 5-12: Create your report using Keynote or Powerpoint to save needing to create another version to show in your findings presentation

A good way to retain your audience's attention is to show short video clips that reinforce your key findings. These can be time consuming to produce but make a big difference as to how your findings will be received and acted upon. Don't forget to pack your speakers for your findings presentation!

A TYPICAL USABILITY TESTING PROJECT SCHEDULE

Timings are hypothetical but use this as a rough checklist to follow (this assumes you have been commissioned to do the work already).

THREE WEEKS BEFORE TESTING

Three weeks before testing, you should:

- Arrange a kick-off meeting and send the agenda to participants
- Hold the kick-off meeting
- Call the recruiter to let them know about the new project
- Book test facilities
- Book resources to help with testing
- Check progress of production of test materials (if applicable)
- Write recruitment brief, get it signed off, and send to recruiter
- Check screener from recruiter, get it signed off, as recruiter to start

TWO WEEKS BEFORE TESTING

Two weeks before testing, you should:

- Check the progress of production of test materials (if applicable)
- Write the draft test plan and issue to client
- Make amends to the test plan
- Check recruitment progress
- Visit test facilities to check everything is as it should be and fix anything that isn't

ONE WEEK BEFORE TESTING

One week before testing, you should:

- Check recruitment progress
- Organize incentives
- Check the progress of production of test materials (if applicable)
- Run a dry run of the test and report back to project team; make necessary changes to test plan
- Check who will attend and book parking spaces and lunch (don't forget to ask about special dietary requirements), and issue maps for the facilities

THE WEEK OF THE TESTING

On the week of testing, you should:

- Check recruitment progress
- Check the progress of production of test materials (if applicable)
- Print off test plans, incentive sign off forms, and respondent lists, and pack incentives
- Check that the kit works and check that you have sufficient disc space to save recordings

DAY OF THE TESTING (ASSUMING IT'S ONLY ONE DAY LONG)

On the day of testing, you should:

- Get to the facility early to set everything up and to check it's working
- Conduct testing and take notes; share these tasks to keep you fresh
- Look after any observers
- Ensure that the spare recruits have arrived and that they stay close to the location

WEEK AFTER THE TESTING

The week after testing, you should:

- Issue high-level findings e-mail as soon as possible, if required
- Pass all incentive sign-off forms to the relevant person
- Drop a courtesy e-mail to your recruiter to thank them for their work
- Thank the testing facility for their help
- Issue a draft report and amend to suit
- Give findings presentation and answer any questions
- Be available for any other feedback from any stakeholders who cannot attend your presentation
- Thank your client for the project and discuss opportunities for future research!

DIFFERENT TYPES OF USABILITY TESTING

Traditionally, usability testing has often been conducted formally in usability labs with two-way mirrors and observation rooms. Over the last five years there has been a move within the industry to identify less formal approaches that are potentially more flexible and faster to perform.

Here are what we feel are the main pros and cons of the most popular approaches so you can choose the most appropriate technique to suit your project. You can also use a blend of these techniques so don't feel you are constrained to just picking one over another.

LAB-BASED USABILITY TESTING

Lab-based usability testing involves inviting users to attend a purpose-built user-testing facility (such as the one shown in Figure 5-13) to take part in test sessions. Typically observers watch via either a two-way mirror, or a video link to a nearby observation room.

Figure 5-13: A lab-based usability test in action

Lab-based usability testing is best:

- When you have a good budget to work with
- When clients wish to observe tests as they happen
- When you don't need to test large amounts of users

Advantages of lab-based usability testing:

- You can immediately question observed user behavior
- Users are generally sourced by a professional recruiter, so care is taken to make sure they match your target users
- Clients can watch test sessions in real-time

Disadvantages of lab-based usability testing:

- Usability labs can present an unnatural environment to demonstrate "typical" behavior
- Formal testing can take a long time to plan, conduct, and analyze compared to more Agile "guerilla" techniques
- Lab testing can be expensive to run due to the time it takes and the facilities it requires

REMOTE USABILITY TESTING

Remote testing is when you and the test participant are in separate locations. Moderated remote testing involves you moderating the test from another location, as shown in Figure 5-14, typically via a screen-sharing tool. Unmoderated testing involves tests happening without moderation; these tests are viewed and analyzed retrospectively.

Figure 5-14: A moderated remote usability test in action, this facilitator is using a phone and screen sharing software to communicate with the user.

When to do remote usability testing:

- When you need to test with geographically dispersed groups
- When you need to test with a larger number of participants
- When time is tight, as you can run unmoderated tests in parallel

Advantages of remote usability testing:

- You can quickly get large amounts of user involvement in a short amount of time
- There is lots of cheap software to run tests with
- Users are typically testing things using their own computers in their own homes

Disadvantages of remote usability testing:

- You are heavily reliant on technology (especially when unmoderated), so expect things to go wrong, such as tests not recording properly
- This technique makes it harder for clients to take part and see for themselves first-hand
- Confidentiality can be harder to enforce as users can potentially save screen shots or save sensitive test materials
- It can be really frustrating when reviewing unmoderated tests, as it's too late to ask users to explain what they are doing

GUERILLA USABILITY TESTING

Guerilla testing is a great technique to use when you've no budget and no time to do it. It is very much a case of doing something being better than doing nothing. It is typically held in informal environments (as you can see from Figure 5-15) and often involves asking people in train stations, cafes, and airport lounges what they think of your design work!

Figure 5-15: Arm yourself with a laptop and plenty of cash to buy people coffee when conducting guerilla usability tests!

When to do guerilla testing:

- When you have little or no time and budget to do more formal testing
- Within more Agile projects with short sprints
- When you need a quick user opinion to help you make a design decision

Advantages of guerilla testing:

- You can gather a surprisingly large amount of useful information in a short period of time
- It is quick and cheap so it offers a good way of introducing usability testing into projects with tight timescales
- You are likely to find yourself testing in some realistic user environments, which is useful as it contributes to your knowledge of their context of use

Disadvantages of guerilla testing:

- It can be really difficult to get the right people to take part, so their opinions and behaviors may not be relevant to your research
- It doesn't present a viable format for clients/project stakeholders to view tests in real time
- You will be limited in how much you can ask people to test in each session, as you are relying on their goodwill

RESOURCES

Don't make me think!: A Common Sense Approach to Web Usability by Steve Krug

Communicating the User Experience: A Practical Guide for Creating Useful UX Documentation by Richard Caddick and Steve Cable

6

GAINING USEFUL INSIGHTS FROM COMPETITOR BENCHMARKING

COMPETITOR BENCHMARKING INVOLVES taking an in-depth look at competing products so that a comparison can be made between them to determine the good from the bad when rated against a predefined set of criteria. Typically, a user experience person will perform a competitor benchmarking exercise because the knowledge it gives them is useful for making design decisions later in the project.

Competitor benchmarking shouldn't be constrained to the same industry. A university, for example, may want to benchmark its website against other universities' websites but may also be interested in benchmarking against business-to-business websites to learn more about how they should talk to businesses.

Typically, you will be asked to benchmark an existing client product with a set of competitor's products. You may also be asked to conduct a competitor benchmark when your client has no product to compare competitors with.

The whole idea of this approach is to conduct an evaluation that makes it easy to compare one product or service with another. To facilitate this comparison, categories are scored. This provides a framework that can be reused to determine whether products have improved or declined based on the original criteria.

WHEN TO PERFORM COMPETITOR BENCHMARKING

Competitor-benchmarking exercises are typically carried out within the early phases of user-centered design projects. Within the early phases other benchmarking activities may be taking place, such as usability testing (see Chapter 5) and expert reviews (see Chapter 10), which are also about determining the current state of a product or service. Competitor benchmarking can also happen on smaller projects, but is typically scaled down to suit such needs.

> Tip: If you have a good working knowledge of a particular market place or industry you will probably already think you know who the main players are and what their strengths and weaknesses are. However, a benchmarking exercise can still be valuable, as competitor offerings change all the time.

When faced with a client who works in an unfamiliar industry, a competitor-benchmarking exercise can be a great way to immerse yourself in an unfamiliar domain. In this instance the outcome of the exercise is very valuable from a UX perspective as it may uncover a set of design patterns that are common within a certain industry.

Competitor benchmarking is a great way to investigate what other people are doing and to get a feel for how well/badly they are doing it. By benchmarking early in the project, you give yourself the best chance of doing something beneficial with the information you have learned to differentiate your product from the competition.

WHY IS COMPETITOR BENCHMARKING IMPORTANT?

This technique gives both you and your project stakeholders an in-depth understanding of your competitors in terms of their strengths and weaknesses. This fundamentally allows you to acknowledge and learn from their strengths and make sure that you offer something that capitalizes on their weaknesses.

The importance of competitor benchmarking varies depending on whether you or your client has an existing product or service that they want to benchmark.

SCENARIO 1: YOU OR YOUR CLIENT HAS NO EXISTING PRODUCT OR SERVICE

With no existing product or service, a competitor-benchmarking exercise is generally used to spot opportunities or gaps in innovation in the marketplace. From a UX perspective these opportunities may be to provide a more intuitive IA, a simpler checkout process, or a more usable registration form than the competition is currently offering.

In this scenario, competitor benchmarking is important because it provides a clear view of what the competition is doing well and badly in terms of the user experience they offer. By spotting weaknesses in the competition and designing a comparatively better user experience, you are giving yourself or your client a competitive advantage.

SCENARIO 2: YOU OR YOUR CLIENT HAS AN EXISTING PRODUCT

When a product exists, you should include it within the exercise as one of the products that is benchmarked. You can still conduct a benchmarking exercise with just one product. This provides a measure of the state of that product, which can then be compared against a future version of itself.

In this scenario a benchmarking exercise is primarily used to get a sense of how good your product's user experience (or any other area of interest) is compared to the competition. This is important, as it identifies areas to focus on in terms of improvements, which makes the most of limited budgets and tight timescales.

GATHERING IDEAS

In many markets beyond the realms of user experience within both the public and private sectors, analysis of the competition is a vital and common activity used to gather ideas. Within the context of user experience design, the approach is often used to get ideas about what to do and what not to do in terms of the way the product works and how the experience unfolds for the user.

Often, when looking across different products such as websites from the same industry or sector, you can spot similarities in the way things look and work. Designers call these similarities *design patterns*.

Examples of common design patterns on websites include interface elements and behaviors such as date pickers, drop-down "mega nav" from global navigation, carousels, brand logos linking to homepages, fat footers, tag clouds, image zooming, and layouts of generic pages such as product pages and search results pages.

You'll read about the typical components of page level design patterns in Part IV of this book.

Design patterns represent conventions that users are used to and already know how to use. A competitor review can help you identify these patterns so that you can reuse them where appropriate. It makes sense to reuse design patterns if they are established within a certain sector or product type. Consider the mayhem if you tried to drive a car where every control was in an unfamiliar place. As a UX designer, you should consider design patterns your friends and use them whenever it is appropriate to do so.

You should use your competitor review to spot these patterns; then you must decide whether they are appropriate to follow given the context and requirements of your client.

HOW TO PERFORM A COMPETITOR BENCHMARK

As with most UX deliverables, the shape of the output or final deliverable depends principally upon what you want to learn from it and how much time you have to do it.

A competitor benchmark is generally of more use to the person who does it than to the person who it is written for as it is generally the case that the person who writes it takes what they learn from it and does something with this knowledge.

Thinking back to how long we typically spend on a competitor review, I can't remember ever having more than two days to do one. More commonly, they are allocated one day in the project plan.

So how should you go about doing a competitor-benchmarking exercise within this tight timeframe? There are no steadfast right and wrong ways of doing one, but this is what works for us.

BE CLEAR ON WHAT YOU WANT TO LEARN FROM IT

The objectives of the exercise may be clear in your mind but may be different in the mind of your client. You must make it clear to them why you are doing this, how long it will take, and when they will see something to show for their efforts.

It is your responsibility as a UX designer to be clear about the methodology and approach to take, but you do need input from your client in terms of any specific areas they want you to examine. Your client may want you to focus on specific features or functionality of competitor sites or seemingly completely random benchmarks.

You should make sure your client understands what the output of the exercise will be and what it will be used for. Show them previous benchmarks you have done if you can so they can see what they will be getting. Once you have their agreement of the scope of the exercise, you can be confident that you are concentrating your efforts in the right areas.

WHO SHOULD YOU BENCHMARK AGAINST?

Your knowledge of the domain or industry within which your client sits determines how much input you have when suggesting good benchmarks. Generally, your client will tell you whom they want you to benchmark against and may ask you for suggestions of other websites or services. If your client doesn't know whom to suggest, try searching for some relevant keywords to see what comes up. This may actually reveal indirect competitors that you client doesn't know about.

> *Tip: It is often a good idea to pick one or two benchmarks from a different industry to include within your analysis. This way, you avoid comparing the same set of competitors again and again and you bring in some fresh thinking regarding best practice from other industries. For example, if your client works in the financial sector, why not include a benchmark from the media sector to provide a totally fresh comparison?*

If you work on intranets it can be hard to get to see to other intranets to benchmark against. Within the public sector you are more likely to be able to share screenshots and may even get a guided tour, but within the private sector this is much harder to do. In this situation it may be better to just benchmark the intranet against itself and then review it over time to see if it has improved.

The amount of competitors you choose to benchmark against is determined by the time you have available and the depth of the analysis you are planning to do. If you have two days to conduct the benchmarking and plan to go into a reasonable level of detail, aim to compare around four or five. If you are planning a more high-level ("has functionality or not") type spreadsheet review, you can easily compare many more.

HOW SHOULD YOU COMPARE ONE COMPETITOR TO ANOTHER?

The answer to this question clearly depends on the objectives you have been given by your client. You may be conducting a review on how good the competitor's information architecture is, so your comparison may focus on how the navigation works, choice of navigation labels, ability to find content, and other information retrieval methods such as search.

In contrast, you may have been asked to concentrate on benchmarking a particular process or piece of functionality such as a checkout process. In this instance a sensible approach is to walk through the whole process on each competitor's site and take screenshots and make notes of interesting observations along the way. Here is an example of the kind of things you might choose to use as points of comparison if you were performing a competitor-benchmarking exercise for a client in the dental insurance industry who wants to redesign their quote form to increase conversion:

How you benchmark one competitor against another depends on the context of your client and your specific project objectives.

- Ranking on common search terms
- Overall look and feel of the site
- Clarity of proposition and price
- Clarity of calls to action
- Availability and clarity on what cover the policy offers
- Ease of contacting insurer
- Ease of accessing quote section
- Clarity of what is needed to complete quote
- What questions are asked?
- Is the progress and length of form clear?
- Length of form and how the form is grouped into sections
- How errors are dealt with

- Is it clear how to progress through the form?
- What is done to engender trust?
- Is it clear how to get help as you fill out the quote form?
- What information is given with the final quote?
- Can the user e-mail or save the quote?
- Is it clear what you should do next?
- Strengths of process
- Weaknesses of processes
- Overall summary of the experience

Once you have identified the criteria with which you will compare the sites (and had them approved by your client), it is simply a case of working through them with each competitor. You can keep your evaluation qualitative, score each criteria, or just provide a final score—it's really up to you to decide what is the most appropriate method based on how the data will be used.

WHAT DOES A COMPETITOR BENCHMARK LOOK LIKE?

Competitor benchmarks can take many forms depending upon your objectives and the time you have to do them. In the past, we have generally used one of three approaches for our final deliverable—a spreadsheet checklist, a detailed analysis, or a set annotated screenshots.

SPREADSHEET CHECKLIST

One approach you can use if you are comparing many different competitors with one another is the spreadsheet. This provides the viewers with an easy format to enable them to make quick comparisons. By its very nature, it won't offer much detail on each specific component and can make it hard to incorporate screenshots, so factor these limitations in if you are considering using spreadsheets. Figure 6-1 shows an example of a spreadsheet checklist.

	Flickr	500px	Photoshelter
Price	$24.95 p.a	$50 p.a	From $109 p.a
Downloads	✔	✘	✔
Social sharing	✔	✔	✔
e-commerce	✘	✘	✔
Galleries	✔	✔	✔
Customization	✘	✔	✔
Video support	✔	✘	✘
Client area	✘	✘	✔
Tagging	✔	✔	✔
24hr support	✘	✘	✔
Prints	✔	✘	✔
Analytics	✔	✔	✔
Custom domains	✘	✔	✔

Figure 6-1: Use a spreadsheet checklist when you need to do a high-level comparison of competitors

DETAILED ANALYSIS

A more detailed analysis is typically documented in Word and can be seen in Figure 6-2. Such an analysis gives a detailed breakdown of specific features, functionality, or content that the website may or may not offer.

This method presents a higher level of detail than the spreadsheet approach and by its nature lends itself better to being presented to project stakeholders. It is likely to take longer than the spreadsheet approach and may make it harder to directly compare one competitor's results with another.

www.flickr.com

Strengths	• Huge user base • Established website with strong brand • Cheap annual membership • Video hosting • Unlimited storage
Revenue generation	Display advertising on free accounts which is removed from pro accounts
Community	Very active community which is propagated through 'Groups', 'Sets', 'Contacts' and "Friends".
Cost	$24.95 per annum
Services	Full integration with many related services such as printing services, photo albums, stickers and framing services.
Usability	Uploading is easy and the user is guided through the process of more technical tasks such as tagging and resizing images. Tagging, search and browse & 'interestingness' facilitate exploration and finding new photographers to add as contacts.
Photo management	'Organize & Create' allows batch operations such as tagging,

Figure 6-2: A detailed analysis can be time consuming, so allow a couple of days in your plan to compare up to three or four competitors

ANNOTATED SCREENSHOTS

When taking the annotated screenshot approach, we typically use PowerPoint or Keynote. This option provides a very good presentation format (as can be seen in Figure 6-3) and is less structured and labor intensive than the spreadsheet checklist or detailed analysis approaches.

This format is quick to complete and easy to interpret because all the comments refer directly to a component of the screenshot. The other benefit of this approach is that it lends itself to being printed and stuck on the wall, which means it's more likely that you will refer to it again later in the project.

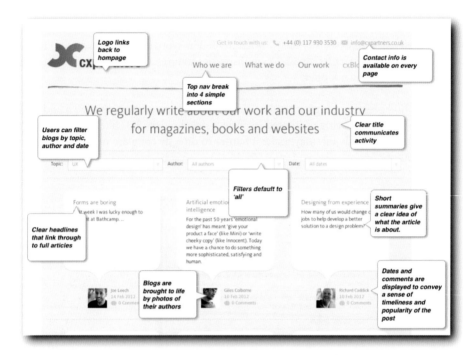

Figure 6-3: Annotated screenshots are the most visually appealing route you can take and are as such much more likely to be read by your project stakeholders

SOURCE: Reproduced with permission of the cxpartners © 2011

RESOURCES

A Project Guide to UX Design by Russ Unger and Carolyn Chandler

Information Architecture for the World Wide Web – 2nd Edition by Louis Rosenfeld and Peter Morville

CONDUCTING EFFECTIVE CONTEXTUAL RESEARCH

CONTEXTUAL RESEARCH INVOLVES getting out of your workplace and conducting research in the real world in the places where your users conduct their everyday tasks. Often this approach is referred to as "contextual inquiry" or "guerilla ethnography."

Contextual research generally focuses on the tasks and processes that people are involved in and helps to uncover what people are doing, how they are doing it, and why they are doing it in that certain way.

It is too easy to stay in our offices and studios when designing. The impacts of such sequestering become clear when you try to use things that clearly haven't been designed with the user's context in mind. They will lack the appropriate features and functionality to suit how they will be used in the real world because the

designer didn't embed themselves in the real world when they designed them.

How should a mobile app behave given that it will be used in all types of environments? How can your e-commerce site design be sympathetic to a busy parent who is trying to shop online at home surrounded by screaming children? When you're answering these questions, it is critical to get out of the office and see these environments for yourself so that you can understand the issues they generate.

By placing yourself in the user's environment and studying its characteristics and constraints you can learn a great deal about where your product is likely to be used. This knowledge is useful in terms of UX because it enables you to make better-informed design decisions and gives you some wonderful contextual insights into real user behavior.

Contextual research can be fascinating as it can open the door to a world you never knew existed. It's a favorite technique of ours because we get to observe some really interesting behavior within an environment that is often totally new. It always throws up all manner of surprises and fascinating behavior and adds a new level of user understanding to the UX design process.

WHEN TO CONDUCT CONTEXTUAL RESEARCH

As with many of the research techniques that have been covered in this book, the earlier you gather information from your users the better. By doing this research early on in the project, you can uncover some interesting user behavior and requirements that feed into all subsequent parts of the project.

Contextual research can be particularly useful when you find yourself designing for users who work in an unfamiliar environment or when designing a particular product or service for a domain that you know little about. The beauty of this approach is that it immerses you within the user's environment so that you experience it first-hand. Experiences like this are much easier to recall during the subsequent design process than other less memorable forms of research, such as reading briefs and findings reports.

The length of time that you commit to your contextual research is likely to vary with the project budget and the nature of what you are studying, but the beauty of the approach is that it doesn't have to be longwinded and expensive. Provided you are researching areas that you can easily gain access to, you needn't allocate huge amounts of time to this activity. You can gain huge amounts of knowledge from a relatively short period of time in the field.

A contextual research approach can suit a project with little or no research budget because it represents a relatively informal approach to research. You can remind yourself of the challenges and constraints of using everyday things such as mobile apps and websites by watching people in easily accessible (and cheap) public environments such as cafes, buses, and restaurants.

More involved contextual research—that involves one-on-one sessions with users—will take more time. Factors such as traveling between users and time spent with users mean that this approach may be more time consuming than other research methods, such as formal lab-based research.

You may also find that you get better insights when you get more time to build rapport with people. This can be really important if you want to see more natural user behavior, so factor this into your planning if you feel it is appropriate for your project because it will take longer to do.

WHY IS CONTEXTUAL RESEARCH IMPORTANT?

Contextual research is an important method for user experience designers for the following reasons.

YOU GET AN UNDERSTANDING OF THE USER'S CONTEXT OF USE

The most important aspect of this technique is that it gives you the most realistic data regarding the users, their behavior, and the environment within which they conduct their tasks. This is critical because you see the reality of how and where people use things and the impacts of these environments upon the use of whatever you are studying. The popularity of mobile devices, such as the iPad shown in Figure 7-1, means that considering context of use is more important than ever.

Figure 7-1: Consider how this environment could affect how the device is used

YOU OBSERVE MORE NATURAL USER BEHAVIOR

Provided your users are conducting their own tasks, this approach presents a set of conditions that will yield more natural user behavior than a user conducting "representative" tasks within a lab environment. This approach can help to reduce the classic mistake seen in more controlled testing environments, whereby users describe what they typically do but that description is often very different from what they actually do during normal usage.

IT ENCOURAGES YOU TO LEAVE YOUR PRECONCEPTIONS AT THE DOOR

We all have preconceived ideas about things or about how certain people behave when faced with specific tasks. The danger of preconceived ideas is that we end up designing products to suit these as opposed to designing for reality. By leaving your desk, you are more likely to base your design decisions around things you have actually observed.

It can also be quite refreshing to remove yourself from your usual working environment and immerse yourself in a new domain. This experience can be an eye opener because often it is so different from what you are used to. You will come back to your colleagues saying things like "How do they get anything done, it's so noisy in there!" and "I can't believe how fast they work; they are so skilled; we must make sure this new interface doesn't slow them down."

IT UNCOVERS CHEATSHEETS, WORKAROUNDS, AND ARTIFACTS

When you're conducting contextual research, you see the users working at their desks surrounded by the tools they use to do their everyday tasks. You will start to notice the various methods that users employ to make the tools and systems that they use regularly work best.

Often, these workarounds will manifest themselves in sticky notes stuck to users' monitors (see Figure 7-2), cheatsheets pinned to the wall, and other such approaches. These are classic signs of usability problems. By questioning why these have been created and what they are making up for, you can learn so much about where and how user needs are not being met.

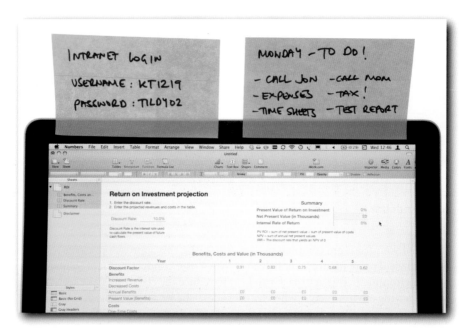

Figure 7-2: Workarounds and reminders can often be symptoms of design problems elsewhere

Clearly you will never see these materials when asking users to come to you for more formal lab research. They are also the types of things that users will not think to mention because they may not recognize that they had to create them because of a flaw in the tool they were trying to use.

Often users will not realize that they behave in a certain way within their own environment. By observing this natural behavior yourself you can get some fantastic insights into the reality of how something is being used and how you can enhance its design to make it easier to use.

GOING TO YOUR USERS SAVES THEM TAKING TIME OUT TO COME TO YOU

Given the simplicity of the approach and the lack of complicated tools needed to conduct the research, there are few places that you can't physically go to, to conduct your contextual research. The flexibility it offers you allows you to fit in around your users. This means that you get to visit those users who may not have been able to spare the time needed to visit a usability lab.

We have conducted contextual research within environments as varied as on trains, in farms, in peoples' homes, in shops, in cafes, on the street, and in airports. Provided the environment is safe and you take sensible precautions, you can get access to all manner of fascinating locations to conduct your research.

HOW TO CONDUCT CONTEXTUAL RESEARCH

Your budget will determine the scope of the contextual research that you conduct. Let's assume that you have the budget to do some fairly detailed contextual research. The following sections pick apart the steps you'll take to conduct your research.

SETTING CLEAR OBJECTIVES

As with all research, it is critical that you set clear objectives with your client at the very beginning of the process. These objectives determine the most appropriate research method to use, so double-check that contextual research is the way to go to get the information you need to fulfill your objectives.

RECRUITING INTERVIEWEES

The recruitment process for contextual enquiry research is very similar to the approach you take when usability testing, except for the additional information you will need to gather about the location of the interviews. The most important aspect of the recruitment is that interviewees understand the nature of the exercise and that you understand the specific nature of the environment you may be working in for health and safety reasons.

It is critical that interviewees understand what you are planning to do so that they can cater to you when you arrive. Make sure they understand the nature of what you are trying to do and, if need be, write a script for your recruiter so you can be sure they are getting a clear brief.

Arranging this type of research is not without its issues. People may be wary of you and your motives. Are you planning to evaluate their performance and design them out of a job? The logistics or arranging a mutually convenient time can be complex and complicated further by health and safety issues. Be prepared for issues such as these and start your recruitment as early as you can in the process.

In less formal contextual research, it is likely that you may not conduct any formal recruitment at all and approach interesting people on the day that interest you. You can also arrange for your client to do your recruitment for you. This can be a very sensible approach, particularly when they need to generate confidential customer lists and have an ongoing relationship with a panel of customers they use for research.

Read more about recruiting users for research in Chapter 5 on usability testing.

PREPARING YOUR RESEARCH

Your preparation for the sessions depends on how you plan to structure the sessions themselves. If you are planning to take more of an observational role when conducting the research you'll need to make a list of the particular things you want to observe and find out more about. For example, if you are observing customer behavior in a shop, you might want to prepare a short set of questions to ask customers as well as a well rehearsed sentence covering who you are and what you are doing.

If you are planning to conduct more of a structured interview, you will clearly need to prepare a set of questions in advance. In this instance, treat the approach more like a usability test, where you have an allocated time slot with people who you can use as you choose.

Planning for contextual research can in some instances be quite difficult because you have no idea what you are going to encounter or what you will see once you are there. I have found that it is good to have a plan in place and then to be prepared to be flexible and adapt to different circumstances as they unfold in front of you.

You should always conduct a trial run of your research. This always identifies issues you won't have thought of and will give you more confidence when you come to do it for real.

CONDUCTING YOUR RESEARCH

In most cases, you have no idea what you will learn and also no idea of the potential importance of what you are being told—you need to record it all! It can be difficult to take notes while facilitating a discussion, so you may need practice your technique before out into the field. You can also record audio from sessions using tools like Pearnote (http://www.useful fruit.com/pearnote/) to save you worrying about getting good notes.

You should always be aware of any potential impacts that your presence may be causing within the environment. I once conducted some contextual research within a small and very busy mobile phone store. I quickly became aware that my presence in the store was distracting customers and I was getting in the salespeople's way. I quickly changed tact and worked in a quieter upper level of the store well away from the busy sales floor. Figure 7-3 shows how you can collect observations and not stop people getting on with their work.

You will also experience people telling you what they think you want to hear. It can take a while for people to relax and to get on with what they actually do, so be aware of this and look out for it happening.

Figure 7-3: Be sensitive to others' main priorities when collecting observations in environments such as peoples' places of work

When working in environments such as shops, it's often a good idea to visit them beforehand and make yourself known to the staff. Your client might be based in a head office and will send a doctrine to the store telling them about the arrangements of your visit. The individual store might not want you there, so make sure you drop in and say hi and explain what you'll be doing to set their minds at ease.

The time you spend in the field is determined by the amount of formal interviews that you have arranged. If you are conducting more observational-based contextual research, it's really up to you to decide when you've seen enough to meet your objectives.

TAKING PHOTOS

Photos are a great way of gathering and recording observations if you feel they are appropriate for the environment within which you are working. Make sure you seek permission before you take any. Photos are useful because they remind you of the environment after the event and also add a wonderful accompaniment to your deliverables. Depending on the context, it may be appropriate to make an audio or video recording of all or some of the sessions as well.

REPORTING YOUR FINDINGS

One of the most time-consuming aspects of contextual research is sifting through your data looking for interesting behavior and then noting repeat instances of that same or similar behavior. Some researchers use codes to help to annotate their findings. Once they observe a pattern, it is assigned a code so that similar findings can be grouped.

The likelihood is that within a fast-paced redesign project, you won't have much time to go through your notes. We often read back through our notes and write interesting observations on sticky notes. Once we have been through all of the sessions, we move the sticky notes around into groups that relate to one another. These groups will then form the sections within a report.

It is a good idea to talk through your observations with someone who is likely to have a better understanding of the system or context than you. If you are gathering data via call center listening, for example, have a chat with the call center staff about your observations to see if they are typical of what they hear too.

Figure 7-4 shows how photos can be used to bring your report to life; photos help your client understand the environments within which their products will be used. You should also embellish reports with important contextual materials that you have collected within the environment, such as scans of leaflets and tickets and examples of workarounds and cheat-sheets. These all help to convey the realities of an environment to the readers of your report.

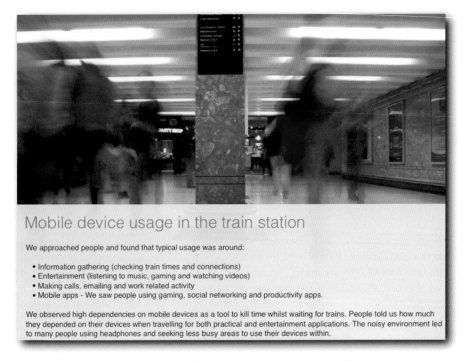

Figure 7-4: Bring your research reports to life with photos of the environment you experienced

RESOURCES

A Project Guide to UX Design by Russ Unger and Carolyn Chandler (pages 99-101)

8

USING ANALYTICS TO UNCOVER INTERESTING USER BEHAVIOR

ANALYTICS HAS BECOME a critical part of solving the puzzle of how digital products are actually being used. The relatively recent proliferation of good, easily available tools such as Google Analytics, has made access to this data easier than ever before.

As a user experience professional, you are often involved in both user research and analysis of analytics, which, when combined can give you a great insight into how something is actually being used.

I like to think of analytics as providing the "what" to which user experience research can provide the "why." By combining the "what" with the "why," you can gain a clear understanding of where design improvements will have the largest positive impact.

A knowledge of the common analytics packages and a willingness to dive into the data to see what is really going on has become a necessary skill set for the user experience professional to master. But rest assured, you don't need to be a master of data analysis to be able to spot interesting user behavior within analytics reports.

WHY ARE ANALYTICS IMPORTANT?

Analytics are important because they give you an idea of how something is being used. You can gather a huge amount of useful information from it that enables you to make better design and management decisions—if you can't measure it, you can't manage it!

Analytics are also important because they allow you to focus on what is important. You can use the data to determine where you should focus your efforts so that the impact of your work is most effective. It is difficult for a group of stakeholders to argue where a project should concentrate its efforts, when they see an analytics report that highlights a major problem such as leaky conversion paths or drop off on product pages.

Analytics provides the "what" for your projects. It shows you what people are doing. Analytics gives you the rationale to form hypotheses, which you can then test in your user research. It is really interesting to sift through the data and form these hypotheses. You never know what you will find and it can be very satisfying to spot some interesting behavior and then use your user research to explain it.

One of the most important aspects of analytics is the metrics that they enable people to define. The subject of KPIs (key performance indicators) and metrics is of fundamental importance to owners of high-value commercial products such as e-commerce websites. It is critical for them to be able to measure performance and also to measure the impact of making changes. Minor changes can have massive impacts. Without analytics, you have no real idea of the impact of the recommendations you are making.

As a UX professional you will probably be very familiar with qualitative research as project budgets and timescales often prevent the use of quantitative methods. Analytics give you a chance to get involved with quantitative data based on statistically significant amounts of data.

Analytics allow you to quickly learn the real impacts of your recommendations from the resulting analytics. Designers usually find it fascinating to see how their designs are actually used in the real world. In what other domain can you launch something to millions of people and then see almost instantaneously how it is being used and where it is working and where it is failing?

WHEN TO USE ANALYTICS

At the beginning of every redesign project we work on, we ask for access to analytics data. Many times, such as when designing new products or propositions, you might have nothing to start with, but make sure you always ask.

You will be likely to use analytics data in different ways depending on the nature of what you have been asked to do.

Here are some common scenarios in which analytics can be useful.

WHEN REDESIGNING AN EXISTING PRODUCT OR SERVICE

This scenario is probably your best chance of getting lots of lovely analytics data. When we are in this situation, we want to learn as much as possible about what is working well and what is working badly. It is critical to have a good understanding of what is working well (such as a high checkout conversion rate shown in Figure 8-1) so you don't remove such aspects from the new design.

Sometimes a redesigned product or service may initially dip in performance as existing customers learn a new version of a previously familiar interface. It's worth warning your clients of this phenomenon to save knee jerk reactions to any early analytics reports. Keep a close eye on the analytics to check that performance returns to expected levels.

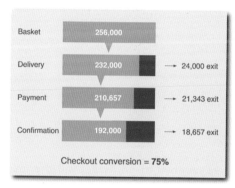

Figure 8-1: Make sure your redesign doesn't negatively impact what is already working well

WHEN DESIGNING A NEW PRODUCT OR PROPOSITION

When designing something brand new, you will not have any existing data to work with. If you are working within a non-competitive environment such as the public sector you may be able to take a look at analytics data from other websites in your sector. You can analyze this data to get a feel for the level of traffic you might be likely to get as well and how these competing services are being used.

Possibly the most important conversation to have with your clients at this point is to ensure they have thought about how they will collect analytics data, and that they have a way of doing this when their new product launches.

WHEN FIXING A SPECIFIC COMPONENT OF A PRODUCT SUCH AS A CHECKOUT PROCESS ON A WEBSITE

You may find yourself being asked to investigate a specific known issue such as a large drop-off rate within a conversion journey such as a checkout process, as shown in Figure 8-2.

As a UX professional you will be expected to be able to contribute to diagnosing where the problem is and then to suggest user research methods to identify why is it happening. You will then need to be able to suggest how the design can be altered to reduce the leakage.

Scenarios such as this make it clear just how broad the skill set of a good UX designer really is. Challenges such as this are pretty daunting, particularly when your recommendations could make positive or negative impacts upon checkout processes that handle hundreds of thousands of dollars.

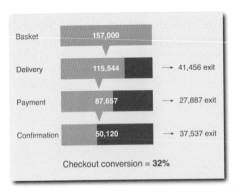

Figure 8-2: Traffic is clearly leaving the checkout process, but why?

In this situation you will find that analytics are your best friend, as they will give you a clear idea of where the problems are. Once you have isolated the problem areas within the checkout process, you will then know where to concentrate your user research.

In some instances, from just a few user tests you can get a clear idea of what is causing the patterns you are seeing in the stats. It may be because users are getting to a point where they cannot answer a mandatory question or they simply don't understand what they need to do next. Bingo—you've found your leak!

Of course, it isn't always this easy. What do you do when your user research gives you no indication of why something is failing? In this instance, it's best to conduct some more research, as it's rare that you will get no indication of what the problem is. Your client then might want to make incremental changes to the checkout process to try to identify the best solution by using tools such as multivariate testing (MVT).

WHEN CONDUCTING AN EXPERT REVIEW

When you elect to or are asked to conduct an expert review, it is often because there is insufficient budget or time to do user research. When you find yourself in this situation, you are often desperate for any kind of insight you can get—this is where analytics can really save your bacon.

Analytics can be useful when conducting an expert review because they will give you some useful insights into how a product is being used. These insights will help you to determine which sections of the product to concentrate your efforts on because it is these areas that will yield the highest value if you can improve them.

> Tip: You will find that you need to make assumptions to explain what you are seeing in the analytics. This can be dangerous and you should be careful to flag any of your assumptions clearly to your clients within your deliverables. This is particularly important when you are making recommendations to change existing interfaces that may have a significant commercial impact if they are modified.

Whenever possible, involve real users to investigate your assumptions. This gives you and your client the confidence that you are identifying and fixing the real issues that are causing problems.

To read more on conducting expert reviews, refer to Chapter 10.

USING ANALYTICS TO HELP SHAPE YOUR OTHER UX DELIVERABLES

To get the most from your analytics work, you need to be clear on why you are doing it, what information you need to gather, and what you'll need to learn to help shape deliverables later in the project.

The following sections list common deliverables and ways that you can modify your approach to get the data that you need.

USING ANALYTICS TO HELP WITH REQUIREMENTS GATHERING

During the requirements gathering phase, you need to identify the areas of the site you are working on that need the most attention to rectify any existing issues. You may find that a client wants to use the redesign as a way of introducing a lot of new features and functionality as shown in Figure 8-3.

In anticipation of this situation, you should ensure that within your analytics phase you get a clear understanding of how the site is being used. This helps you to influence the prioritization of business requirements that emerge later in the project. Your knowledge of the site's priorities from the analytics insights will help you steer the redesign to the areas of the site that need it the most.

To read more on requirements gathering techniques, please see Chapter 4.

Figure 8-3: Analytics can help you to prioritize requirements

USING ANALYTICS TO HELP WITH TASK MODELS

There are various inputs to task models from qualitative data such as user research to quantitative data such as analytics. From your analytics, you should be able to spot usage patterns and paths within the product you are evaluating. You can then use these paths as the basis of your task models, such as the one shown in Figure 8-4, analytics analysis will indicate different usage patterns that in turn are indicative of different user tasks.

Figure 8-4: Use analytics as the basis for your task models

You might find later that these separate paths are actually part of one larger task. You may also discover usage paths that map to new tasks that haven't previously been considered. Either way, the patterns in the data can be a great starting point for you task modeling work later in the project.

To read more on creating task models, read Chapter 12.

USING ANALYTICS TO HELP WITH PERSONAS

I have a love-hate relationship with personas. The personas I love are full of useful insights (see Figure 8-5) are based on data that you can use to make decisions. The ones I hate tell you how many cats someone has, what their names are, and what they like to eat. That's all well and good but not very useful when it comes to making design decisions!

Figure 8-5: Analytics can be useful ways to add behavior insights to persona profiles

Analytics can help you with your personas because they uncover usage patterns that you can build a persona around. This is great because it means that your personas will actually represent something important that is actually happening (based on real data and not on a designer's imagination). The other advantage is that you will be converting something people find tricky (data analysis) into something people understand (representations of real people in persona form).

To read more on creating personas, please see Chapter 14.

USING ANALYTICS TO HELP WITH WIREFRAMING AND PROTOYPING

When constructing wireframes and prototypes you must be confident that every component you are adding has a useful role. If you have spent the time understanding the analytics, it makes it much easier to be able to justify and prioritize the elements of a wireframe or prototype, because you know how important it is to the overall effectiveness of the site. Consider how you could use analytics to justify the components of a wireframe such as the one shown in Figure 8-6.

If you know which element of a wireframe or prototype is contributing to a key site metric, you can ensure that the element is represented in a way that maximizes its performance. This focus can make the evaluation of wireframes, prototypes, and final designs more straightforward and less subjective. It becomes less about whether a client likes the look of something and more about how it will maximize performance against the key metrics.

To read more on creating wireframes, see Chapter 17. For more information on prototyping, see Chapter 18.

USING ANALYTICS TO HELP WITH YOUR USER RESEARCH

Analytics start to become really powerful when combined with qualitative techniques such as user research (as shown in Figure 8-7) because it is at this point that you can discover the reasons for the patterns in the data. Your analytics will give you the hypotheses that become the foundation of your research. These hypotheses then become the objectives of the research—the goal being to try and uncover why people are behaving in the way you are observing in the data.

So you can now see how everything ties together. The people you recruit for your research are based on your personas, which are modeled on the behavior you have observed in the data. The tasks you set for the user research are based on the task models that in themselves are based on the data. Everything is data driven. You can base all of your design decisions on cold, hard real data, which in itself represents actual user behavior. Beautiful, isn't it!

To read more on conducting user research, specifically usability testing, see Chapter 5.

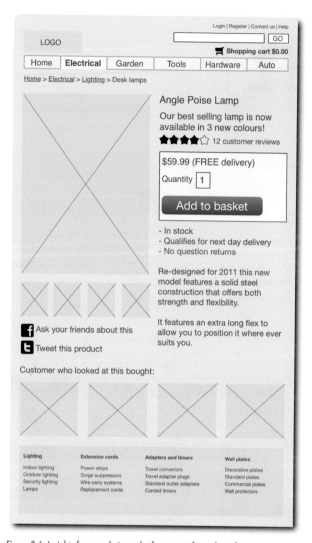

Figure 8-6: Insights from analytics make for more informed wireframes

Figure 8-7: User research provides the "why" to the "what" you learned from the analytics

DIFFERENT TYPES OF ANALYTICS YOU CAN USE

When people think of analytics they generally turn to the common analytics software tools such as Google Analytics or Omniture, but there are some other less obvious analytics options you should consider that can uncover fascinating user insights.

CLASSIC WEB ANALYTICS

"Classic" in this case refers to using tools such as Google analytics. You'll need to find out which analytics package/s your client uses (if any) and spend some time to understand their idiosyncrasies. The good news is because of their popularity there will be lots of good advice online to help you to get the best from them.

You'll need to determine which metrics you want to investigate and how that tool reports on them. Buckle up, it can be a bumpy ride. Fear not, though, we tell you how to get the most from these tools later in this chapter.

SEARCH LOG ANALYSIS

Search logs from in-site search engines uncover all manner of hidden insights into what people are really looking for. They are often forgotten during the UX design process. Get a hold of the logs and look at the type of information people are after, the frequency of these requests, the language people are using, and what content is available for the most requested items.

Does the site have anything to cater for those frequently requested items? What terms are people using to find the information they want? This information is a really important to the design of your IA because it helps you to match your labeling with the language that users actually use.

A/B AND MULTIVARIATE TESTING

The market for tools that help to determine the optimum combination of content by testing with statistically significant sample sizes has grown hugely over recent years. In some ways, it can be seen as a challenge to the UX profession, as people think surely they can just launch a series of pages and then optimize them over time using these tools without time-consuming user research.

In many ways these tools are your friends. As a UX professional, you can use them to understand what performs well and then use more qualitative techniques to find out why. You client may decide they no longer need you because their multivariate tool is giving them all the answers, but without the reasons why these things are occurring, they can't learn from these changes.

You should expect to be challenged by the data that these tools uncover. For example, users once told us how much they hated a particular feature, and how it had no impact on their likelihood to buy. The analyst then told me that when this feature was shown on the site the analytics showed that the conversion rate increased. To make a clear recommendation in a seemingly contradictory situation like this, you need to have a good grasp of the variables involved and work with the analyst to get to a final UX recommendation.

Patterns noted using these tools can form the brief you are given as a UX practitioner as thus they actually generate work for you. Your client may have seen one variation of a page perform better than another or one particular label perform particularly well and they will want you to uncover the reasons why.

Analytics tools can uncover bad news, too. What happens if, when following your redesign project, metrics such as conversion just fall off a cliff? Are you accountable for finding out why and fixing it? Are you solely responsible or are there just too many variables involved to prevent the blame being directed at you? You should be prepared for these situations and develop suggestions that you will offer to a client in this scenario to rectify the problem.

As a UX professional you will be making design recommendations that will likely have huge financial impacts on your client's bottom line. You should be using analytics tools to inform your design decisions and also to refine them. Spend time understanding what they do so you can work out how to make them work for you. You will not only learn what works but also why it works. That knowledge will make you very valuable to your current and future clients.

HOW TO USE ANALYTICS TO UNCOVER USER BEHAVIOR

Let's imagine you have been allocated a fixed period of time—say two days—to dig into your client's analytics on an existing site. Your client (who runs an e-commerce site) is concerned that they are losing traffic through the buying process and they want you to identify and fix the problem.

SET YOUR OWN OBJECTIVES FOR THE TIME YOU HAVE

Within the fairly limited time you have, you need to not only find your way around the analytics tool but you also need to work out what you want it to tell you. In this situation, you should identify what you want to learn first so that you remain focused on the outcome you need.

Typical outcomes for this exercise might be to:

- Identify where people are coming from and how they are moving through the site
- Uncover the purpose of their visit
- Identify at which point of the buying process they are leaving the site
- Identify whether user behavior is different depending on a unique factor such as device used, acquisition method, or path taken through the buying process

By listing your objectives like this, you can allocate a suitable chuck of time to each one depending on their contribution to your overall objective. Once you have allocated chunks of time, you can focus on working out how your analytics tool will give you the information you need. Put them somewhere visible, as shown in Figure 8-8, to help you to keep on track.

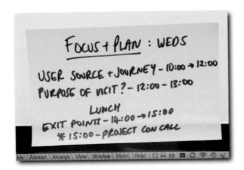

Figure 8-8: Make sure your objectives are clearly visible to help you to focus on them

GET TO KNOW THE ANALYTICS TOOL

If you are lucky enough to be familiar with the specific analytics tool that your client happens to use, you are one step ahead. When you find yourself presented with a new tool, you need to become acquainted with it quickly.

If you ask around, you can often find a client-side analytics expert who can give you a quick, guided tour of the tool. This saves you time, gives you the opportunity to ask "stupid" questions, and also a offers a chance to see any customization of the tool that the client may have done themselves, such as setting up custom reports.

Custom reports will often be set up based on key metrics that you will also be interested in. Always ask your clients which reports they regularly run and why. This can uncover some valuable data and will also help you to focus on what is important to your client.

I remember the first time I was introduced to an "enterprise-level" analytics tool. My client told me that it was very comprehensive and that I would have "fun" getting to grips with it. That is always a bad sign! I had limited time to understand how it worked let alone how to make it tell me what I needed to know. Learn from my mistakes. Identify as early as possible in the project which tools are available and get access to them as soon as possible in order to familiarize yourself with the way they work. It'll save you many potential headaches further down the line.

WHAT SHOULD YOU BE MEASURING?

Different measurements seem to come in and out of favor, all depending on your client's experience with analytics. Some may ask you to focus on really odd metrics such as "time on site" and "page views." We have had many a senior manager tell us how they want to make their site as "sticky" as possible. They wanted users to stay on it for as long as possible. But what if users could come and get what they need and then go off and do something more important? Surely that would represent a more successful user experience than being stuck on the site!

You should focus instead on using analytics to uncover as many of the "what" questions as possible. You'll then identify the "why" in your later qualitative research phase. Set yourself the task of identifying what people are doing in relation to your specific objectives. Remember, you are likely to have limited time and may need to produce a deliverable to convey your findings, so you must stay focused.

Remember to keep an eye on the clock. It is easy to get lost in the data and start trying to uncover new patterns that don't contribute to your overall objectives.

In relation to the specific objectives this chapter has identified, let's take a look at how you might go about uncovering data that will help you find out what is going on.

Objective 1: Identify Where People Are Coming from and How They Are Moving Through the Site

You will need to work out how your analytics tool will allow you to segment traffic (based on the source) and then how you can isolate these segments and follow the paths they take through the site. Are the majority of successful visits coming from e-mail campaigns, SEM/PPC, or organic traffic? Can you cross-reference these with their corresponding conversion rates?

You may find that the source of traffic has no relationship to the path they take to achieve their goals. You should document these discoveries as you go, as it's always good to feel that you are progressing with your findings report if time is tight.

Some analytics tools will allow you to overlay "click density" data on top of pages. This can be useful because the data is displayed in context to the page itself. This can make the analysis easier than when wrangling with endless pages of numbers, tables, and charts. Figure 8-9 shows an example of how this may look in your analytics package.

Figure 8-9: View click density data to get a useful visual idea of what is happening

Analytics tools are great at showing you the main paths that users are taking. Many also allow you to apply sophisticated filters, which will allow you to further interrogate these patterns.

Objective 2: Try to Uncover the Purpose of Their Visit

You should be very careful when trying to infer the purpose of a particular visit from analytics alone. In reality you will only be actually making an informed guess regarding a user's primary goal. If you have access to the search logs, this may give you a very clear idea of what they came for, but browser-based data will be much harder to unpick.

Much of the job of uncovering the actual purpose of a visit is best postponed until you do your qualitative research. There is nothing wrong with using the quantitative research to develop a hypothesis that you can then either prove or disprove at a later stage.

Objective 3: Identify at Which Point of the Buying Process They Are Leaving the Site

Is all of the lost traffic leaving at the same point? Are there any patterns between where traffic is coming from and where users are leaving? Is one path particularly more or less efficient than the others? How does the conversion rate vary depending on the path taken? The answers to these questions will start to uncover some prime areas for your qualitative testing sessions.

It may be the case that you have a single point of failure (such as a registration page) or you may see leakage throughout the process.

Objective 4: Identify Whether User Behavior Is Different Depending on a Unique Factor Such as Device Used, Acquisition Method, or Path Taken Through Buying Process

Once you have identified where you are losing traffic, try to determine if you can identify any reason or pattern behind this behavior. Are there any other interesting behaviors that you have seen that you would like to try to explore in your qualitative research? Which A/B or multivariate tests have yielded the best results and how do these relate to the data you are looking at? Is it simply the case that the majority of traffic is leaving from one area in particular, regardless of any other variable?

So many questions and so little time to find the answers! You can see how easy it can be to get lost in the data. In reality, you will be able to uncover the answers only to some of these questions.

With longer-term client engagements, you can regularly spend time looking at the analytics to get a feel for trends and "normal" usage data. The reality of a UX project is that you will rarely get the time you want, so plan for this and make the most of the time you have.

COLLATING THE DATA AND PRESENTING IT BACK TO CLIENTS

The last thing you should be presenting back to your client is a load of data that looks like it is in the same format as the analytics tool that you plucked it from!

Your skills as a UX designer are vital here because you need to identify the interesting data, make sense of it, and present it back to your clients in a format that is simple, clear, and engaging. Figure 8-10 shows how you can present data back in context to the area of the site it relates to. This approach makes it really easy for clients to interpret what is really going on.

Figure 8-10: Keep your report clear, concise, and easy to use

Your focus must be to report back only on your original primary objectives. State these at the beginning of your report, report back on them, and then tell your client what you are going to do with what you have learned in the rest of the project. You should also state which questions remain unanswered and how you are going to answer them later in the project.

RESOURCES

Web Analytics: An Hour a Day by Avinash Kaushik

CHAPTER

DESIGNING, LAUNCHING, AND ANALYZING A SUCCESSFUL SURVEY

SURVEYS ARE A very popular method of data collection that are used (and abused) to collect information such as opinions, preferences, and ideas, both online and offline.

It has never been easier to design and launch a survey. This has led to surveys becoming a popular way of gathering information but has inevitably also led to some very poor surveys being published.

This chapter concentrates on the online survey. We have all been invited to complete a badly designed survey. The endless questions, the huge free text entry boxes, and the confusing questions cause many people to head straight for the Quit button.

So when should you use surveys, how should you design and launch them and what should you do with the results?

WHEN SHOULD YOU LAUNCH A SURVEY?

Surveys can be a great tool to get a large amount of feedback over a relatively short period of time. They are great for gathering peoples opinions, ideas, and feelings about things. They are cheap and easy to set up and also easy to promote, which allows you to start receiving results soon after you launch them.

Surveys are not good for gathering specific insights about peoples' actual behavior. This is because what people say they do and what they actually do are often two very different things. If you base your design decisions on what people tell you they do, and not what they actually do, your product will not be designed to support actual user behavior. If you are trying to find out how something is actually used, don't use surveys. Usability tests are much better in such situations (see Chapter 5 for more on conducting usability testing).

> Tip: In our UX projects, we are generally more likely to use surveys early on in a project as a formative, or idea-generating technique. We then typically use evaluative techniques such as usability testing later, when we need to act upon observed behavior as opposed to self-reported behavior (which is what a survey will likely give you).

Surveys can be used as a cheap method of screening potential recruits for usability testing. Provided you have a clear idea of your recruitment criteria, surveys offer a perfectly acceptable guerilla method of generating a list of potential recruits if your budget won't stretch to professional recruiters.

We have launched surveys when we needed people's opinions on specific things such as who we should invite to speak at a conference, what people thought of an event we held, and which topics people thought we should publish more information about. In these examples, we used surveys to help us to make decisions. Often, this was because we felt we weren't in a position to make that decision ourselves and needed some user input to help us.

Surveys can be useful for getting a general opinion or feeling about certain topics. The information that a survey generates is often used to help make decisions, to benchmark a product or service, or to influence how something is developed.

A survey doesn't have to consist of a long list of questions. A survey could be as simple as one question with as few as two possible responses such as the one shown in Figure 9-1. These "quick polls" are often used on newspaper websites, whereby journalists try to encourage user engagement with stories and also to canvas reader's opinions. These polls typically provide the users with instant feedback.

The types of surveys covered in this chapter follow a different model than polls. Surveys are typically made up of more than one question and do not provide the users with any idea of how others have responded to the questions. Some surveys do offer to share the results with people who participate as a way of trying to encourage people to complete the survey.

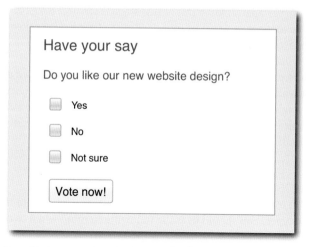

Figure 9-1: A survey can be as simple as a quick poll

Surveys are a popular method because they are quick and easy to put together and launch. Often they are used in the situations whereby a company has no time or money to involve users. This is better than nothing of course, but good surveys take time to plan and design, and when hurried, they can easily fail to deliver your objectives.

HOW TO DESIGN AN ONLINE SURVEY

As with any piece of research, it is critical to identify exactly what your objectives are before you launch a survey. This doesn't need to be an arduous task; just focus on what you want to discover and you'll find it much easier to design your survey as a result.

Once you have identified exactly what you want to learn, write down some example questions. You should approach this much as you would when doing some sketches before you commit to wireframing. By listing your questions in Word or by even writing them out on paper, you will get a feel for how well they are worded and whether one flows into the next.

The next thing to consider is how the questions break down. You might want to offer a set of possible answers for people to choose from. This helps the recipients and gives you data against specific responses. Again, sketch out the likely break down of the responses for each question (when relevant); your survey will start taking shape.

Once you have your first draft, send it to a friend to read through. This reflects a mini user-centered design process. Do something rough, get some feedback, and then improve it. This will save you time in the long run; it's better to get it right on paper before you spend time building the survey using an online tool.

Once you have your questions, consider how long it will take people to fill out the survey. If you were to respond to it, how would you feel? Is it written in plain English? Have you used any industry jargon or acronyms? Are any of your questions ambiguous? Are all of your questions related to your objectives? Do all of the questions apply to all respondents?

You should try and pull the survey apart. Doing this at this stage is sensible because you haven't committed much time to it yet so you'll be more willing to fix what is broken. Challenge yourself to cut as many words from your questions as possible. Be succinct!

It is easy to fall into the trap of prejudicing the wording of questions with your own preconceptions. They then become leading questions that will be likely to influence the respondent's answer. A leading question might ask "How much did you enjoy your visit to our website today?". This assumes they enjoyed it in the first place, which of course they may not have. Your questions must be neutral!

PROS AND CONS OF DIFFERENT QUESTION TYPES

Online survey tools allow you to choose from many different question formats, but they will broadly fall into one of three types. You should bear the following in mind when selecting question types for your survey.

Objective Questions

An objective question has a definite answer. An example of an objective question is "What is your job title?"

Pros:

- Answers are short and succinct
- Answers are factually correct

Cons:

- Answers lack depth
- Answers rely on respondent remembering specific details

Subjective Questions

A subjective question has no "right" answer. A respondent's answer will reflect a feeling or a subjective judgment. A subjective question will generally offer the respondent a choice of answers from which they will pick one or more responses that match how they feel about something. An example of a subjective question is "Please rate the following areas of our website."

Pros:

- Respondents can choose from a range of options
- Answers are easy to analyze

Cons:

- Respondent may choose best-fit answer, which might not be exact answer
- Respondents may choose neutral or middle choice if given the ability to do so

Open-Ended Questions

An open-ended question is one whereby the respondent is not given any options to choose from to form their answer. Typically, this question is followed by a free text box, into which respondents can type whatever they like. An example of an open-ended question is "Please tell us how you think we can improve our website."

Pros:

- Respondent has the flexibility to tell you what they want
- You are providing an unconstrained response format

Cons:

- Time-consuming to analyze
- Responses are interpreted by an analyst, who can interpret/misinterpret the responses in the way they choose
- Harder for people to fill out because it makes them think

When you start building the survey online, you will be offered all manner of different question formats, from simple yes/no-type questions to free text entry responses and multiple-choice answers. Familiarize yourself with the question format options that are available and use a selection within your survey. However, don't go crazy with using all of the different question formats; this can be disorientating for respondents.

Questions with a fixed set of answers lead to a set of responses that are easier to analyze and represent in charts and graphs as they are controlled and are comparable. Questions that allow free-text answers will take much longer to analyze and may not be comparable with one another.

Sometimes the question itself will determine the type of question format you offer. If you are asking someone's opinion it may seem restrictive to just give them a set of options. A question that can only have a few possible answers (such as your gender) suits a restricted question format such as a set of options from a drop-down menu.

As with anything, the more time you spend designing the survey, the better your responses will be. One critical point to consider is that you should design your survey in a way that makes your analysis easy. Adding lots of questions with free text answers will seem like a great idea until you need to analyze thousands of words of user feedback.

Once you have planned out the number of questions you will have, what those questions are, how they break down, and in which order they will appear, you will have done the hard work of designing your survey. This would be a great time to send it to another friend and fine-tune your ideas. Again, this doesn't have to be time consuming. You can get to this point from having done nothing easily in one day.

Remember that completing surveys can be boring unless respondents are motivated to fill them out. Please do everyone a favor and make it as short and sweet as possible. Your users will reward you in the quality of their responses.

Timing is interesting when it comes to surveys. They are relatively quick to put together but can take ages to gather the volume of responses you need for a useful dataset. This makes them a tricky tool in some respects, as you will never really know how long it will take to get what you need. This isn't a scenario that the project manager will enjoy. All you can do at this point is design it well, promote it, and offer a good incentive to maximize the chances of people completing it.

HOW TO BUILD A SURVEY USING AN ONLINE TOOL

As with many other UX research techniques, there are many different survey tools that are available to use online. Our most recent experiences have been of using SurveyMonkey (see www.surveymonkey.com), so this section uses it to illustrate how easy it is to design an online survey.

CREATE A NEW SURVEY

Simply click the Create New Survey button from the My Surveys page of SurveyMonkey.

This will load the Create Survey page, where you will be asked to name your survey. Give the survey a meaningful name, as it may appear as a link to the survey once the survey is published. See Figure 9-2.

Click Continue to load the Edit Survey screen. From here, you can add questions and select from different custom themes. Let's assume that you have your list of finished questions to hand. To add your first question, click Add Question and select the question type you want from the drop-down box, as shown in Figure 9-3.

Click through each question type and see what they offer. Your may not be familiar with the names of the different question types but you will quickly recognize the ones you want from the list of available formats. See Figure 9-4.

Your survey should have an introduction, which explains how long the survey will take and how the results will be used. Reassure respondents of their anonymity when presenting results and that their responses will be kept confidential (if this is the case). To add an introduction, just select the question type called Descriptive Text from the drop-down menu.

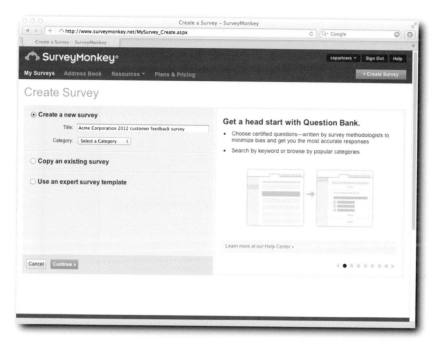

Figure 9-2: Name your survey and then click Continue

SOURCE: Reproduced with permission of SurveyMonkey, LLC (www.surveymonkey.com) © 2012

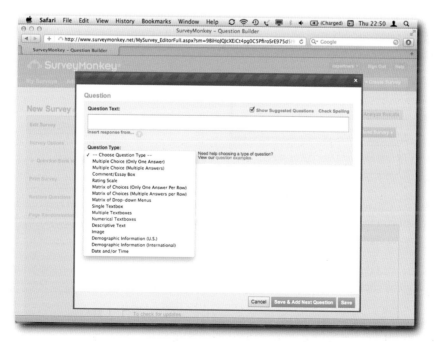

Figure 9-3: Select the question type you want from the list of options

SOURCE: Reproduced with permission of SurveyMonkey, LLC (www.surveymonkey.com) © 2012

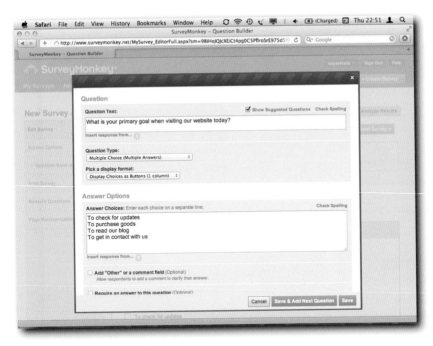

Figure 9-4: Add your question text and your answer options

SOURCE: Reproduced with permission of SurveyMonkey, LLC (www.surveymonkey.com) © 2012

Continue adding your other questions. When adding questions with multiple answers, remember to check the Add Other or a Comment Field option to allow for more flexibility for respondents answers, as shown in Figure 9-5.

Figure 9-5: Let respondents add their own responses too via the Add Other option

SOURCE: Reproduced with permission of SurveyMonkey, LLC (www.surveymonkey.com) © 2012

Click Save Changes and you see how question will look when presented to respondents. If at this point you realize that you chose the wrong question format, you can simply click Edit Question to change it.

Click the Add Question button to keep building your survey. Regularly preview your survey as you go by clicking the Preview Survey button in the top-right of the screen (see Figure 9-6).

You can customize the survey via the Survey Options navigation option on the left side. We recommend that you show a progress bar that illustrates the percentage completed. It is important that respondents have a clear idea of how much more they need to do to complete the survey (see Figure 9-7). Click Save Changes to return to the Edit Survey page.

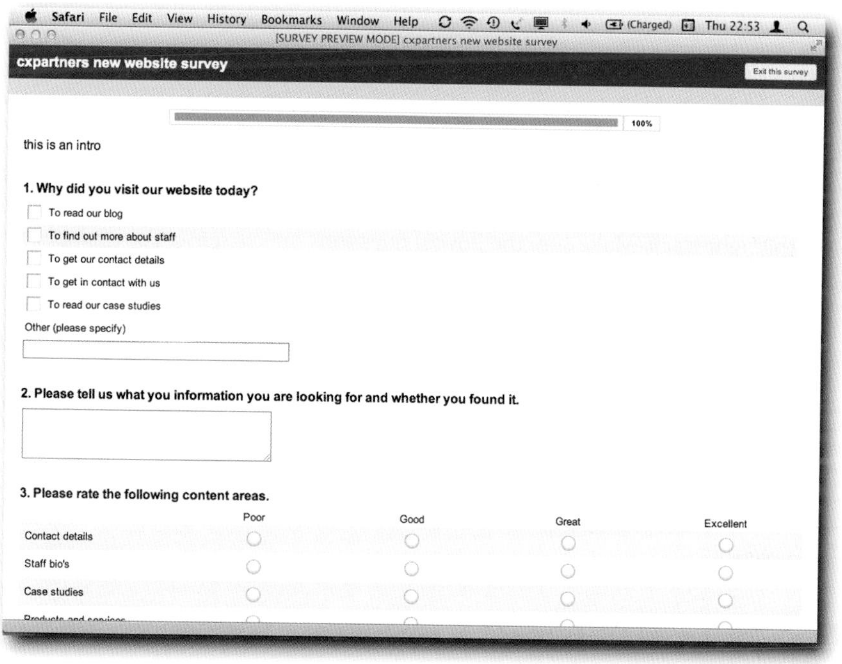

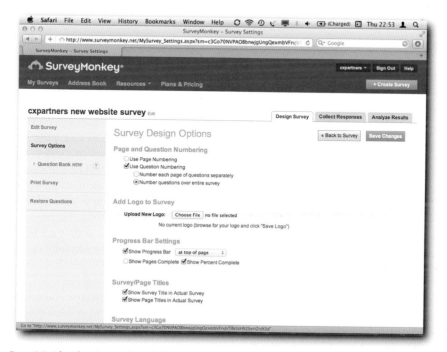

Figure 9-6: Regularly preview your survey; it feels good to see it progressing nicely!

SOURCE: Reproduced with permission of SurveyMonkey, LLC (www.surveymonkey.com) © 2012

Figure 9-7: Select Show Progress Bar and Show Percentage Complete from the Survey Options menu

SOURCE: Reproduced with permission of SurveyMonkey, LLC (www.surveymonkey.com) © 2012

When you are happy with your survey, run through the following checklist as a final check:

1. Make sure it is realistic for your users to answer your questions; will they know the answers? Don't ask them question that require a lot of work to calculate the answer. Keep the questions simple and straightforward.

2. Check that the narrative of the questions reads as naturally as possible. If a question sounds like a conversation and the tone is right for the nature of the content, you will be on the right track. Make sure the flow of questions makes sense. For example, are responses to some questions related to other questions? Are they being asked in logical order? If not, reorder them to make them flow more naturally.

3. At the end of the survey, make sure that you thank the respondents and remind them how valuable their contributions are to you.

4. Once you are happy with the survey, preview it and give it a read through. Check for typos. Then read it again!

5. Once you feel that it is ready, ask a friend to fill it out. Ask them to try to pull it apart. Ask them if they feel the incentive is suitable for the amount of effort that is required to complete it.

HOW TO LAUNCH YOUR SURVEY

When you are happy with the survey, choose Send Survey. This will generate a URL for you to send to respondents. SurveyMonkey gives you loads of options to share the URL, including by e-mail, Twitter, Facebook, and MailChimp, among others (see Figure 9-8).

Make any incentive suitable based on what you are asking people to do. Can you offer an incentive that users can redeem immediately? This will often make people more likely to respond.

When publicizing your survey, you should explain who you are and why you are doing the research. Most importantly, tell people if you are offering an incentive for their involvement.

We have found Twitter to be a particularly effective way of promoting surveys, even though the character limit can cause issues. You can also launch surveys via pop-ups on your client's website. These can work well despite how disruptive they can be to users. Bear in mind that you will need to speak to technical colleagues to find out how the survey will be launched. You may also be able to trigger the survey to show to users who are doing certain tasks if you need to segment respondents in any way.

E-mail newsletters can also be an effective way of promoting surveys as they are being delivered to an interested audience. This format also allows more space to fully explain the motives for the survey, which will help to encourage participation.

If you need to target a particular audience for your survey, this will likely influence your strategy for seeking appropriate respondents. Your client is likely to have some great ideas about how to target respondents, as they will be doing this all the time already.

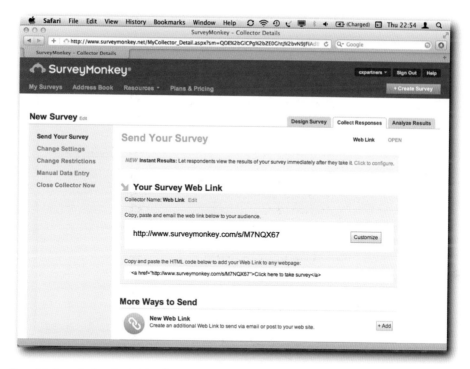

Figure 9-8: SurveyMonkey gives you lots of options to promote your survey to potential respondents

SOURCE: Reproduced with permission of SurveyMonkey, LLC (www.surveymonkey.com) © 2012

The number of results that you will need to make your responses significant is an interesting point. We suggest setting a target with your client and then do everything you can to hit that number. This target will depend on the nature of your client's business. If they need huge numbers, you may need to enlist the help of a specialist to get the number of responses that you need.

HOW TO ANALYZE THE RESULTS OF A SURVEY

Once your survey is live, you can check the data you are collecting whenever you want by clicking the Analyze Results tab at the top of the page. It is great watching the responses come in and the graphs on the page take shape, as shown in Figure 9-9.

SurveyMonkey allows you do all sorts of things with your responses, such as filter them, compare responses to the same questions, and browse them in full. You can also download them in your format of choice to do what you want with them in your favorite analysis tool, as shown in Figure 9-10.

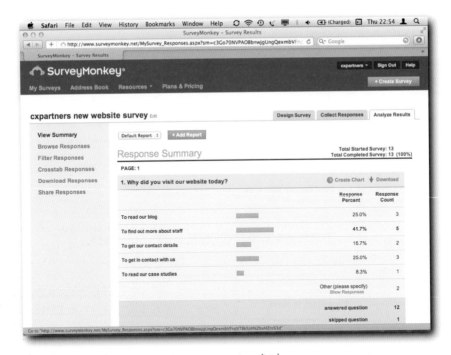

Figure 9-9: You can watch responses coming in to your survey immediately

SOURCE: Reproduced with permission of SurveyMonkey, LLC (www.surveymonkey.com) © 2012

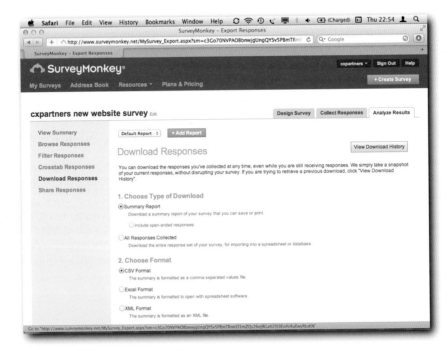

Figure 9-10: Download your responses in the format that suits your needs the best

SOURCE: Reproduced with permission of SurveyMonkey, LLC (www.surveymonkey.com) © 2012

After putting so much effort into promoting your survey, you will probably feel overwhelmed with the amount of responses you have gathered.

What will you do with the 1,500 different responses to the free text entry question that asked people what their job titles were? How can you quickly analyze this to turn it into a format that both you and your client can understand? This can get quite overwhelming very quickly, particularly if the responses relate to a domain you know little about.

> Tip: If you are working in an unfamiliar domain, enlist the help of a subject matter expert to help you interpret the results. If you do it on your own, there is a danger that you will misinterpret free text answers and miss any nuances they may contain.

It is at this point that we recommend revisiting the original objectives that you set for this method of research. Focus on analyzing the responses that help you to meet your objectives. Do this first at the very least, and then consider any secondary objectives you may have.

When you are deep in the analysis you will love the questions you set with fixed answers, as the survey tool does the analysis for you. The questions that offer free text answers will take the most time to analyze. You might it useful to identify a group of recurring themes and code responses that fit with each of these themes. For each new theme you discover, create a new code to suit. You can then visualize these groups of similar answers using graph and chart tools in packages such as Numbers and Excel.

REPORTING YOUR FINDINGS BACK TO YOUR CLIENT

Despite all of the painstaking number crunching, data analysis, endless reading, and analysis, your job for the client report is to present everything in a simple format that shows clearly what you found.

As with any UX research findings, you must identify what you learned in a format that your findings can be acted upon. You should highlight the patterns and trends that you observed, the data that answers your original objectives, and the anomalies that you didn't expect.

Put yourself in the position of your client. What do they want to learn from this? What decisions will they have to make from your research? Which aspects of what you discovered will contribute to the next stage(s) of the project? The answers to these questions will help you design a killer findings presentation, which will do justice to all the hard work you put into designing and analyzing your survey!

10

CONDUCTING A USEFUL EXPERT REVIEW

AN EXPERT REVIEW is a low-cost method for understanding an existing product's key usability issues. An expert review is simply an evaluation of an existing product based on a set of usability guidelines, the target users, and their tasks.

We find that conducting an expert review is an excellent way of immersing ourselves in a product at the beginning of a redesign project. If we're working on a project that's designing something from the ground up (with no existing product to reference), competitor benchmarking (Chapter 6) is similarly useful.

WHY ARE EXPERT REVIEWS IMPORTANT?

Expert reviews are important because they are the cheapest and easiest tool in your UX evaluation armory. They are not as thorough and rigorous as usability testing (Chapter 5), but they are quick and require no resources beyond your own time.

To conduct an expert review, you step through the existing product, imagining yourself to be a novice user. Before you start, list the main user groups and tasks that the product must allow the users to complete. Are you able to complete the tasks easily? Are you able to understand the progress you have made? Additionally, evaluate the product against a set of good practice guidelines in order to catch non-task-based usability issues.

The term *expert review* is perhaps a misnomer. You don't need to be a UX expert to conduct one. Even a novice can produce useful findings—it is the act of stepping through the product with the user in mind that uncovers the usability issues.

What Is an Expert Review?

Our approach to the expert review is essentially a hybrid of two different human-computer interaction techniques: heuristic evaluation and cognitive walkthrough.

A heuristic evaluation is a method for evaluating a product against a set of UX design guidelines. Heuristic means "rule of thumb" in this context. Jakob Nielsen and Rolf Molich first developed heuristic evaluations in the early 1990s, and many people still use the 10 guidelines they developed to evaluate against. These Ten Usability Heuristics can be found on Nielsen's website at www.useit.com/papers/heuristic/heuristic_list.html.

A cognitive walkthrough is a method for evaluating a product based on how easy it is for new users to complete tasks on the system.

Both methods require the product to be evaluated by several researchers in order to reach consensus and to catch a majority of usability problems.

The expert reviews described here are not designed to be conducted by several researchers—the cost is generally prohibitive in real-world projects. However, if you have the resources available, it is certainly desirable to use more than one researcher. The use of a single-person expert review is sometimes questioned within the UX community as different "experts" will have different opinions and spot different usability issues. This type of expert review is not an exact science. More importantly, actual users are not involved in the process. So, if your expert review uncovers usability problems, you would be wise to verify these issues via some other method such as usability testing.

WHEN TO CONDUCT AN EXPERT REVIEW

An expert review is the perfect starting point for any redesign or usability review project. It immerses you in the product and its users and provides valuable insights. For example, if you need to write a test plan for usability testing, an expert review will identify areas you should concentrate on. If you find that a task is particularly difficult, it makes sense to test that hypothesis with real users. If you're embarking on a redesign project, you need to understand what is working well and badly in the existing product and an expert review is a cheap and quick way of achieving this. If you have no time and budget for research with real users, an expert review is an invaluable method for placing a user focus on your thinking.

An expert review is most valuable at the very beginning of a project. Conduct your review before you've learned your client's jargon, design rationale, and internal politics. This will allow you to make your observations with a clear mind—it will be much easier for you to step through the product as a novice user if you *are* a novice user.

HOW TO CONDUCT AN EXPERT REVIEW

To conduct a successful expert review, you need to establish some information about the product's users. You also need to set some best practice guidelines (heuristics) to evaluate against.

WHO ARE YOUR TARGET USERS?

If you are to step through the product, imagining yourself in the place of a novice user, you need to know who that user is. Try to get some details of current users from your client. If you're working on a redesign that's aimed at a new set of customers, find out information about them too.

Write down a list of target users. For an online fashion shoe store they might be:

- Women aged 25-45 with a good disposable income who are keen followers of fashion
- Women aged 18-24 with a limited disposable income who are keen followers of fashion
- Men aged 25-50 buying for their female partners

In this example, it may be that women aged 25-45 are the only user group you need to consider as they are the only primary user group, with the others being secondary. In this case, you know that the primary user group is keenly interested in fashion, and thus an expert in the product's domain. However, you may need to consider whether the user base for your product has a poor understanding of the subject.

WHAT ARE YOUR USERS' KEY TASKS?

Now, write down the tasks that your users must be able to complete using the product. Do this for each primary user group. For the online shoe store's primary user group of affluent women aged 25-45, there is a single key task—to purchase a pair of shoes.

This single key task must be broken down into a series of tasks that add up to a purchase:

- Browse for suitable shoes
- View details of shoes
- Decide which shoes to purchase
- Choose correct size of shoe
- Arrange delivery
- Pay for shoes

Other tasks for this user group may include:

- Return unwanted shoes
- Compile a short list of desired shoes to consider or share with friends
- Browse for suitable shoes
- View details of shoes
- Share shoe details with best friend
- Decide which shoes to purchase

Additionally, it may be necessary to consider the secondary user groups—the male users of the site and the younger women with less disposable income—and add another couple of tasks:

- Buy a gift voucher
- Find a fashionable bargain

CONTEXT OF USE

Where will your users be when they are using your product? At work during lunch hour? On a phone on the train home from work? Curled up on the sofa with a tablet or laptop with half an eye on Facebook and Twitter? All of these are likely scenarios for a fashion shoes website, yet none of them imply 100% concentration on the product you are evaluating. Think about your users' attention when they complete their tasks—are they likely to be distracted and, if so, does the product treat them kindly? Another issue to consider is whether your users will be time pressured. This may be an unlikely scenario for users of a fashion shoes website, but consider an online supermarket or business hotels website.

UX GUIDELINES

Now you have a list of key tasks, and an idea of who is likely to be completing them in what context. Next, you need a set of best practice guidelines to evaluate the product against. This will help you establish usability issues that are not directly related to the tasks you have identified.

There are plenty of existing heuristic evaluation checklists, not least Nielsen's Ten Usability Heuristics. There are also ISO standards, which can be applied here. ISO 9241-110 covers ergonomic principles that apply to the design of dialogues between humans and information systems.

The heuristics described here are based on these sources and on our experiences of designing and usability testing for real-world projects.

First Impressions

How does the product feel at first sight? Does it look professional, trustworthy, easy to use, or appealing? Does the terminology make sense? Does the product draw you in?

Navigation and Information Architecture

Does the navigation use natural language? Is the product organized to meet user's needs? Does the navigation and IA speak the user's language, not that of the organization? Is the navigation consistent throughout the product? Is it clear where in the product the user is at any time?

Consistency

Is the product consistent throughout? Think about graphic design, color, fonts, and tone of voice. Are the same words used for the same concepts and screens within the navigation, headings, and copy?

Also consider consistency with the wider world. This is particularly important for websites, where Internet design conventions and patterns are well established. For example, there are conventions for date selectors and shopping carts. If the website has chosen not to use these conventions, can users still understand what to do?

Content

Is the copy easy to scan and read? It should not be too wordy, broken up with headings and sub-headings, and it should use appropriate imagery. Is the tone of voice appropriate for the audience and subject matter? Are novice users supported without patronizing experts?

Trustworthiness

Do you feel safe providing personal information? Does the product trick users into signing up for e-mails they don't want? Does it bombard them with intrusive advertising from disreputable suppliers? Is the content accurate and well written? Is there a clear indication of who runs a website? Can they be contacted, preferably by phone? Even small things like broken links on a website can go a long way to undermining trust.

Forms, Transactions, and Feedback

Are forms easy to understand and complete? Are form fields grouped logically? Are form fields named with natural language? Are there strong calls-to-action and a clear indication of how to proceed? Is the process ordered to match users' expectations or to match the underlying database?

Are security measures for online payment clear (without scaring the user)? How much use of legalese and jargon is there?

Does the system remove the need to remember items between screens? Does the system support users who may be distracted or short on time? Can they save their progress and come back later? Does it provide clear feedback that an action has been received by the system? For example, has the item been placed in the shopping cart or has the credit card been processed?

Error Handling

Does the product prevent errors from occurring? Does the product help users recover from errors, for example with clear messaging? How does the product deal with "help" information? Is it provided contextually or must the user search hidden FAQs for answers? How does the product deal with null search results? Does it provide suggestions and alternatives or simply leave the users wondering what they did wrong? Does the system support undo and redo, where appropriate?

Time and Complexity

How many steps must users go through to complete their tasks? Is the product long-winded? Does it feel complex? Are users able to complete key tasks in a reasonable amount of time?

"Accessibility" Issues

This book is not about accessibility, so this is not a full list of accessibility considerations. For a comprehensive list, see the W3C's Web Content Accessibility Guidelines. However, "accessibility" issues are about much more than needing assistive technologies to access websites and applications.

Is the contrast between background color and text high enough to be legible? Contrast is important for an ageing population—just watch someone who needs reading glasses struggle with standard-sized type in dark gray on a light gray background.

How about color blind users? Around 8% of the male population is color blind in one form or another (red/green is the most common). *(Source: http://en.wikipedia.org/wiki/Color_blindness.)* Is there a clear contrast between text and background if the user is red/green color blind? Is color-coded information also available without the use of color? There are plenty of color-blindness simulators available on the Internet. See Figure 10-1.

Figure 10-1: The *Smashing Magazine* homepage filtered for red/green and blue/yellow color blindness

SOURCE: Reproduced with permission of Smashing Magazine (www.smashingmagazine.com)
© 2012 Smashing Media GmbH

Is the font size legible to someone with mildly long sight? Is it possible to increase the font size if required? Is whitespace used to improve legibility or is the screen busy and crowded?

Use of complex language will affect more than just users with learning difficulties. The average reading age of the population as a whole is surprisingly low. We recommend that generalist content for the web aims for a reading age of 12. Although the reading age of copy is notoriously difficult to measure, there are formulae such as the Flesch Reading Ease scale (available within Microsoft Word) that can be used to evaluate English copy.

For websites, can the site be used on a variety of different contexts and technologies? Desktop machines and mobile devices such as phones and tablets with different operating systems? Mobile devices may have a slow or intermittent Internet connection as well as small screen size.

CONDUCT YOUR REVIEW

You have a list of users, their key tasks, and a set of heuristics to evaluate the product against. Now you need to conduct your review. Take notes throughout the review so you can write them up accurately later: don't expect to remember everything you thought at different parts of the process. Don't forget to note positive as well as negative comments. Take screenshots of the product as you go so you can annotate them later.

Fire up the application or website you are reviewing. Note any first impressions, such as how appealing or trustworthy the product appears to be.

Cognitive Walkthrough

Start with the *cognitive walkthrough* part of the exercise. A cognitive walkthrough is simply a review of any existing product, whereby you imagine yourself in the place of a user. What are the user's key tasks likely to be and are they able to complete them using the product?

Pick your primary user group and their primary task. Imagine you are a member of the user group coming to the product for the first time, wanting to complete the task. Don't forget to consider whether your user is distracted or perhaps using a mobile device.

In the shoe shop example, you might be a 30-year-old woman, wanting to buy some new shoes for work at an advertising agency. They need to be fashionable but comfortable to wear all day. You have a UK size 6 foot that's a little wide, making buying shoes tricky. You'll see we've fleshed out the user and their task. For a cognitive walkthrough, it's important to have a picture of what your users know and don't know when they come to the product. In this case, the user knows why they want the new shoes (for work); they know their size (6, wide); they may have made some style decisions already (a mid-heel); they may have idiosyncrasies that make purchase decisions more complex (wide feet); they will also have personal tastes (fashionable, doesn't like blue).

Now use the product to complete your chosen task. Do you know where to go next? Does the product provide enough information for you to continue? Why? Why not? Does the product behave as expected? Does the product assume knowledge that the user may not have? Is information carried from one step of the task to the next? Does the product use language that the user will understand? Do users understand whether the action they took has been completed? Make notes on every screen and consider how the journey feels. Is it short and smooth or long and complicated?

Keep going until you've completed all the tasks on your list. How successful were you? Did the product support all your tasks? If not, how serious were its failings? The complete inability to complete a key task with the information available is an extremely serious failure, whereas a small amount of confusion about how to select a shoe size is clearly less so.

Heuristic Evaluation

Now it's time to perform a second pass of the product. This time, you don't need to worry about putting yourself in the place of a particular user group. Review key screens against the UX guidelines listed previously. Note any potential problems or anything the product does well. Not all of the guidelines will be relevant to every screen, but the act of going through the checklist may uncover different usability issues than those identified using the cognitive walkthrough.

If you were looking at the example shoe website, you might find that it feels elegant and fashionable. However, the navigation structure changes from page to page and doesn't highlight your position within the site, leaving you feeling lost. Although you found that you could complete your task to purchase some shoes during the cognitive walkthrough part of the exercise, the form-filling process felt long-winded and complex.

ANALYZING AND REPORTING YOUR FINDINGS

You should now have a number of screenshots and a set of notes relating to them. We find that annotated screenshots are the most impactful way of documenting our findings. We generally use PowerPoint or Keynote, which means we can easily present the report in person. Also, it's great for printing out and sticking to a wall to prompt further discussion and analysis (sticky notes and felt tips help here too).

You need to distil your notes into something that's useful to you and useful to your client. What will your report be used for? You may want to identify *quick wins*—small fixes that will improve usability without a full redesign. You may be interested in areas to explore further with user testing. You may be looking at a complete redesign and want to be sure you understand what works well as much as you need to understand what works badly. Where possible, include recommendations for improvement, not merely descriptions of problems.

Start your report by documenting what you were evaluating against: user groups, their tasks, and your set of heuristics. This will help your client understand the thinking behind your review.

For each screen you have a comment on, make a new slide. Place the appropriate screenshot on the slide and annotate it with your comments. We find that numbered notes work best, with the notes down one side and numbers over the screenshot where applicable. Figure 10-2 shows an example expert review write up.

Figure 10-2: Putting an expert review slide deck together in PowerPoint

For each usability issue, a severity rating can help clients understand how important it is to fix (see Figure 10-3). For example, if you were unable to complete a purchase, the severity rating would be extremely high, whereas as slightly ambiguous navigation item would be low. If the client needs to identify quick wins, it may be that the navigation item is much easier to fix than the purchase path. You could also comment on how likely users are to encounter the problem.

Figure 10-3: Annotated screenshot with severity ratings

When you have documented all your notes against screenshots, ask yourself if any themes emerge. Is there a story that your report really needs to tell? If so, make sure that the order of the slides and annotations help to tell that story. Add a summary at the beginning of the deck and you're done.

TIME TO ALLOW

Allow yourself a day or two, but you can learn lots in an hour if you don't need to write it up as a report.

RESOURCES

User Focus - Usability Expert Reviews: Beyond Heuristic Evaluation: http://www.userfocus. co.uk/articles/expertreviews.html

ISO 9241-110: *2006 Ergonomics of human-system interaction -- Part 110: Dialogue principles*

Web Content Accessibility Guidelines: http://www.w3.org/WAI/intro/wcag

Techniques and Failures for Web Content Accessibility Guidelines 2.0 http://www.w3.org/TR/WCAG20-GENERAL/#G17

Neilsen's 10 Usability Heuristics: http://www.useit.com/papers/heuristic/heuristic_list.html

Human-Computer Interaction by Alan Dix, Janet Finlay, Gregory Abowd, Russell Beale (in particular the chapter on evaluation techniques)

Vischeck color blindness simulator: www.vischeck.com

Etre color blindness simulator: www.etre.com/tools/colourblindsimulator/

UX DESIGN TOOLS AND TECHNIQUES

11

PLANNING AND RUNNING SUCCESSFUL IDEATION WORKSHOPS

IDEATION WORKSHOPS ARE a collaborative design method. They help you and your client decide which design solutions are suitable for the project. Which are unsuitable and why? Conducting an ideation workshop will bring these questions alive. Run a successful ideation workshop and you and your client will have a shared understanding of how your product will work.

WHY ARE IDEATION WORKSHOPS IMPORTANT?

Ideation workshops are a great way of generating ideas and discussing which ones should be pursued. A successful ideation workshop identifies the design questions associated with your product, along with possible design solutions. What *could* your project do? What *should* it do? Now is the time to come up with lots of ideas and discuss them with your client.

The really important thing here is that your client will get an insight into user-centered design thinking. They will see how to go about making decisions by asking what is important to the users of the product. You will make decisions together. This will make the sign-off process for your next design deliverables (be they wireframes or graphic designs) much easier.

Ideation workshops can be seen as another method of fleshing out your project brief. Your client may have a really clear picture in their head of what they want from the project. They may not be very good at articulating their vision, but they'll be the first to tell you if you've got something wrong. Some people are particularly bad at visualizing something that does not exist. Others may have come up with design solutions that are flawed or don't meet the core business and user needs. Different stakeholders may have different ideas of what they want.

Running an ideation workshop will surface these types of conflicts. It will allow people unused to talking about design to have their say on an equal footing. It provides a platform for discussing all the issues and coming to a consensus. It generates a real feeling of teamwork with the client. You should leave the workshop with a clear direction for the next steps in your design process.

WHEN TO RUN AN IDEATION WORKSHOP

We like to run an ideation workshop for any design project we undertake. It doesn't always turn out that way, which can be a cause of regret if design sign-off proves to be tricky. It can seem like a big thing to ask of new clients—to give up at least half a day of their time—but successful workshops lead to a concrete shared understanding of design decisions. Hence no nasty surprises later. They can prevent significant amounts of rework.

HOW TO RUN AN IDEATION WORKSHOP

To run a successful ideation workshop, you need to do a bit of preparation up front. You need to decide on suitable activities and make sure you invite the right people.

PLANNING AN IDEATION WORKSHOP

First, work out how much time you can ask of your client. We prefer to run full-day ideation workshops, but this is not always possible. You'll need a minimum of three hours to decide on anything useful.

Now you need to choose activities to fit into the available time. If you have the luxury of a full-day workshop, this shouldn't be too difficult. If you only have a few hours, you will have to limit yourself to one or two activities.

It's not always easy to judge in advance which techniques will be best for the client team you are working with. Some people are delighted to have the chance to get the pens out and do some drawing; others are terrified at the prospect. Some people are great at explaining what they want; others need an example to point to. Some will have very clear ideas of project outcomes right from the get-go; others have very little idea. Some people will expect you, the designer, to do all the work; others will be desperate to collaborate. You often don't know before you turn up what type of people your clients are, so having alternative techniques up your sleeve is a good plan.

WORKSHOP ACTIVITIES

The important thing when choosing activities is to understand the information that will most help your project move forwards. Plan the workshop to elicit this. Figure 11-1 shows a list of some of the workshop activities we use. There are lots of other workshop techniques out there—try them and adapt them to meet the needs of your projects and your clients.

You Need To...	Workshop Activities
Agree on project functionality	Competitor benchmark review Functionality prioritization exercise Template prioritization exercise
Generate design ideas	Competitor likes and dislikes Competitor benchmark review Rapid sketching exercise
Design key screens	Content prioritization exercise Collaborative wireframing
Design the navigation structure	Group card sorting User journey exercise

Figure 11-1: Ideation workshop activities

Going into an ideation workshop, you need to understand the goals of the project. If you and your client do not have a clear understanding of the project goals, consider running an *elevator pitch* exercise (described in Chapter 4 on requirements workshops) at the beginning of your ideation workshop.

Competitor Benchmark Review

You should run this exercise if you need to understand the functionality your product should have. Reviewing competitors will draw up a list of potential functionality and generate discussion on whether the project should support such functionality. Additionally, you can stimulate debate on design look and feel and tone of voice.

Conduct a competitor benchmarking exercise (Chapter 6) with a focus on functionality and perhaps look and feel. Make sure you include screenshots of the competitors you are discussing. Bring the results of this to your workshop. You could bring your presentation on a laptop and project it to the workshop participants. Alternatively, print out the results on poster-sized and stick it up on the walls.

Stick each new sheet up and talk about your findings. What do the other workshop participants think? Record any comments as you go along. This could be in marker pen or on sticky notes straight onto your printouts. It can help to use one color of sticky notes for positive comments and another for negative.

When you've been through all your printouts, the walls will be full of images of competitors and notes. Now is the time to review the discussion and identify themes. Summarize your discussions by listing outcomes on the whiteboard. If you are running the exercise to agree on project functionality, write up the list of functionality that has emerged. If you are running the exercise to generate design ideas, this list might also include notes on desired look and feel or tone of voice. For example, when discussing a new holiday website, you may find that workshop participants like competitor sites with large imagery and a relaxed tone of voice. Or for a law firm's website, an informal tone may be unsuitable. Review your list with the workshop participants and make changes as necessary. Don't forget to photograph the whiteboard and annotated printouts before you move onto the next exercise.

Allow at least an hour for this exercise. More time may be required if you have a hefty competitor benchmark report to get through, although you should try to limit this to keep it manageable. Don't forget to give yourself enough time to conduct the review and get prints made before your workshop.

Functionality Prioritization Exercise

This is a perfect exercise to run if you have lots of candidate functionality and need to understand which is a must-have, which a nice-to-have, and which can be discounted or put on a long-term backlog. It works beautifully as a follow-up to a competitor benchmark review (discussed previously).

First you need to list all possible functionality. You can prep a lot of this beforehand, by writing your own list of options. This is particularly easy to do if you have completed competitor benchmarking. If you choose to prepare a list in advance, boldly write each item on a strip of paper or index card.

Ask the workshop participants to call out potential functionality. Write everything on the whiteboard or on an index card as it is mentioned. At this stage, you're capturing everything without making value judgments. If you came prepared with functionalities on index cards, make sure you have plenty of blank cards, so you can add in new functionality as it comes up. Don't stop listing functionality till you're sure you've considered everything. As the workshop facilitator, it's your job to make sure that everyone has had their say—some personalities are naturally dominant, but that doesn't make them always right.

Now that you have a long list of potential functionality for your project, you need to prioritize it.

If you wrote your functionality as a list on the whiteboard, start with the must-haves. As a group, decide on the functionality that your product has to have. Get a different colored whiteboard pen and write "1" next to everything that is first priority. If you are struggling to agree, return to your project goals. Does the candidate functionality help meet the project goals? If not, it's not priority 1. Next move onto functionality that is nice-to-have, but not core to the project. Write a "2" next to these items. What's left? Is there anything here that your project must not do? Put an "x" next to these items. Is anything still unallocated? Put a "3" next to these items—your project won't consider them but they are worth considering for future releases of the product.

If your functionality is on index cards, call them out one at a time and stick them to the whiteboard under headings. The headings should be something like "must have," "nice to have," "must not have," and "future releases." For the functionality on each card, discuss which heading it belongs under and stick it there. Again, if you are struggling to categorize a piece of functionality, examine it against the goals you have for your project. If discussion is pro-tracted, and you really can't agree, you can always park the conversation and note that you should come back later.

As you conduct this exercise, you may find that some functionality moves from one group to another. This is fine—you want to make sure everyone's happy with the final list. You also want to make sure that the "must haves" list is manageable. Do you think you can design all the functionality in the time available? If not, it makes sense to further prioritize the "must haves" list. Which is the most important must have item? Write a "1" next to it (in yet another color if you are not using index cards). What about the next most important? Write a "2" next to this one. Carry on until you get to the end of your "must haves" list. Discuss whether you can group this essential functionality into manageable phases. Figure 11-2 shows a functional-ity prioritization exercise in progress.

Figure 11-2: A functionality prioritization exercise

Allow an hour or two for this exercise. It is extremely important to get right.

Template Prioritization Exercise

If you have a clear understanding of the required functionality, but need to decide what you must work on for this project, a template prioritization exercise (as described in Chapter 4) is a good activity to run.

Competitor Likes and Dislikes

This is a variation on the competitor likes and dislikes exercise described in Chapter 4. It is targeted at specific screens (such as product pages or home pages) rather than competitors' entire products. Run this exercise if you want to generate high-level design ideas for key screens.

Before the workshop, think about what these key screens should be. For the imaginary ShoeUX.com website, they may be the homepage, a shoe product page, and a shortlist page. Ask everyone to bring to the workshop printed screenshots of competitors' versions of these screens that they like or dislike. In this example, "competitors" may be wider than online shoe vendors. Examples of good and bad online shortlists will be equally useful. When it comes to product pages, bringing it back to shoes may be sensible.

Ask each participant to try to bring along at least one good and one bad example for each screen you'll discuss—not too many to be daunting, but enough to provide plenty of discussion points. Don't forget to include yourself in the exercise.

On the day, ask everyone to share his or her choices and rationale. If no one's talking, go first yourself to get things warmed up. Which screens do they particularly like and why? Which do they hate? Pin the printouts to a wall or whiteboard where everyone can see them. It is sensible to record the key like or dislike on sticky notes attached to the printouts. Group the printouts by screen (for example, put all the homepages next to each other).

When everyone has shared his or her thoughts, discuss each screen. Do any themes emerge? If so, record them on sticky notes or on the whiteboard. For example, you may find that everyone has been raving about 360° views for the shoes product page, but that several people hate a competitor's shoe size availability widget.

This exercise is a great way of getting a feel for what your client wants from individual screens. What does a successful screen look like to them? What must it not do? A group discussion will dive a lot deeper into the rationale behind your client's choices than a simple list of likes and dislikes would. Don't forget to photograph the results of your discussions, or take them away with you, for later reference.

Allow around 15 minutes per workshop participant for this exercise, but cap it at an hour and a half.

Rapid Sketching Exercise

This rapid sketching exercise is derived from Leah Buley's sketching workshops that she gave when she was working at Adaptive Path. We think it's a brilliant way of rapidly generating lots of ideas.

Give everyone (including yourself) a sheet of paper and a pen. You could use one of several sketching templates available on the Internet (including on Leah Buley's website, ugleah.com/ux-team-of-one/). Alternatively, simply divide plain paper into six equal rectangles—what you need here are six small areas to fill with ideas (see Figure 11-3).

Figure 11-3: cxpartners' rapid sketching template

Now comes the fun bit. Ask everyone to fill each of the six rectangles with an idea for the project you are working on. You may say that people can choose any combination of screens from the project. Alternatively, it may make more sense to concentrate on a few key screens or a particular user journey. Reassure the group that this is about generating ideas, not good drawings. Let people know they can draw whatever they like—the ideas don't have to fit into any existing product or user flow. Set a timer and allow 20 minutes for sketching.

Next, ask everyone to talk through what they drew and pin it to the wall. If no one's particularly vocal, describe your sketches first to get people talking.

When everyone has described their ideas, you need to discuss them. It may be that, in order to digest everything, people need five minutes in front of the wall that the sketches are pinned to. Now you should lead a discussion on the relative merits of the ideas. There is something leveling about sketches pinned to the wall—it should no longer matter whether the idea came from the boss or a lowlier team member. Did any themes emerge? Perhaps lots of people thought of a 360° shoe viewer or a shortlist. The aim here is to identify ideas worthy of further exploration. Figure 11-4 shows the output from a rapid sketching exercise to generate ideas for ShoeUX.com, the imaginary online shoe emporium.

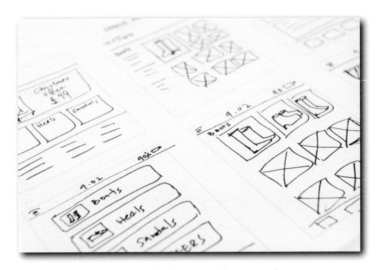

Figure 11-4: A rapid sketching exercise for the imaginary ShoeUX.com website

Leah Buley's original exercise calls for the group to move on to higher fidelity sketching—choosing one idea to elaborate on. This is a great way of understanding which ideas the group likes. However, we have found that a group unused to sketching sometimes struggles with this. One alternative is to ask each participant to talk through his or her favorite ideas from the wall. They could choose their own ideas or those of others. Use sticky notes or small round colored stickers to mark the ideas that were liked. When everyone has spoken, review the sketches that have been marked. Use the whiteboard to list desirable features and themes.

If you were discussing ShoeUX.com, you might find that most people thought a shareable shortlist was important, along with a directional fashion lead to the homepage content and large product photography. Ideas around street style were liked, although no clear direction was identified. Figure 11-5 shows the results of a rapid sketching exercise for ShoeUX.com.

You should now have a good idea of the themes you need to go away and explore during the project's design phase.

Allow 30 minutes for setup and sketching, plus around 10 minutes per workshop participant for this exercise.

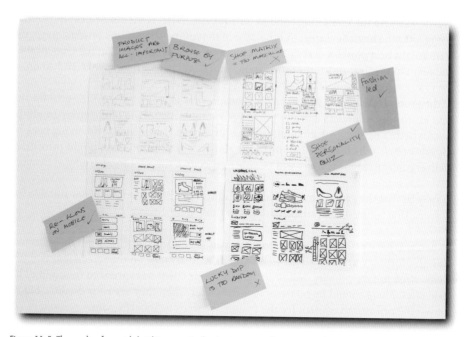

Figure 11-5: The results of a rapid sketching exercise for the imaginary ShoeUX.com website

Content Prioritization Exercise

This exercise is brilliant for examining ideas for key screens. For an online shop, often the product page is the most important screen to examine here. Other likely candidates are a homepage or product listing.

Start the exercise by identifying the main business goals for the screen you are examining. For a product page, this is clearly "buy the product," whereas a homepage might have several including, "signpost relevant products" and "communicate brand values." Also of use here is any vision or elevator pitch you have for the product.

As a group, list any content that could potentially live on your chosen screen. Use a white-board so everyone can see what's been thought of. Don't make any decisions at this stage— write down everything that's proposed. For a shoe product page, candidate content might include a main product photo, additional product photos, the price, a product description, a Buy Now button, product reviews, a size selector, and more. If there is an existing version of the page, its contents are a good starting point.

Now you need to prioritize this candidate content. There are several ways to do this, including dot-voting, where everyone is given five small round stickers and they use them to vote for content by placing one or more stickers next to items they think are the most important. A simpler alternative is to have a group discussion. Firstly, agree on *hygiene factors*: content that the screen simply cannot exist without. In the example of a shoe product page, this might be a product photo, a size selector, the price, and a Buy Now button. Using a different colored whiteboard pen, put a tick against all the hygiene factors.

Next, prioritize the remaining content on your list. What is the single next most important thing after the hygiene factors? In the case of the online shoe store's product page, the next item might be a product description. Write a "1" next to this item on the content list and move on to the next most important item, which will get a "2" next to it, and so on.

If the group is struggling to reach consensus, review the items against the goal for the screen and against the product's elevator pitch. For example, members of the group might be arguing over whether delivery information is more important than reviews. Referring back to the elevator pitch, which states that the target audience is short on time, might prioritize the delivery information, as users will be able to specify a timeslot for delivery.

It may be that the group decides that some of the candidate content is not suitable for the screen. That is fine—just put a cross next to these items.

When you have prioritized all the content, you have a wonderful start to the wireframing and design process. You know all the items you have to arrange on the screen and you know which items need to take priority. Not only that, but your client has agreed to the content and the priorities. There should be no nasty surprises later when they see your designs. Figure 11-6 shows the prioritized content for the imaginary website ShoeUX.com.

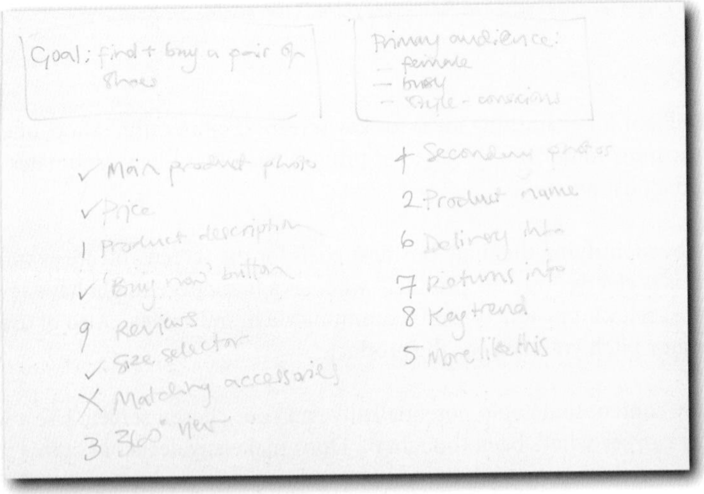

Figure 11-6: The results of a content prioritization exercise for the imaginary ShoeUX.com website

Allow 45 minutes to an hour per screen for this exercise.

Collaborative Wireframing

Collaborative wireframing is a perfect complement to the content prioritization exercise (discussed previously). In fact, a list of prioritized content is imperative as an input to collaborative wireframes. You'll need another whiteboard for this, as participants need to see your content list as you draw.

Think of your clean whiteboard as the screen you're examining. Look at your prioritized content list—start with the hygiene factors and the top few prioritized items. Start to draw boxes on the whiteboard to represent them. The visual hierarchy of boxes should represent your content priorities. You may find that some items need to be visually grouped, even though they have very different priorities. For example, you might find that delivery information needs to be visually grouped alongside product reviews, even though delivery information was deemed to be much more important. Figure 11-7 shows the results of a collaborative wireframing exercise for the example website, ShoeUX.com.

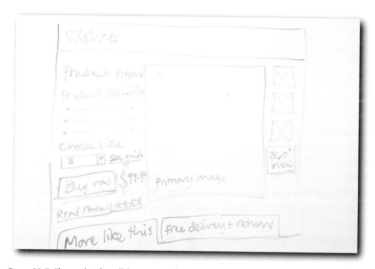

Figure 11-7: The results of a collaborative wireframing exercise for the imaginary ShoeUX.com website

The benefits of doing this on a whiteboard with your client are clear. You can erase a content block as easily as you have drawn it. Your client can take the whiteboard pen and draw their thoughts. You can thrash out discrepancies between visual groupings and agreed priorities. You and your client will leave the workshop with a really clear picture of what your key screens will look like. All that head-scratching that you often do in a room on your own with OmniGraffle or Photoshop or your other design weapon of choice will have been done in advance. You will be free to sweat the details. Your client will have made the key design decisions alongside you, so shouldn't pipe up with awkward comments later.

Allow half and hour to an hour for each screen for this exercise.

Group Card Sorting

Card sorting is an activity more commonly run during usability testing. It is a method for uncovering users' understanding of a domain. Card sorting with users is covered in Chapter 15 on information architecture. The basic premise is that you provide index cards with different content items on them and ask people to put them into logical groups. The way people group the cards and the reasons they give helps form the main navigation structure of a website.

It is sometimes useful to run a group sorting exercise in ideation workshops. The danger here is that groupthink comes into play, or that everyone bows to the boss's views. However, it can also be a quick way of uncovering your client's expectations of how to design the project's information architecture. If you have already run card sorts with users, it may be more appropriate here to simply run through the results of these sorts with your clients. Alternatively, if you are planning to run card sorts with users later in the project, a card sort with your client will identify candidate group labels to verify in usability testing.

Before the workshop, prepare index cards with the main content areas that need to be grouped to form your project's information architecture. If you are working on a redesign project, the existing sitemap is a good place to start. For ideation workshops, you need to run an open card sort—provide cards for the content and blank ones for the content group names.

Use a big table to move the cards around, or stick them to the wall with Blu-Tack putty. Start by grouping like content. Maybe "women's high heels," "women's sandals," and "women's flats" form one group, whereas "men's lace-ups" and "men's boots" form another. If you find that one item needs to live in more than one place, write it on a second card. When you have put all the content cards into groups, you need to name the groups. We've chosen an easy example here—"women's shoes" and "men's shoes" spring to mind. However, there are plenty of situations where this will generate lively discussion. If agreement is proving difficult to reach, it's fine to park the discussion and agree to return later. Perhaps there's some user research or digging through server analytics that will help solve a dispute?

When you have your cards sorted and labeled, don't forget to photograph the results for later study. Figure 11-8 shows a card sort for the example ShoeUX.com website.

Figure 11-8: The results of a group card sort for the imaginary ShoeUX.com website

Allow around an hour for this exercise—more or less depending on how many cards you need to sort and the likelihood of a dispute arising.

User Journey Exercise

Another way of gaining insight into your project's information architecture is to run the user journey exercise as described in Chapter 4 on requirements workshops.

WHO TO INVITE

You'll notice this list is very similar to the attendees for the requirements workshop. They are your project's key stakeholders. In fact, we often run hybrid workshops—requirements in the morning and ideation in the afternoon.

> *Tip: We like to keep our ideation workshops to fewer than eight people, as it keeps the decision-making process simple. However, we know of UX practitioners who delight in running huge workshops with up to 60 people. They have developed special techniques to facilitate useful outcomes, generally involving teamwork.*

The techniques described here work for a client workshop, but also work for your own design and development teams—they are a great way of making everyone feel heard. With clients, they are a great way of identifying themes and outliers. Does everyone in the room reach consensus easily? Does one person have a series of madcap ideas that everyone else discounts? These workshops can do an excellent job of defusing the potentially tricky situation of a boss with a terrible idea. It's much easier to collaborate on an alternative than it is to discredit it.

Consider inviting:

- The project owner (likely your project contact)
- The project sponsor (the person with financial responsibility for the project, often the project owner's boss)
- A representative of the technical team
- A representative of the graphic design team
- A representative of the content or copywriting team
- A representative of the internal UX team
- A representative of the product or merchandising team (someone who knows all about the products your project will sell)
- The project manager

BEFORE THE WORKSHOP

Plan your workshop activities and write an agenda, including timings. Don't forget to include lunch and coffee breaks—thinking is hungry work! Figure 11-9 shows an example requirements workshop agenda, focusing on generating ideas and co-designing key screens.

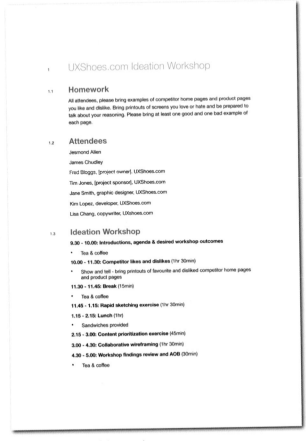

Figure 11-9: Ideation workshop agenda

If you are running the workshop at your client's offices, ask for a room big enough for all the attendees to move about in—you want everyone to have a chance to grab a marker pen and contribute. You'll need a room with a whiteboard or two and a flipchart. It's also useful to be allowed to stick things to the walls with Blu-Tack. If you're planning on running a rapid sketching exercise, make sure you have a table in the room or something for everyone to lean on. This is a good excuse to invite the client to your offices as you can control the environment.

Take the kit you'll need with you:

- The agenda
- Printouts (competitor benchmarking, competitor likes and dislikes, and/or rapid sketching templates)

- Index cards (completed for group card sorting or functionality prioritization and blank for labeling and anything you haven't thought of)
- Blu-Tack putty (for sticking up printouts and completed flipchart sheets)
- Whiteboard pens in different colors
- Flipchart stand, paper, and pens
- Sticky notes
- Small round colored stickers for dot voting
- Camera to record whiteboard contents before erasing

RUNNING THE WORKSHOP

Start the workshop with introductions and a quick run-through of the agenda and aims of the workshop. It's your job to facilitate discussions—you want to find what your clients think, not to tell them what to think. Some really valuable information you can come away with is an insight into your client's team. Who has lots of good ideas? Who doesn't? Who from the client team must you listen to?

If you have to clear a whiteboard to make space for more workshopping, photograph it before you wipe it.

Wrap up the workshop by reviewing your work—reiterate the findings from the day's activities. Did any themes emerge? You should now have a good sense of how to progress your design work and a strong sense of teamwork with your fellow workshop participants.

AFTER THE WORKSHOP

After a successful ideation workshop, you and your client should have a shared set of design ideas. You will have discussed possible design routes and agreed on which to explore further.

Share your photographs of whiteboards, card sorts, and workshop walls with your client. It's important to have a shared record of decisions for everyone to refer back to.

If possible, spend some of the next day writing up your notes from the workshop. You'll have a clear idea of your next steps in the design process by now, and it makes sense to share these with your client. It is a great way of setting realistic expectations. Ask your client to comment on your notes—this will verify that your understanding of the workshop outcomes is the same as theirs.

RESOURCES

Alan Colville's "A Shared Vision" slides: http://www.slideshare.net/ alancolville/a-shared-vision-the-coordinating-force-behind-great-ux

Undercover User Experience Design by Cennydd Bowles and James Box

Gamestorming: A Playbook for Innovators, Rulebreakers, and Changemakers by Dave Gray, Sunni Brown, and James Macanufo (The games are also available online for free at http://www.gogamestorm.com/?page_id=234)

Leah Buley and Brandon Schauer's "Good Design Faster" slides: http://www.slideshare.net/whatidiscover/good-design-faster

Leah Buley's personal website: http://www.ugleah.com

12

CREATING TASK MODELS AND USER JOURNEYS THAT CONVEY REAL USER BEHAVIOR

A TASK MODEL IS a description of the activities users perform in order to reach their goals. Task models can represent both real-world and digital activities. They help you understand how your product can fit into the users' lives. User journeys are a method of expressing the ideal route for your product to facilitate these activities.

The task models and user journeys described in this chapter are ultimately derived from the academic study of task analysis within the field of human-computer interaction. Our approach is rather less formal and examines tasks at a much less granular level. This approach is designed to strike an appropriate balance between research time and useful insight.

WHY ARE TASK MODELS AND USER JOURNEYS IMPORTANT?

The aim of producing task models is to ensure that your product matches users' expectations of how the system works. Usability problems occur when there is a discrepancy between what the user wants to do and the way that the system requires them to do it. Conducting user research and developing a task model is extremely useful in helping to make design decisions later. If you produce a task model as part of your requirements-gathering activities, you can evaluate your subsequent designs against it. At every stage you can ask whether the design supports the task model. This can help you prioritize user flows and interface elements. It is useful to refer back to if there are difficult choices to be made.

The aim of producing user journeys is to ensure that users' tasks are streamlined and easy to accomplish. User journeys can be produced with or without first developing a task model. A user journey is something to think about when designing the flow of your product. Which user journeys are most important? How can you structure your product to ensure these key journeys are smooth?

WHEN TO DEVELOP TASK MODELS AND USER JOURNEYS

The typical aim of a task model for the projects we work on is to understand the decision-making process involved in making a purchase. What is known at the outset, what must be learned on the way, and how can the product best support the process?

Do your users tend to make a snap decision? Make sure they have all they need at their fingertips. Are they likely to go away and consult someone else? Make the information easy to share and come back to; make it easy to save progress. Do your users know some but not all of the information they need to make a decision? Make it easy to specify the known quantities while handholding through the unknown.

Task models help you to understand how your users will need to interact with the information provided by your product. Match your product design to the way your users already work and your product will fit seamlessly into their lives.

A task model can help you choose features for your product. (Is a shortlist useful? How about a sharing widget or a comparison table?) It can help you to design your information architecture. (Does this content fit at this point in the user's task flow or at another? Which attributes should a user be able to filter by?) It can help you design specific interactions. (Should the user choose color or size first? Might it be necessary to save a form and come back later?) A task model can identify gaps in users' knowledge and underpin the design of contextual help for your product.

Simple user journeys are easy and useful for every project. At their most basic, they help to sanity-check an information architecture. Can users complete their primary tasks in as few steps as possible? A user journey analysis can help you to make rational choices about optimizations. Which items belong in the top-level navigation? Which steps in the journey should expert users be able to bypass?

As a designer, you must choose which steps a user must go through in order to complete their tasks. Producing task models and considering user journeys helps you to produce better designs that closely match users' needs.

HOW TO DEVELOP TASK MODELS

In order to develop a useful task model, you need to do two things:

- Understand how your users think about the task at hand
- Represent this understanding in a way that helps you to make design decisions later

If your project were to create a shoe website, you would want to understand how your target audiences go about browsing and buying shoes. What is their motivation for purchase? Do they enjoy browsing or is it a chore? Are they likely to go away and come back again or will they buy straight away? What do they know about what they need from a shoe? Its purpose (work or partying)? Its size? (If a particular shoe is not available in the customer's size, they simply will not buy it.) Its fit? Shoes need to be tried on, and may not be comfortable even if they are the correct size, so return policies are likely to be vitally important. Talking to real users of competitor products in order to generate a task model will help focus the project.

UNDERSTANDING USERS' TASKS

There are a number of methods for generating a picture of your users' tasks. User testing is our preferred method, but it helps to get another perspective, say from stakeholder interviews or contextual research.

User Testing

The best source of information for developing a task model is user testing (Chapter 5). If you are running user testing at the beginning of a project, devote some of the test to developing a task model. Focus this part of the test on users' current behaviors. Ask your test participants to describe the last time they did the task you are interested in. Don't ask them to speculate on how they would like to do it—memories are much more indicative of likely future behavior than imagination.

For example, if you were designing a website that sells shoes, you might ask your test participants to consider the last time they bought shoes. Ask them to tell you what prompted the purchase and how they went about selecting the right pair and buying them. You might find that this transaction was completed entirely offline. This is fine—you may still find out some useful information. However, your next question would be to ask about the last time the participant bought shoes online. For this example, you would likely have recruited test participants who had bought shoes online in the last year or so. Now you want them to show you how they went about their task. You are interested in the following:

- What prompted the purchase?
- What influenced their choice of vendor (friend's recommendations, newspapers, magazines, favorite vendor, a Google search, or something else)?
- Which websites or apps were used for research or purchase? In what context were these digital products used (on a laptop at home, on a desktop PC at work, on a smartphone on the train)?
- Did they find what they wanted and buy it straight away? Or did they think it over for a while?
- Did they need to consult someone else before a decision was made?
- Were there any problems along the way?
- Were there any moments of delight along the way?

Ask the participant to replicate their journey as you watch, telling you about what was good and bad along the way. Don't expect them to start at any existing website or app—give them a blank browser as a starting point. They may go straight to a favorite URL or they may begin with Google. It is interesting for you to see where the users begin their task.

> Tip: As you watch a number of users go through this process, you should see patterns develop. Perhaps shoe buyers all know why they want the shoes before they look for them, or maybe several participants would only purchase from an online store offering free returns. These patterns are task analysis gold dust. You will use them later to devise your model.

Unfortunately, it is not always possible to run formal user testing at the beginning of every project. Interviewing real users is the best way of generating an accurate task model. However, there are other methods that can both supplement and replace user testing in task model generation.

Guerilla Testing

In place of recruiting users to come to structured user testing sessions, ask your friends and family. Many projects center on subjects they will understand—if they have experience of the focus of your project, they will have something to teach you.

Ask them the same questions as outlined under user testing. If they can show you what they did on a computer, all the better.

Stakeholder Interviews

Ask your client how their customers currently go about their tasks. If you are running stakeholder interviews (Chapter 3) as part of your requirements-gathering process, you could ask this question to a number of senior members of your client's team. It is always interesting to see if there are any discrepancies in understanding! Asking people to draw a flow diagram can be useful here.

Contextual Research

Are you able to access your client's customers in any way other than user testing? Contextual research (Chapter 7) may be useful here. Can you visit a bricks-and-mortar store and observe customers browsing and making purchases? How do they make decisions? Under what circumstances do they seek assistance? Your client's store is best for this—your client can ask the store manager to make you welcome. However, if it is easier get to competitor stores, you may well learn plenty from hanging around for half an hour or so.

Another way of getting access to real users is via call center listening. If your client runs phone-based customer services, ask to listen in to customer calls for a few hours. Additionally, interviewing call center staff is a great way of identifying patterns in customer interactions with the company.

IDENTIFYING PATTERNS

The most important component of task analysis is gaining a deep understanding of the goals people are trying to achieve. A thorough understanding of user's goals and tasks will allow you to break those goals down into smaller sub-goals and sub-tasks.

The next step is to identify patterns and groupings that apply across different users. One way of doing this is to write each individual sub-task or sub-goal on an index card or sticky note. Step through your notes from user testing, stakeholder interviews, and/or contextual research and write each task or goal you come across on a new sticky note.

For example, for online shoe purchases, you might review your notes from the first test participant and write:

- Want to purchase shoes for work
- Visit website recommended by friend
- Investigate returns policy (must be able to return items for free)
- Find shoes suitable for work (black, mid heel, not too flamboyant)
- View detail on selected shoes
- Decide which shoes to buy
- Order chosen shoes in a size 7

The notes from your second participant may produce:

- Bored at lunchtime
- Visit favorite online shoe vendor
- View saved shortlist
- Send link to best friend for second opinion (the friend likes them!)
- Order chosen shoes in a size 6

Once you have done this for all your observations, you'll have a big pile of cards or sticky notes. Now you need to make sense of them. Lay them out on a table or stick sticky notes to the wall. Start by grouping duplicates and extremely similar items. In a moment, you'll remove the duplicates, but it's important to see which are common and which are less so first. Note the large groups before removing the duplicate sticky notes or cards.

The next step is to impose some order. Try to organize the remaining cards. Chronological order is usually the best system, but there may be another useful pattern to work with. It helps to have some headings to group the cards under. For the online shoe shop example, you might have the following order.

Trigger:

- Want to purchase shoes for work
- Bored at lunchtime
- See shoes featured in a magazine

Entry points:

- Visit website recommended by friend
- Visit favorite online shoe vendor
- Visit URL from magazine

Browse shoes:

- Find shoes suitable for purpose
- Color, heel height, materials, style, brand, and so on
- Find affordable shoes
- View detail on selected shoes
- View saved shortlist

Decide:

- Decide which shoes to buy
- Send link to best friend for second opinion
- Are they available in my size?
- Investigate returns policy
- Investigate shipping destinations and costs

Purchase:

- Order chosen shoes in a size x
- Order chosen shoes in several sizes to try fit
- Order several different pairs in size x

Figure 12-1 shows an example set of grouped sticky notes.

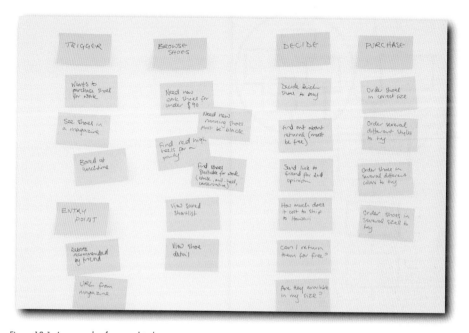

Figure 12-1: An example of grouped tasks

PRODUCING A TASK MODEL DIAGRAM

Now you should have an arrangement of sticky notes that does a good job of describing your users' tasks. All that remains is to distill this into a diagram. The aim of this is to describe how your users want to behave, clarifying and formalizing user requirements. The finished diagram should underpin your design process.

Figure 12-2 shows an example task model for buying shoes. Imagine that your research had found that most people know what they want the shoes for at the beginning of the process. For some people, the next consideration is price, whereas for others it is one of several factors that can be grouped under "appearance" (heel, color, style, brand, material, and so on). Shoes with the right appearance and price are candidates for purchase. At this point, some users said they would ask a friend's advice or mull the decision over for a day or two. Others would make a decision straight away. Once users had decided on a pair of shoes, they checked to see if it was in their size. Once they had added it to their basket, they checked how to return items and investigated their shipping options. Figure 12-2 shows these findings in a simple, easily referred to format. It's not based on real research with real shoe buyers, so don't rely on it!

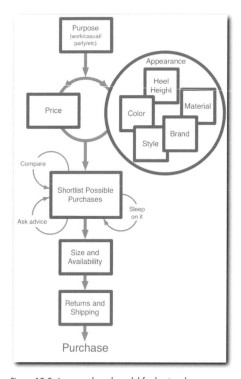

Figure 12-2: An example task model for buying shoes

Layers of Information

Once you have your basic task model diagram, there are further layers of information you could add to it to make it even more useful. Figure 12-3 shows layers of information added to the example task model. Think about adding:

- Entry points—Where do different types of users enter the system?
- Content needs—Notes on product content and functionality to support the task.
- Failure points—Areas where existing products fail the users. These should be opportunities for your new product to improve the situation.
- Personas—If you have developed personas (Chapter 14) for your project, layering them onto your task model will bring it to life.

WHAT NEXT?

The really important thing here is what happens next. How will you use your task model throughout your UCD process?

The first thing to do is discuss it with your client. If you and your client share an understanding of the customer's needs and tasks, your design job will be all the easier.

The usefulness of a task model becomes clear when design work begins. Look at your model when designing your information architecture. The shoe example might imply that top-level navigation includes some way of segmenting by purpose, so you might have "Women's shoes" subdivided into "Work shoes," "Casual shoes," and "Party shoes." On further reflection this may not work too well as different customers will have a very different idea of what "Work shoes" or "Party shoes" look like. A more appropriate subdivision may be by style, such as "Boots," "Shoes," "Sandals," "Slippers," and so on. The importance of purpose to users could be reflected in editorial, say with features on "Perfect party shoes" near Christmas, "Classic office shoes" or "Shoes for the great outdoors." Other aspects grouped under appearance may not be top-level navigation, but certainly imply ways to narrow product listings down to a manageable number. The fact that users were found to list potential purchases directly implies "shortlist" functionality within the new site, possibly with the ability to compare a number of shoes side by side. Additionally, returns and shipping information should be clearly displayed throughout the buying process.

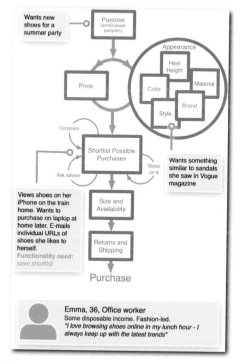

Figure 12-3: An example task model for buying shoes, with extra layers of information added

Task Models for Different Purchases

Consider two very different examples of very different purchases. Typically, we see different timescales for small purchases to large purchases. For example, someone may decide they need a new T-shirt in their lunch hour, browse for something they like, and purchase it immediately. A sofa or family holiday, on the other hand, will take longer and likely involve more than one decision-maker. There will be joint decisions around budget and preferences, research phases, and the sharing of candidate purchases. A final decision leading to purchase could well happen months after the first discussions on the subject. Task models that are useful to such different processes have different requirements. For the T-shirt purchase, your task model should reflect the information that users typically have at the beginning of their task (T-shirt size, budget, work or casual, and so on). Your task model can capture decisions the users need to make on the way (color, design, and so on). A task model that successfully conveys that information might lead to design decisions allowing users to first choose size and budget before having to select color. The sofa task model, on the other hand, would need to reflect a more complex interaction over time. From the first thought—I need a new sofa—the research phase may start with "how much money do I need to spend to get a sofa I like?" and continue with "which suppliers have sofas I like?" There will be discussions around the need for a sofa bed, the color, the fabric, the size. One stakeholder may find something they love and want to share it with another stakeholder. Finally, a decision to purchase will be made, and the users may come back online to order. Or they may visit a local store to make the final decision based on bouncing on the cushions. This task model might imply that you should design shortlists, easy sharing of candidate purchases, and a seamless journey from online to offline and back again.

HOW TO DEVELOP USER JOURNEYS

User journeys are particularly useful at two different stages in a user-centered design process. First, they are a useful way of evaluating an existing system prior to redesign. Secondly, they are something you should consider when designing a product's information architecture (Chapter 15). When you examine actual user journeys on an existing product, you should be looking for optimization opportunities. When you are considering the user journeys associated with a new information architecture, you should be interested in designing the ideal journey.

For all user journey analysis, you first need to identify the key journeys that you want to examine. These will typically align closely with the business goals for the product. In the shoe shop example, the primary business goal is to sell shoes. A secondary business goal might be to facilitate returns, as this will reduce the load on the call center. So, you might decide that the two journeys you will focus on are:

- Purchase shoes
- Return unwanted shoes

USER JOURNEY ANALYSIS ON AN EXISTING PRODUCT

There are a number of ways of evaluating user journeys on existing websites or apps. Testing with real users is always our preferred method of gaining insight, as it is unbiased and reflects customer needs rather than business needs.

User Testing

If you are running user testing (Chapter 5) at the beginning of a redesign process, try to add some tasks to help with user journey analysis. At this stage in the project, user journey analysis and task modeling are extremely similar. The difference is that your user journeys focus on the existing system and the routes people use to complete their tasks on it. Task models encompass the wider world and what people want to do to complete their tasks.

During the test, ask your participants to complete your key journeys using the existing product. Use a think-aloud protocol—ask participants to tell you what they're thinking as they step through the task. Note down the pages or screens they visit along the way, including any jumping back and forth between screens and any dead-ends. These notes will form the basis of your user journey diagram.

Analytics

Another great source of real customer data are an existing website's server statistics. Ask your client's statistics analyst to talk you through the key goals and journeys. Look for pages with high exit numbers in order to identify potential pain points.

Expert Review

If you do not have access to real users via testing, the next best thing is an expert review (see Chapter 10). Consider your key tasks and step through the site trying to complete them. Note the pages or screens you visit along the way. Again, note anything that feels long-winded, complex, or leads to a dead end.

User Journey Diagram for an Existing Product

Pull all your research and analysis together in a user journey diagram. For each task, produce a separate user journey diagram.

The easiest way to get started is to write the name of each screen that users typically visit to complete the specified task on a sticky note. Then, stick the notes to a whiteboard in the order that they are visited. Draw directional arrows between them to show a typical journey. This may result in arrows that start at the homepage and continue to confirmation with no deviation. Or you may find that there are detours and circular routes along the way. Figure 12-4 shows this activity in progress.

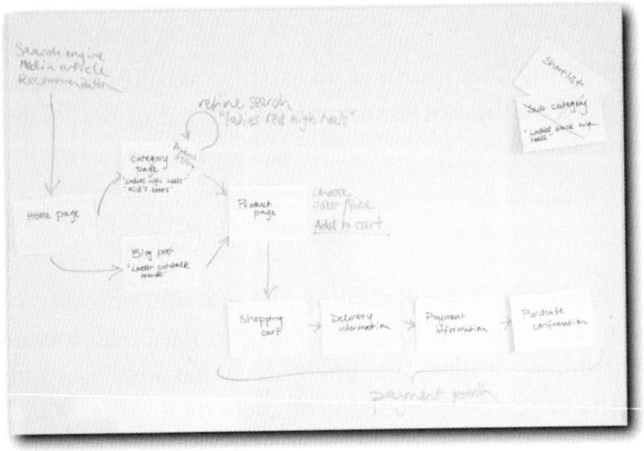

Figure 12-4: Working out a user journey diagram on a whiteboard

Once you have your basic diagram, you can add useful comments and observations. Interesting things to note include:

- Jumps back and forth between pages. Can the redesign provide information to help users make decisions on one page without having to jump?
- Detours from the expected journey. For example, if people are using a shopping cart as a shortlist, there may be extra functionality that could be designed to make this process easier.
- Pages with unexpectedly high drop-off rates in the analytics. Can the redesign address the problem?
- Any other pain points, such as onerous registration requirements or the necessity to wade through long terms and conditions.

Figure 12-5 shows an annotated user journey diagram for the imaginary ShoeUX.com website.

When you come to your redesign work, you can think about the following issues:

- Are there any pages that could be skipped?
- Is there extra information you could provide to prevent the need for jumping back and forth between pages?
- Are there any shortcuts needed?
- Is any extra functionality needed?

USER JOURNEYS AND INFORMATION ARCHITECTURE

User journeys should always be taken into consideration when designing a new information architecture. When you have a candidate architecture, evaluate it against your key user tasks. If you developed task models and user journeys at the requirements gathering phase of your project, refer to them when you design your information architecture.

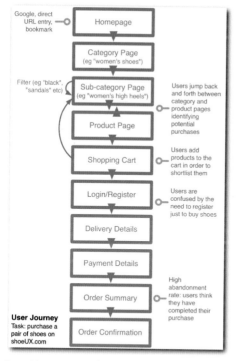

Figure 12-5: An annotated user journey diagram for an existing product

Task Models

If you've developed a task model, make sure that your new product design supports that model. Referring to a well-researched task model will allow you to design your information architecture in a manner that matches your user's understanding of the system. Prioritize and streamline your user journeys based on your task model.

If the journey your users take through your product matches their expectations, it will be seamless. If you break their expectations, they will find the journey to be difficult and jarring.

Stakeholder Interviews

Another method for identifying ideal user journeys is to discuss them with your client stakeholders. Refer back to the collaborative user journey exercise in Chapter 4 on requirements workshops.

USER JOURNEY DIAGRAM FOR NEW INFORMATION ARCHITECTURES

Now you need to document your user journey as it relates to your new information architecture. The best way to do this is to superimpose the key journeys onto your sitemap diagram.

Figure 12-6 shows the key journey to purchase a pair of shoes superimposed on an example information architecture for the imaginary website, ShoeUX.com. It shows that the journey from homepage to purchase is simple and uninterrupted. It includes lessons from the task model:

- It is possible to filter products by price, heel height, color, style, brand, and material.
- Shortlist functionality has been added.
- It is easy to share individual products and the shortlist.
- The need to register before completing the purchase process has been removed.

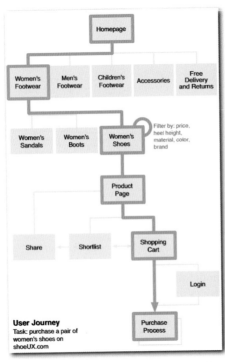

Figure 12-6: A user journey superimposed on a sitemap diagram

RESOURCES

Communicating the User Experience by Richard Caddick and Steve Cable

Mental Models by Indi Young

Usability for the Web: Designing Web Sites that Work by Tom Brinck, Darren Gergle, and Scott D. Wood

100 Things Every Designer Needs to Know about People by Susan M Weinschenk (see the chapters on mental models and conceptual models)

User and Task Analysis for Interface Design by JoAnn T. Hackos and Janice C. Redish

Human-Computer Interaction by Alan Dix, Janet Finlay, Gregory Abowd, and Russell Beale (see the chapter on task analysis)

Human-Computer Interaction by Jenny Preece, Yvonne Rogers, Helen Sharp, David Benyon, Simon Holland, and Tom Carey (see the chapter on task analysis)

Simple and Usable: Web, Mobile and Interaction Design (2010) by Giles Colborne

13
CREATING CUSTOMER EXPERIENCE MAPS TO HELP VISUALIZE THE USER EXPERIENCE

A CUSTOMER EXPERIENCE MAP breaks a product or service into its constituent parts and visualizes how well or badly user and business needs are being met along the way.

A customer experience map will typically consist of both a user and a business/system layer. The user layer generally identifies user needs but can also highlight user questions and anxieties for each point of the customer experience. The business/system layer identifies what provision is made to meet that user need, again at each point of the customer experience.

Customer experience maps are used by product owners to visualize how well their product is supporting the needs of the business and of their customers. They are used as strategic documents to help to prioritize improvements and to spot opportunities to innovate their products.

In the context of user experience design, customer experience maps are great way of making you think more deeply about the way users see the world. As a UX deliverable they present a very clear and simplified visualization of something that is otherwise often unseen and difficult for people to visualize.

WHEN TO CREATE CUSTOMER EXPERIENCE MAPS

Customer experience maps are typically delivered by UX designers in the form of a visual representation (see Figure 13-1) that maps how users expect to go about doing something (such as planning and booking a family holiday) against the way that a website or service actually allows them to go about doing it. It is common for the digital product of interest to only map to a particular portion of the wider experience map.

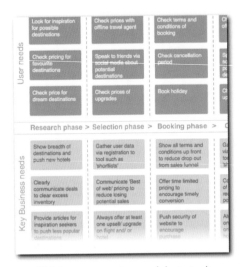

Figure 13-1: A customer experiencemap helps to visualize user
and business requirements in one diagram that is easy to interpret

Customer experience maps are used by designers within UX projects to map out the questions, information needs, issues, and anxieties that users have when passing through a process. In addition, they show where a system falls short of meeting user needs and thus provide a useful strategic document or roadmap for planning future improvements.

Customer experience maps are typically created early on within large user-centered design projects once some research has been conducted, such as set of benchmarking usability tests. You may also be asked to create customer experience maps as a project in itself; you will typically deliver them to summarize some form of research activity that you or a third party has conducted.

Customer experience maps are generally created when you are faced with one of the following scenarios.

YOU WANT TO UNDERSTAND MORE ABOUT HOW USERS GO ABOUT DOING A PARTICULAR ACTIVITY

This is the classic scenario when UX designers create customer experience maps because they are an ideal way of charting user behavior within a domain that, as a designer, you may not be familiar with.

Imagine you have been asked to research how people go about researching a booking holidays online. You can get a fair way to a model based on your own experience and that of your colleagues.

Imagine your client wanted to break into a new unfamiliar market with their holiday booking website. They may come to you to help them to understand how people in this market go about this process, which you may not know anything about. In this instance you would need to conduct some user research to build your model from.

In both instances a customer experience map provides a very accessible summary of user behavior that illustrates clearly how people go about doing a certain activity or process. This provides the foundation around which you then design the experience.

YOU WANT TO UNDERSTAND HOW WELL A WEBSITE IS MEETING THE NEEDS OF ITS USERS

This scenario may arise for many reasons, including someone seeking to identify priorities when spending a budget to improve a site or service, or when a new manager is employed to run an existing service and wants to understand how it is performing.

A customer experience map is a good tool to use in this instance because you can map out user needs at different points in a process and see how well a site or service meets those needs. The end result is essentially a gap analysis, which highlights where work needs to be done to meet user needs that are currently being left unfulfilled.

You can also illustrate different types of users or different stages of user engagement such as a customer moving from being a new customer to a longer-term customer on your customer experience maps. Within the map you can chart how their needs change over time and what the site or service needs to offer to retain and reward their patronage.

YOU WANT TO CREATE A STRATEGIC DOCUMENT OR ROADMAP TO DEFINE THE FUTURE DEVELOPMENT OF A WEBSITE OR SERVICE

The type of map you create in this situation is similar to the "meeting user needs scenario" discussed previously, but differs slightly in that in this scenario, you'll often add suggestions for new site content, features, and functionality that would satisfy both current user needs and also could provide for future needs.

In this type of customer experience map it is also useful to provide a sense of priority against which gaps you feel should be addressed first.

A customer experience map provides an ideal roadmap because it is easy to read and understand by non-technical audiences. They have proved to be most effective when printed on large paper and stuck to walls in busy parts of offices to ensure they are noticeable and accessible to everyone.

The visual format of a customer experience map can be very effective because it is rare that a client will see a visualization of essentially how their digital product works and where it is failing. As a large printed document, it can be taken to meetings and easily shared. People can simply point to the problems and discuss how they will fix them.

Essentially, a customer experience map provides an ideal strategic tool because it simplifies a set of behaviors and needs that are incredibly complex, unknown, and highly conceptual. To many strategic thinkers, it provides a better format for strategic planning than spreadsheets and PowerPoint slides.

WHY ARE CUSTOMER EXPERIENCE MAPS IMPORTANT?

Within the context of user experience, customer experience maps are clearly important because they help you understand how your users see the world. From this understanding, you can optimize your designs to match your customer experience maps.

THEY HELP YOU DESIGN MORE USABLE PRODUCTS AND SERVICES

Often things are not designed to meet user needs. A website or service may be designed based on constraints of the software or hardware or typically the priorities of the business that is operating the service. In this situation, the way the system works is often described as the *system model* and it is when this doesn't match the customer needs that websites and services fail to deliver the optimum user experience.

As a designer, it is likely that you have an understanding of how people want to go about doing something. If you are basing your designs heavily on your perceived knowledge as opposed to knowledge based on actual user behavior, it is likely that your *designer's model* will differ from your perception of how something works. This leads to the classic scenario where designers can't understand how people find using their designs so difficult often exclaiming, "It's obvious; who are these idiots!"

THEY HELP YOU UNDERSTAND HOW OTHER PEOPLE SEE THE WORLD

One of the most fascinating aspects of user experience design is getting insight into how people behave and understand the world around them. Every project will uncover some unique behavior that you could never have anticipated and these present a continual source of challenges for the designer to cater to.

User behavior and understanding of how to do something is a difficult thing to articulate and communicate to project teams. Often it is something that, as a UX designer, you will understand and carry within your head. However, it is critical that you can share this in a format that other people will understand. Customer experience maps provide a great way of sharing this knowledge in an easily accessible format.

THEY HELP YOU COMPARE DIFFERENT CHANNELS

Users often use a variety of channels to fulfill their needs, such as a website, a call center, and a mobile application. You can use a customer experience map to map how each of these channels is performing against specific user needs.

THEY HELP YOU SPOT CONTENT AND FUNCTIONALITY GAPS

During the mapping process, it can quickly become apparent where there is a user need that a product or service is failing to fulfill. These gaps are then prioritized and are used as a roadmap by development teams to improve the product or service.

Customer experience maps can also be important when planning a completely new product or service as they can be used as a to-do list to ensure that each stage of the users process is provided for within the product or service that is being designed.

HOW TO CREATE A CUSTOMER EXPERIENCE MAP

There is no right or wrong way to create customer experience maps and many different examples can be found via a quick Google search. What is critical is that you know why you are using this technique and you know what you want to get from it. The answers to both of these questions will determine the approach that you take and ultimately the resulting format of the map.

You should always show your clients and project stakeholders examples of previous customer experience map you have constructed in order to give them a clear idea of what you are working toward. Their reaction to what you show them will also help you to decide which approach is the most appropriate for you to take.

As with every aspect of UX design, context is critical to what you do and how you do it. Therefore, consider an example that illustrates how you could go about creating a new customer experience map from scratch.

Imagine you have been approached by a online photographic retailer and asked to research how people go about buying a new camera and how well their website currently supports this behavior. You have decided to create a customer experience map as a final deliverable. Within the map, you plan to illustrate the process that users take and also highlight where the site succeeds and fails to meet users needs.

STEP 1: CONDUCT SOME RESEARCH WITH REPRESENTATIVE USERS

There are many different types of research you can conduct in order to get the information you need for the customer experience map, including contextual research (see Chapter 7), user surveys (see Chapter 9), and task modeling (see Chapter 12), but my chosen approach in this scenario is to hold some usability tests.

Usability testing is a great approach in this example because it will mean you'll get to meet the people face to face. Such face-to-face contact, as shown in Figure 13-2, helps to build empathy and a greater understanding of their needs. It also means you can question behavior you find interesting and as thus be flexible around test plans to investigate unanticipated user behavior.

Figure 13-2: Usability testing in action

In this example, I would give users the simple task of researching and attempting to purchase a new camera online having deliberately recruited people who were currently in the process of doing exactly that.

You should ensure that your test plan is broad enough to capture user needs and behavior across the entire spectrum of the task, from the very earliest tentative searches for recommendations to the actual point of purchase. Don't stress if you can't get everyone through the process, as you will construct the experience map from indicative behavior you see across all of your recruits.

Remember the objective of the exercise. You are trying to uncover people's expectations and experiences of researching and buying a new camera. In this example I would write my test plan to ensure I got some great insights into the following questions I wanted to get answers to such as:

Where do people start? Where do they go? What do they search for? What are they worried about? What features are important to them? What causes them problems? What helps them with their tasks? How do they make decisions? What influences their choice? At which point do they fail or give up? How did they get to their final choice? Which patterns do you spot in user behavior?

It is likely that your client will also have a set of specific questions that they also want insights into. By planning the questions you want answers to, you can ensure that you ask the most useful questions that will contribute the most valuable insights to your map.

STEP 2: ANALYZE YOUR RESULTS AND BUILD THE USER LAYER

The easiest way to analyze the results of the tests is to pull out specific observations, behaviors, quotes, and issues and write each of them onto individual sticky notes. In this example, the logical way of ordering these is to map them to sequence of events that users followed during the testing.

Before you start make sure you have at least 4 or 5 meters (12 to 15 feet) of free wall space; this will give you enough space to get all of your sticky notes on the wall and also enough space to move them around. It is also advisable to stick some huge bits of paper to the wall first so you can roll up the whole finished map and transport it to clients.

The contents of the sticky notes can either be user questions or quotes that convey what users were trying to do at that particular time (see Figure 13-3). You may have groups of similar sticky notes that make different observations about the same thing; just pull these together and label them with a useful title such as "Researching Purchase" or "Choosing Between Options." Rationalize the sticky notes as you go, removing any duplicates or anything you feel is not representative of your findings.

Figure 13-3: Write user quotes, requirements, and questions on
sticky notes and add them to your wall

> *Tip: If you deliberately tested with different user groups (such as experts versus mainstreamers), you can differentiate them by using different color sticky notes. This allows you to represent the models of different user groups within one map, which might be useful if your client's product or service has many user groups who are distinctly different.*

Once you are happy with what you have added, walk a colleague along to see if you have missed anything obvious. Once you are happy with it, take a few photos. At this point, you should ideally walk your client through the map to get their input and also to ensure they are happy with the direction you are heading.

STEP 3: ANALYZE YOUR RESULTS AND BUILD THE BUSINESS LAYER

In some instances you may just need to tidy up your output from Step 2 in a drawing package such as OmniGraffle and your map is finished for the time being. In the camera shopping example, the client has asked for a critique of how well the website supports the users, so you need to add a business layer to the customer experience map.

This is simply a case of going through each individual stage of customer experience map and evaluating how well or badly the current website addresses that specific user need, question, or requirement. You may also want to identify the performance of different channels that the user may have encountered during their task. This will often highlight user goals and business goals that are in clear conflict with one another, which leads to a point of failure within the process.

To help interpret your map, you can convey how well or badly a specific user need is met by identifying the provision of features, functionality, and content, as shown in Figure 13-4.

Figure 13-4: Map your business layer to each set of user requirements

STEP 4: DOCUMENT THE MAP IN A FORMAT THAT CAN BE EDITED AND SHARED

The software you choose is up to you—we use a tried and tested OmniGraffle template, but use whatever works for you. Bear in mind that however you do it, it's going to end up being printed on very large bits of paper. Therefore, make sure you set your document up properly before you do too much work on it.

The key to a customer journey map is that it is essentially a living document as it represents something that changes over time. Your clients and stakeholders may not wish to update the document and are possibly more likely to want you to do it, but be sure to check with them as this might determine the tools you choose to draw up the map.

Once you have a good draft map together, print it out on large paper and hold a review meeting with your project team (see Figure 13-5). Ask people to go through it and annotate anything they want to change or add.

Figure 13-5: A stakeholder amending a draft customer experience map

At the end of the session gather up the printouts and make all necessary changes to the v1.0 map. The benefit of this approach is that you are involving your clients in the creation of these documents. They therefore not only understand them, but also will be more likely to buy in to the research and the approach you have taken.

As well as supplying your client with a PDF of the final map like the one shown in Figure 13-6, send them some large format printouts. Out of all of the deliverables we give to clients, customer experience maps seem to be the ones they like to stick to their office walls, as they generally look fantastic!

The key point here is that the visual format of these deliverables is what makes them so successful. They do a great job of highlighting gaps in a service offering to busy people who do not have time to read lengthy reports or attend findings presentations. Display them in communal areas and watch how people just can't help but check them out and start to address the problems they identify.

Be careful when adding a title to the final customer experience map. Customer experience map as a term is meaningless to many people so why not just keep it simple and call it something like "How People Research and Buy Cameras Online."

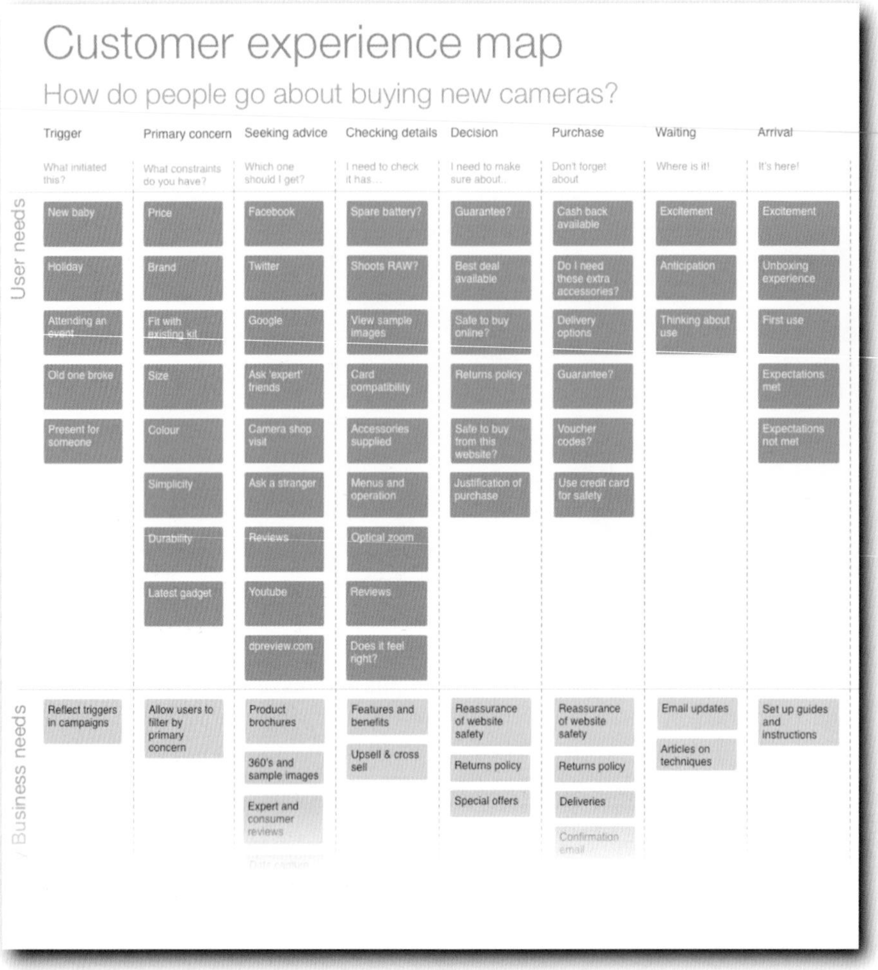

Figure 13-6: A simplified example of a customer experience map final deliverable

RESOURCES

Mental Models: Aligning Design Strategy with Human Behavior by Indi Young

The Anatomy of an Experience Map by Chris Risdon of Adaptive Path: http://www.adaptive-path.com/ideas/the-anatomy-of-an-experience-map

CHAPTER

14

CREATING USEFUL PERSONA PROFILES

PERSONA PROFILES ARE a representation of a digital product's users. They are used to keep the user front and center throughout the design, development, and maintenance processes. A persona is a short, vivid description of a fictional character that represents a group of the product's users.

Personas bring the product's users to life in an easily understood, memorable, digestible, and sharable format. They help production teams to prioritize user needs and core tasks.

Alan Cooper introduced personas in his 1998 book *The Inmates Are Running the Asylum,* as part of his goal-directed design methodology, describing user-centered design methods aimed at developers.

WHY ARE PERSONAS IMPORTANT?

A persona is a representation of the goals and behaviors of an actual group of users. They are derived from research with real users, so they have a strong grounding in fact. A set of persona profiles embodies a detailed understanding of real people.

A persona is a short description of a fictional character that illustrates a known group of a product's users. The character is named, pictured, and given biographical details. Their behavior patterns, needs, and goals when interacting with the product are outlined. Although some of this detail is made up, the underlying data is based on real user research.

A good set of personas helps product teams empathize with their users. Digital production teams (with their bias towards young males) often have lifestyles very different than their product's users. Personas aid those teams to put themselves in the place of their users as they make UX decisions. In short, personas are used to help the organization understand their customers.

Personas aid discussions on what users want—they provide a basis in fact and help prevent individuals from projecting their own needs onto an abstract "user." A persona provides a specific, consistent understanding of a particular audience group. They help production teams focus on primary audiences rather than getting bogged down in edge cases.

Personas can help with the evaluation of design solutions and the prioritization of features—"would Bob understand this form?" or "would Mary use this widget?"

The number of personas generated for any single product will differ just as user bases differ. However, there are usually somewhere between three and eight different personas. Fewer than three is unrealistic and more than eight may become unwieldy. However, the actual number should be based on user data and not decided in advance. It is often the case that a single persona will represent a product's primary audience, with others representing secondary audiences.

WHEN TO DEVELOP PERSONAS

If you plan to develop personas for your project, do it early. Personas can be used to inform requirements, ideation, user journeys, wireframes, visual design, development, and ongoing product maintenance. In short, pretty much every aspect of a digital product's UX. They are typically generated from the same types of research that are used for generating task models (see Chapter 12), so they can easily be scheduled around the same time.

It is imperative that personas be integrated within the ongoing design and development team. In order to be effective, they need to be a living, breathing part of the team's knowledge base. This means you cannot simply show the team the personas after you have developed them. You must involve the team in the process: invite them to the user research, show them your workings, and ask for their input. Consider running a workshop to develop the personas from research into named characters with biographical detail.

WHEN PERSONAS DON'T WORK

Personas can be a controversial tool in the UX armory. As external consultants, we have seen a fair few personas that are clearly just made up. We have been asked to produce others that we know will never go on to be used by their intended audience—the production team. However, we have also seen personas doing a great job of including users at every decision point. Here's when personas don't work so well:

- When they're just made up and don't represent genuine user groups, based on real data. It is unwise to make critical design and business decisions based on made up stories.
- When they were developed externally and have no meaning for the teams who must work with them. Personas created with in-house teams as part of the user requirements gathering process are much more likely to be useful design tools.
- When they are seen to replace the need for ongoing research with real users. This is a big one—nothing can beat actual user research as a validation technique.
- When they contain too much superfluous information. Too many biographical details can get in the way; it's better to focus on behavior patterns and goals. However, a few personal touches can really help bring a persona to life.

If you don't have any real user data, and no budget to obtain any, what should you do? First, don't create personas. A persona implies that the information is based on research. However, any time you spend considering and documenting the product's likely users is useful. Just don't pretend it's something it isn't. You could always use any time you might have spent making up personas on some guerilla testing.

HOW TO CREATE PERSONA PROFILES

Personas start with user research. The persona generation process goes something like this:

1. Understand your product's users with research and statistics
2. Examine your data for themes and patterns
3. Distill those patterns into individual characters that embody your findings
4. Bring the characters to life with biographical information and imagery

Generally, a persona is a one- to two-page description of a fictionalized character. It captures such things as user behavior patterns, goals, skills, attitudes, and environments. It makes sense to provide personas in a visually rich manner—something compelling that can be printed out large and live on the production team's walls.

INPUTS TO PERSONAS

When producing personas, it is best practice to use more than one data source. This removes bias and provides a richer data set to draw from. Consider using two or more of the following methods to gather information for your personas.

User Testing

User testing is the best way of starting persona development. You need a good amount of qualitative data on which to base realistic personas. Use one-to-one depth interviews to understand participants' backgrounds and answers to specific questions. Use the "think aloud" protocol to examine the use of existing and competitor products. You'll uncover a wealth of information about user goals, needs, and attitudes. There's more on user testing methods in Chapter 5. For realistic persona development, it makes sense to interview more than the minimum five users recommended for a standard usability test. Ten would be a good starting point.

Analytics

Existing website analytics is another goldmine. What areas of your product are currently most used? Where are users leaving? Can you infer any segmentation from site stats? There's more about analytics in Chapter 8.

Customer Data

Data on any existing customer base is great for suggesting demographic information for your different personas. If 70% of your existing customers are female (and the business is happy to maintain that proportion), around that proportion of your personas should be female. This type of data can also imply location, income, and family status.

Some businesses will have detailed customer segmentation analysis. This will likely belong to the marketing department, and you should ask to see it, if it exists. Customer segmentation is often provided in a very persona-like manner. However, it's important to realize that it is likely to have a different focus than the user needs portrayed by a persona. Use the information when you can, but don't rely on it to provide all the data you require.

Customer Surveys

If your client does not hold detailed demographic information about their customers (or does not yet have any customers), consider running a survey. There's more on surveys in Chapter 9. A little quantitative information will help ground your personas in reality. The types of information you should consider gathering here includes gender, age, income, marital status, number of kids, location, competitor products used, and attitude to the proposed product.

Social Networks

Analyze behavior on social networks and online forums. What are users saying about your client's business and products?

Contextual Research

Contextual or ethnographic research can take a number of forms, including home visits to users, store visits, and call center listening. There's more on this in Chapter 7. The aim of this type of research is to provide a clear understanding of the context of use and the opportunities and constraints implied by this context.

The aim of home visits is to put user observations in context: where are your users when they interact with your product? Are they relaxed, under time pressure, juggling 10 things at once, using their cell phone on the bus, or something else?

Store visits and call center listening will help to paint a picture of existing interactions with the business. What are users' common pain points and anxieties? How do they go about deciding between products? What do sales assistants do to assist purchase? Where are there opportunities to delight? Interview staff to get their take on patterns and themes within customer interactions.

DEVELOPING PERSONAS

You've gathered lots of user information, so what do you do with it? In order to distill useful personas from reams of data, you need to identify recurring themes and patterns.

Examine the information you have and write down candidate behavior variables. For a shoe retailer, these might include frequency of shopping, attitude to high fashion, willingness to return unwanted items, and need for good value. These can often be represented as two ends of a sliding scale. Alternatively, you may want to use sticky notes to record and group attitudes.

Now see if you can map your user test participants against the variables you have come up with. If this proves tricky, you may need to go back and come up with revised variables. Look for clusters of users with similar attitudes. Here's where you'll see some candidate personas emerging. In the shoe shop example, you might see "the fashionista"—people who want all the latest trends, who buy lots of shoes, and are happy to return any they are not totally satisfied with. Another cluster might represent "the bargain hunter"—people who are equally trend led, but don't have the disposable income to support large numbers of purchases. Figure 14-1 shows example behavior variables for the shoe website example, with the attitudes of seven user test participants mapped against them. Candidate personas have been identified. Note that a real-world example would require a greater number of variables and participants.

Keep at this exercise until you feel you have identified all the major groupings. The data should reveal how many personas you need to develop. The example in Figure 14-1 identifies two personas—the fashionista and the bargain hunter—but there is a weaker third cluster of more infrequent, practicality-led customers. This would perhaps imply a third persona, perhaps called "the classic dresser." Other projects may throw up very different groupings, perhaps along more demographic lines, for example "busy working mom," "homemaker," or "enjoying retirement." Different projects again may find that the job title is an important differentiator. Different personas often represent people with different attitudes and access to technology. For example, one persona might represent someone who is highly anxious about online purchases whereas another might describe someone with almost constant connectivity.

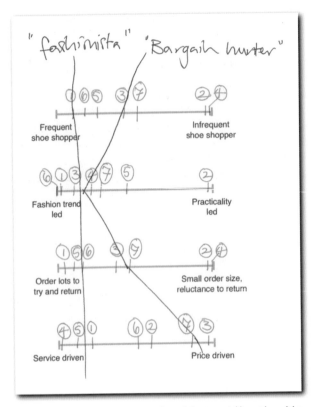

Figure 14-1: User test participants mapped onto behavior variables, with candidate personas identified

WHAT SHOULD YOU INCLUDE IN YOUR PERSONAS?

Now you've synthesized all your information into candidate personas, it's time to add the details that will bring them to life. You should include information that's relevant to your project. Too much detail will be unhelpful and difficult to wade through, but you need to provide enough to paint a vibrant, believable picture.

When adding demographic information to your candidate personas, use supporting data from customer surveys or existing customer segmentation. Try to represent the spread of known customers in the demographic spread of your personas. There is an exception to this: If your project is intended to shift to new user groups, it is these new users whom your personas should represent.

Here are some details to consider including in your personas. To use all of them would be to provide too much information, so pick the ones that are most appropriate to your project.

Name and Gender

Include a name for all personas. It humanizes the persona and helps team members refer to it. Make sure you don't choose names of people known to the team or specific user test participants, as the persona will not represent them in their entirety. Choose a name that also implies gender. Some people choose to use alliteration (for example, "Fashionista Fran" or "Bargain Hunter Bella"), but others feel that this leads to personas that cannot be taken seriously. Make a judgment based on the your client's office culture.

Image(s)

Provide a portrait of the persona. This could be a photograph of someone from the right demographic, or perhaps an illustration. Additionally, example descriptive images are often used. Examples of descriptive images include photographs of the persona's desk or other working environment, or drawings of important aspects of their lives or the technology they commonly access. Images should represent key behaviors and attitudes, not just demographic data such as age, gender, or affluence.

Images can be tricky to source. Consider using stock photography libraries, but beware of images that are obviously stock photos. Consider using your friends and acquaintances, as long as the production team doesn't know them. Another place to look is Flickr, with photos licensed to use commercially under the Creative Commons scheme.

Lately, we have seen lots of personas that use far more photography and illustration than words to describe the users.

Age

Including the persona's age adds authenticity and aids empathy.

Biography

Bring the data to life by weaving it into a (very) short biographical story. Marital status, number of kids, or education level may come in here.

Location

Including a location can imply many aspects of the persona's life, including social attitudes, costs of living, and access to services.

Occupation

Giving a persona an occupation helps envisage their daily lives, including social contacts, commute time, income, and access to technology.

Salary

Disposable income may well be important to your project. Are customers looking for good deals over better service? Are they likely to make impulse purchases? Salary, household income, or some other indication of affluence can imply answers to these types of questions.

Personal Quote

A user quote or guiding principle can do a great job of encapsulating a persona. Some of the best ones come from actual user testing quotes.

Description of User Segment

These might be the descriptions of the first candidate personas you came up with. They might be "businesswoman," "stay at home mom," "fashionista," "present buyer," or any one of a myriad other descriptors.

Attitude to Technology

Does the persona represent someone who happily embraces new technologies and is never parted from their iPhone? Alternatively, maybe they are someone who only uses the Internet when they have to. Are they comfortable with the devices they use? Do they spend a lot of time on social networks? Does television or print media heavily influence them?

Context of Use

Where would this persona be when they use your product? Would they only ever use it on the laptop at home, or would they use multiple devices, including cell phones or tablets? Are there any likely distractions while using your product? Are there others present who would be involved in any decision-making processes?

Customer Segmentation Data

It can be useful to include quantitative data, such as the percentage of actual customers represented by this persona.

Key Drivers

What are the persona's reasons for using your product in the first place? What would trigger them to interact with your product?

Key Goals and Needs

For example, "I need to know that they offer free delivery and returns—I can't afford to pay to return ill-fitting shoes" or "I want to have access to the latest fashions without having to spend half my life in shops." These can include experience goals like "I don't want to feel stupid," "I want to have fun," or "I want to be a member of the fashion in-crowd." What must the system do in order to meet these needs? What must the system never do for this user? For example, "don't overwhelm him with choice" or "never appear to offer unfashionable products."

Pain Points

What causes anxiety or pain for this persona? How can your product address this?

Figure 14-2 shows an example persona for the fictional shoe website ShoeUX.com.

Figure 14-2: An example persona for the fictional shoe website ShoeUX.com

WORKING WITH PERSONAS

Personas are of use only if the team adopts them, and they go on to be used throughout the development and maintenance of the product. Here are a few areas where personas can be useful.

DESIGN

Use your personas when you design new screens and user journeys. Which features are most important to your users? Which calls to action will be most compelling? What content is required to support key tasks?

STRATEGY AND PRIORITIZATION

Personas can be really useful when you prioritize your backlog or decide on new features. Which features will help the most users complete their key tasks? Will the feature be useful to many customer groups or just one? Personas represent the users who are most strategically important to a business. If a proposed feature doesn't meet the needs of the users represented in your personas, it is unlikely to be a development priority.

CONTENT CREATION

Refer to your personas when you write your content—what content do the users represented by your personas require? How should you write in order to help them complete their key tasks? What would "Fran" like to read about this product?

EVALUATION

Does the product meet the needs of users? Does it speak their language? Do they know how to complete their goals? It is important to note that evaluating against personas should never replace actual user testing. Evaluating against personas can be done at every design decision, but testing with real users is where you uncover issues and opportunities.

Personas should never replace actual user testing.

Once you have generated personas from an initial round of user testing, they become useful for recruiting for future testing. Use your personas to inform your recruitment brief, to specify key lifestyle and demographic requirements.

Smashing UX Tools and Techniques for Creating Personas

To generate the data required to produce personas, we typically run user testing (Chapter 5) with 10 or more participants.

Supplement the information from user testing with one or more of the following: stakeholder interviews (Chapter 3) to uncover what the organization knows about its customers, contextual research (Chapter 7) to understand more about users' interactions with the organization, analytics (Chapter 8) to evaluate existing product use, or customer surveys (Chapter 9) to generate rich customer data.

RESOURCES

Communicating the User Experience by Richard Caddick and Steve Cable (2011)

The Inmates are Running the Asylum: Why High-tech Products Drive Us Crazy and How to Restore the Sanity by Alan Cooper (2004)

A Project Guide to UX Design by Russ Unger and Carolyn Chandler (2009)

About Face 3: The Essentials of Interaction Design by Alan Cooper, Robert Reimann, and David Cronin (2007)

Getting from research to personas: harnessing the power of data by Kim Goodwin on the Cooper.com blog: www.cooper.com/journal/2002/11/getting_from_research_to_perso.html

Persona template available to download from cxpartners.com/ux-resources

15

DESIGNING USABLE INFORMATION ARCHITECTURES

THE INFORMATION ARCHITECTURE of a product or service as the design behind the design. It is the craft that defines the experience, the thinking, and strategy that underpins the final graphic design. The information architecture determines how a digital product will fit together, how people will move within it, and essentially how it will fulfill its intended purpose.

A good information architecture will allow people to find what they want without really giving it much thought. Great information architecture is invisible to users. They don't pay it much attention (or care about it) because they are too busy getting on with their tasks.

As the amount of information grows within a site, the importance of designing a logical and scalable architecture to house it becomes more and more important. Search typically brings users to your site and your IA defines what they do from there on in.

Information architecture as a discipline is often discussed generically as "UX" work so it is likely that you will be performing many IA tasks within your work. It is a critical component of the design process and provides the foundations for every successful and usable digital product.

WHAT DOES INFORMATION ARCHITECTURE ENCOMPASS?

The information architecture of a digital product, as well as the UX designer who designs the IA, is typically responsible for the following areas.

GATHERING REQUIREMENTS

The information architecture must be designed to deliver the objectives of the client. A detailed requirements-gathering phase underpins every successful information architecture. The designer must consider the following issues:

- What are the objectives of what I am designing and how can I design it in such a way to meet those objectives?
- How can I use what I know about users to design this in such a way to support their behavior?
- How can I design something that will persuade people to do what the client wants them to do?
- How can I make this better than the competition?

Figure 15-1 shows just how simple requirements gathering can be. Just take the time to sit down with people to understand what they want and why they want it.

Figure 15-1: A thorough requirements-gathering process is critical to a usable IA

THINKING ABOUT USERS

The most critical component to usable IA design is an understanding of who will use the product and what they will use it for. Typical questions you will need to consider include:

- Who will be using this?
- What will they be trying to do when they use it?

- What constraints will they have when they use it?
- What is their context of use? Are they in a hurry? Is it a critical task?
- What device will they be using?

DEFINING AND DESIGNING PROCESSES

The IA will determine the order in which information is presented to the users. The IA will also determine what information set is presented within each individual step of the process. This is documented within process flows that define the logic of how a process works.

PLANNING CONTENT

A UX designer requires information to architect! When designing information architectures, designers need to answer questions such as the following:

- What content do we have? How much is there? What different types of content are there?
- What content do we need?
- What is the most intuitive way of organizing this content?
- How will people want to move through this content to complete their tasks?

Content requirements are often determined by performing content audits to better understand the quantity and quality of the content that needs to be organized.

DESIGNING STRUCTURES TO HOUSE INFORMATION

This process involves the definition of a site's component sections, the organization of content that sits within those sections, and the labeling used to describe those sections.

This is documented in the form of *sitemaps.* Users are typically involved in the sitemap design process by way of research activities such as *card sorts,* which are discussed later in this chapter.

DESIGNING NAVIGATION

The navigation design answers the following questions:

- How many levels of navigation will there be?
- Where will it appear on the different pages?
- Where will it appear within the interface?
- What will the specific navigation labels be?

The answers to these questions are documented within sitemaps and are also illustrated in wireframes and page sketches.

To read more on designing navigation, be sure to read Chapter 19.

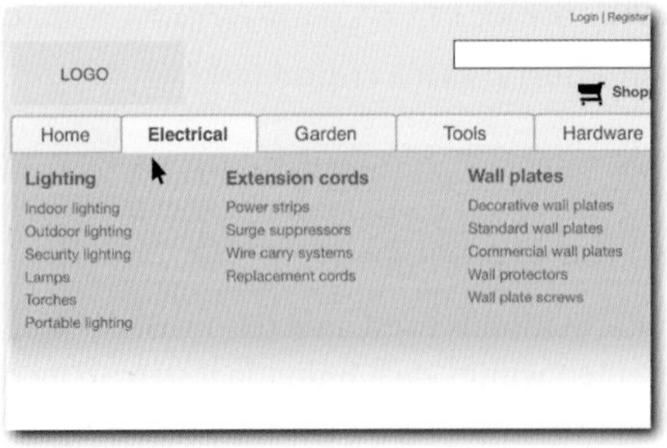

Figure 15-2: Navigation design is a critical component of the
IA process

DESIGNING PAGES, PAGE COMPONENTS, AND FUNCTIONAL ELEMENTS

A significant amount of time and effort is required to define the individual page components of a digital product and how they should be presented in the most effective way. The UX designer needs to consider what the user can do and see from each individual component of the product and must consider questions such as:.

- How will this be presented to users and in what order within the screen?
- What are the different page states that make up an interactive experience?
- How will the page deliver its commercial objectives?

The pages and components of digital products are typically documented within sketches (Chapter 16), wireframes (see Chapter 17), or prototypes (see Chapter 18).

DESIGNING THE SEARCH EXPERIENCE

As search is such an important way of finding information, the UX designer must consider the following questions:

- How will users access the search?
- How will the search results be presented?
- What happens if no results are found?
- How will users be able to refine their searches further?

To read more on designing search, be sure to read Chapter 22.

The answers to these questions will be documented within wireframes and prototypes. The scope of the IA of a product or service is broad and covers a wide range of the tasks performed within UX design. During your projects you may find that many different people with different job titles are involved in performing IA tasks. Information architectures were always typically designed by information architects. Now many information architects call themselves *UX designers* because the scope of their responsibilities are much broader.

In terms of your overall tasks when designing usable information architectures, consider these as your fundamental objectives:

- To define how a product or service will work by creating an overall vision that defines how it will fit together. Then design, in detail, each component part.
- To design an information structure that makes retrieval of information and usage as easy as possible.
- To design an information structure that maximizes the commercial potential of a product or service.
- To design a scalable architecture that can grow over time to cater to new content and functionality requirements without compromising the user experience.

WHY IS INFORMATION ARCHITECTURE IMPORTANT?

One of the main complaints users have when using the Internet is the sheer amount of information they have to wade through before they find what they need. People describe themselves as "drowning" in information and suffering from modern day problems such as information overload. Figure 15-3 illustrates the effect that this can have on some people!

Figure 15-3: Stress from information overload is a modern problem in a connected world

Information architecture helps to solve this problem. It is important because it tries to structure the masses of online information and create order from chaos. Search has made locating information so much easier, with sophisticated tools such as Google changing the way that people find information online. Information architecture seeks to maintain this ease of finding information and completing tasks within the specific website or application of interest.

Information architecture is becoming more important as businesses flex the technological capabilities of the web. Websites are becoming more and more complex and are serving multiple experiences to different customers. Architecting these systems is becoming more and more complex given the diversity of usage scenarios they need to support.

In terms of user experience, the information architecture of a website or app is critical because it forms the foundations of the experience. It defines the options a user has and when they have them. It defines how they move through a product and how easily they will be able to find and act upon what they are looking for.

From a commercial perspective, information architecture is critical. Good information architecture makes it easy for users to find suitable products as well as other alternatives. If done well, it makes things easier to buy. A well-designed information architecture makes something easier and more enjoyable to use. This encourages repeat visits from your users and help to maximize sales.

Good information architecture can also make your product or service more visible to search engines thus improving the chances of obtaining traffic. Once users visit your site from search a well-designed navigation will help them to do what they need to do, thus making the experience as easy as possible.

HOW TO DESIGN A USABLE INFORMATION ARCHITECTURE

The approach you take to designing a usable information architecture will vary upon a variety of factors such as what you are designing, how long you have to design it, and whether a version of the product already exists.

DISCOVERY TASKS

Before you start designing, you need to understand the context within which you'll be working. This phase is all about immersing yourself in your client's world and also the world of your client's customers. It is often the most fascinating of the project phases because it uncovers the insights that end up as the innovations that you design into your final information architecture.

Re-Read the Brief

Do you remember that document you skimmed over when you were pitching for the project you have just won? That was the brief. They always differ in quality, but for the time being it's all you have to base your approach on, so go through it in detail and make a list of questions to follow up with the client and your project team. It is likely that it will contain a few juicy little requirements that will determine the approach you take, so make sure you know it inside and out before you progress.

Gather Business Requirements

The brief you received from your client will be likely to contain some high-level requirements that you can explore further during the business requirements-gathering phase.

The key consideration when gathering requirements is often whom you should meet with and how long you will get with them. This is often determined by your client, who will have a view on who they want to involve, and for how long. It is likely that you will need to meet senior stakeholders, so make sure that you plan the sessions thoroughly to make the most of the limited time you will get with them.

Chapters 3 and 4 cover the tools and techniques to use when gathering business requirements in detail, It is likely that you will want to identify answers to questions such as:

- What is your role and stake in this project?
- Why are you doing this? What are your objectives for this project?
- What are your measures of success?
- What is your vision for this project?
- Who are your main competitors?
- Given your role, what are the key success factors of this project for your department?
- What will make this service unique? What is your unique selling point?
- Will you have any personal KPIs that might be affected by this project?
- What specifically must this product allow your customers to do?

It is likely that your script will differ from the previous questions, but whatever you do, prepare a script and try to stick to it as much as possible. You will find that stakeholders are likely to have their own agenda and may want to ignore your questions and tell you all about what they want you to hear. Remember that you need to get the answers to your questions, so be prepared for some diplomatic redirecting of questioning!

> *Tip: We like to do the business requirements before the user research. The business requirements will identify the goals and objectives of the project that you can use to inform your approach and questioning within your user research. We often find ourselves thinking back to business stakeholder interviews when conducting user research and asking questions that we know that stakeholders would want to be answered. If you do your user research first, something is bound to come up in the business requirements that you won't get a chance to ask users about until much later in the project.*

The output of the business requirements phase will be some form of documentation that you can work on with your client to prioritize the individual requirements based on their importance and feasibility for phase one. You may have a business analyst on your project who will be tasked with documenting each individual functional requirement. Clearly this person is vital, as you'll need to understand what's in scope so that you can design something that encompasses every necessary piece of functionality.

Gather User Requirements

Don't forget that you are not the user and you will learn a lot from real users that can contribute to your final information architecture. This is important no matter how well you feel you know the topic or subject you are working on.

A great way of collecting user requirements is to run some usability tests (as shown in Figure 15-4) of existing and/or competitor services to get an understanding of how people behave and what is important to them when trying to perform a particular task.

Figure 15-4: Remember, you are not the user! Great user insight is fundamental to designing a great IA

Typical objectives of user research might be:

- To understand how good/bad the information architecture of competitors is
- To understand how users go about doing a particular task
- To gather user requirements around a particular activity
- To understand what a broader set of user tasks might be
- To identify content, features and functionality that would give your client's site a competitive advantage
- To identify any design patterns that users are accustomed to within a particular domain
- To learn more about the type of language and labeling that is typically used on the sorts of websites you are interested in

If you need a guide to conducting usability testing, check out Chapter 5 for all you need to know to get started.

The output of the user research is likely to be a report that outlines your findings, but you could also generate a more focused list of prioritized user requirements, which you can use later as a checklist for your subsequent IA tasks.

Speak to Key Project Stakeholders

You will make decisions during the IA phase that are likely to have a huge impact on other stakeholders who are working on your project. Although you shouldn't be constrained by technology, it makes sense to chat to your developers throughout the IA phase to let them know the direction you are taking. This will flag anything that they may need to think about and can often result in the developer making suggestions that improve the resulting IA.

It is likely that you will also need to work closely with Search Engine Optimization (SEO) specialists. They will be interested in how you are planning to structure your site, as this is likely to have an effect on the way that the content will rank with search engines. We've learned from experience that you need to chat to these guys early in the project to hear their point of view, as it could save you a considerable amount of pain later. Read more about working with SEO experts in Chapter 2.

Be prepared for client stakeholders from departments such as advertising and editorial to become your new best friends. They will have a huge amount to gain/lose based on your decisions. Are you planning to strip out the banner adverts to improve the UX? Will you be prioritizing the editorial above the product listings, as the client thinks the users love it? Welcome to the political world of IA!

What's the Big Idea?

The IA of a website or service is often a direct reflection of the proposition of the service. If your client has their proposition clearly worked out, it is likely that there is at least one potential way of structuring the content that seems to be the most sensible approach to start with. You may have noticed from your competitor review that all of the competitor sites use a similar structure; ask yourself whether it makes sense to deviate from this convention.

As an IA, you will often find yourself designing how offline propositions can be translated to work online. This is a challenging but very rewarding activity because your client is relying on your knowledge to design something from scratch that will present a compelling and profitable experience. Before you start organizing content, you might find that you need to outline how the site will work at a higher level; this is sometimes called the *concept map* and it helps to ensure there is a shared vision for how proposition for the site will work.

One of my favorite concept maps is the one shown in Figure 15-5 that shows how Flickr works at a conceptual level.

It's the kind of thing that you can imagine someone quickly documenting after a spark of inspiration. It might be useful to sketch these out when you are designing something that is completely new or doesn't fit a conventional pattern or structure. They can be useful when you need to convey what you have in mind before you spend hours determining the detail of how it all fits together.

You may not need to create something as grand as a concept map to communicate your ideas. Imagine how someone communicated the concept of Twitter before it existed. They could try and describe it but they may have needed to communicate the big idea in broader terms first to get others to understand the concept. Perhaps it looked something like Figure 15-6?

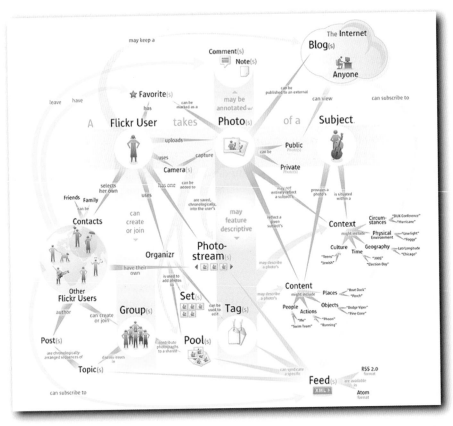

Figure 15-5: A concept map for flickr.com courtesy of Bryce Glass (http://www.flickr.com/photos/bryce/58299511/in/photostream/)

SOURCE: Reproduced with permission from Bryce Glass © 2012

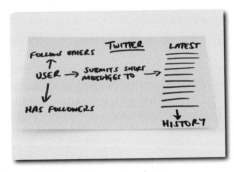

Figure 15-6: A potential concept map for Twitter

Make sure that your clients and colleagues spend time going through your concept map. I once had a client tell me an idea I communicated in a concept map was absolute rubbish. I was gutted at the time but on reflection that was the deliverable doing its job. It allowed me to change direction and not invest a huge amount of time in pursuing something that didn't meet my client's objectives.

Be mindful when sharing concept maps as others may not have your conceptual thinking skills. You may be able to picture the solution clearly in your own mind but others may struggle. Just because you present them with a concept map don't expect them to understand it. This is an example of a deliverable that you should always talk someone through and never just e-mail it off to them without an accompanying discussion.

Understand Your Context

When you ask anyone who works in IA/UX or usability how a particular problem should be solved they will often respond with an answer of "it depends." As annoying as it may be, this response is often totally appropriate. Until you fully understand the context of a product it's very difficult to give an accurate and useful answer.

Gaining an understanding of context is absolutely critical to good design. As a UX designer, you need to immerse yourself in the world of your client and their users. This is why working on projects that map to your hobbies and interests feels easier because you already get it.

To gain an understanding of context, check out the competition (see Chapter 6 to find out how), speak to friends and family who use products like the one you are designing, and familiarize yourself with the client's websites and services. You will suddenly notice your client or their competitors everywhere and this is a good sign that you are immersing yourself into your project.

Get Under the Bonnet

It is likely that your client will have some sort of analytics package that—if you are lucky—you might get to look at. You better have a pretty good idea what is working and what isn't within an IA before you start redesigning it. From spending time analyzing the analytics, you can get a good idea of what people are doing and where they are going on the site.

We've noticed that most clients will have set up specific reports they regularly track within their analytics tools. These are interesting because they indicate what is important data to your clients. Ask for an explanation of how these work and why they are tracking that specific activity.

We've learned the hard way how complicated some analytics packages can be and have struggled to get enough time to find our way around them fully. It is likely that your client can introduce you to a colleague who can give you a quick-guided tour, which can save you hours of fruitless exploration.

The main benefits of this activity is that it always identifies interesting patterns of usage that you will want to find out more about in your user research. You may notice that users are all following a particular route through the site or all may be leaving from an unexpected part of the site. The analytics gives you the "what," to which you can use user research to provide the "why." To find out more about analytics, please see Chapter 8.

Understand What You Need To Organize

One of the most critical tasks you will face is getting a good understanding of the content that you will be organizing into an intuitive, usable, and coherent IA. The greatest problem I've found is that often in big redesign projects at this stage no one knows what the content will be. It sounds crazy but I've often been trying to create an IA without any 'I'!

If the website already exists, you can conduct an audit of what they already have so that you can understand what you need to organize. But beware—the content inventory task can take a long time and for large sites can become quite onerous. You need to set out an audit plan and see how long it takes you to get through a representative sample of the site. It's okay if you don't get through everything in detail; your time allotted for this task may only allow you to get a good overview. See Figure 15-7.

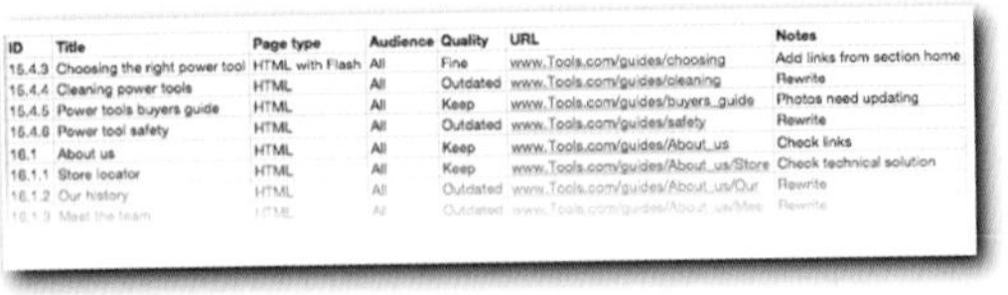

ID	Title	Page type	Audience	Quality	URL	Notes
15.4.3	Choosing the right power tool	HTML with Flash	All	Fine	www.Tools.com/guides/choosing	Add links from section home
15.4.4	Cleaning power tools	HTML	All	Outdated	www.Tools.com/guides/cleaning	Rewrite
15.4.5	Power tools buyers guide	HTML	All	Keep	www.Tools.com/guides/buyers_guide	Photos need updating
15.4.6	Power tool safety	HTML	All	Outdated	www.Tools.com/guides/safety	Rewrite
16.1	About us	HTML	All	Keep	www.Tools.com/guides/About_us	Check links
16.1.1	Store locator	HTML	All	Keep	www.Tools.com/guides/About_us/Store	Check technical solution
16.1.2	Our history	HTML	All	Outdated	www.Tools.com/guides/About_us/Our	Rewrite
16.1.3	Meet the team	HTML	All	Outdated	www.Tools.com/guides/About_us/Mee	Rewrite

Figure 15-7: Content audits are the best way to fully understand what content you need to organize

For more detailed content-auditing tasks, we often use a spreadsheet with headings such as:

- **Unique ID**: Useful so you can refer to a particular thing in a separate document such as an e-mail or requirements document.
- **Page URL**: So anyone can easily click through to see what you've audited.
- **Page Title**: To remind you what the page was about.
- **Page Type**: Is it a simple HTML page or a PDF download, a Flash micro site, or something unique?
- **Audience**: If you know the audience well, you can determine whether the content is relevant to any of the intended audiences.
- **Quality**: Some people like to apply the ROT principle to decide whether content is **R**edundant, **O**utdated, or **T**rivial. It's a tough call for you to make as an UX designer. A content specialist who knows the content and the audience well may be better placed to judge content using this method.
- **Notes**: The page may contain some functionality that may be discontinued or you might want to flag something to be usability tested in the future.

The trick with a content audit is to provide enough detail to be useful but not so much that the task becomes too huge to complete efficiently.

If you are designing something completely new then you will find yourself designing an IA to house content that probably hasn't been written yet. The type of content you require will come from your user and stakeholder research. There may be a content plan that you can use to base your IA on if you are lucky, but you may find that your IA becomes the content plan! If the content is yet to be written, now is a good time to investigate how that process will work because the earlier it starts the better.

DESIGN TASKS

Having completed some discovery activities, you'll be raring to start designing an IA that's going to meet your project objectives. The discovery phase will give you all the background knowledge you'll need to start putting together a draft IA.

Design Your IA

The best way to plan out an IA is to get a few pens, a massive stack of sticky notes, and a large space on the wall. The sticky notes give you the flexibility to move things around until you get a structure that starts to make sense. Remember to take loads of photos as you go. You will change stuff, realize that the old stuff was good, realize there is no Undo button in real life, and curse! Digital photos are free; take them liberally and often!

Be sure to take loads of photos of your IA design as you go. You will change your mind often, and there is no Undo button in real life.

There are some well-established ways of organizing information that you might be able to make use of. I first came across them as being referred to as the *five hat tricks of information,* which were first developed by Richard Saul Wurman and are featured in my all-time favorite UX book *Universal Principles of Design.* The five hat tricks—or ways to organize information—are as follows:

- **Location**—Organize by physical geography or by position within a space of a location.
- **Alphabet**—Categorize information by alphabetical order, such as names in an address book.
- **Time**—Organize information in chronological order, such as ordering news articles by latest published.
- **Category**—Group objects or content by similar attributes, such as music albums grouped by musical genre.
- **Hierarchy**—Group by magnitude, such as the largest to the smallest or such as the "view cheapest first" sort options on e-commerce search results.

It is more than likely that your IA will use a combination of these approaches to organize the information it contains. The vast majority of content-rich websites organize their content by category. But you might wonder how to determine what categories to use and how to label them.

When designing an IA, you have two choices. You can either come up with a draft IA to test with users or you can get users involved early on to help you design a draft IA. The route you take depends largely on the time you have. The ideal situation is to involve users when creating your IA and then involve them again to test your results. Card sorting is a commonly used technique that you can use to do exactly that.

Use Card Sorting to Involve Users in the IA Design Process

Card sorting is the classic technique used to get user involvement in the IA design process. It's a relatively straightforward technique that involves asking users to organize a deck of cards, each labeled with a different category or content object, into groups. The groups represent "buckets" that users feel contain similar things. This grouping exercise allows you to understand how users expect things to be grouped, why they feel they should be grouped together, and how they would label that group. How users group the content and the reasons they give reveal their mental models of the subject area and helps ensure that the design is aligned with how users think about things. See Chapter 13 to learn more about how mental models can be developed further into customer experience maps.

We have run card-sorting sessions with as many as 15 participants in the past to get a good data set, but online tools such as Optimalsort and Websort allow you to involve many more people. Before you embark on the online route, remember how useful it is to get the explanation from users as to why they are grouping things the way they are. You just don't get this level of insight from an online method. As ever your choice is determined by factors such as the amount of objects to be organized, time to do it, client sensitivity to qualitative versus quantitative data, and budget.

So how do you run the kind of a card-sorting exercise shown in Figure 15-8? The following sections list some tips for running successful cards sorts.

Figure 15-8: A card sort in action

Organize the Sessions As You Would for a Usability Test

You need to ensure that you recruit representative users and plan for when people don't show up in the same way as you do for a usability test. For hints and tips on how to do this, check out Chapter 5 on usability testing.

Warm Up First!

Prepare a set of cards with the names of common fruits and vegetables and get participants to sort them into groups. Be sure to chuck a tomato in there to initiate a conversation around what to do when a card doesn't seem to fit into any available group. Having done this, your users will understand the game and will be raring to start the main task.

Consider How You Capture Results

At the end of each session, you need to record the final groupings of cards. If you are asking users to organize a large number of cards, this could take some time so give yourself time to do this between sessions. You can also give each card a unique ID so you call out numbers for a colleague to record into a spreadsheet or record them straight into an analysis tools such as xSort (Mac only – http://www.xsortapp.com). There is a great analysis spreadsheet that converts your raw data into some useful outputs available at http://www.boxesandarrows.com/view/card_sorting_a_definitive_guide.

Closed vs. Open Card Sorts

A closed card sort is one that gives users a set of top-level categories to sort cards into. An open card sort has no top-level category constraints and involvers users creating their own categories. Closed sorts are constraining as they assume the top-level categories are correct. By limiting the sorting options, closed sorts make analysis easier. Open sorts offer more scope for users insights into groupings and labeling, as they are not constrained. However, they can make comparison of different users sorts incongruous, so analysis can be tricky.

Qualitative vs. Quantitative

Ideally, you need enough users to see some interesting variation but not so many that you have too much data to be able to crunch in the time you have available. As with all user involvement, doing anything, no matter how small, will dramatically increase your under-standing of how users see the world. If your budget can stretch to a day's worth of card sorting and you get through five or six, you will learn more than enough to create a good draft IA.

The value of being able to ask people to explain their choices cannot be overstated. We once saw a user create an additional category in a card sort that he labeled "the Internet"! He needed an extra category to act like a miscellaneous section, but his choice of labeling was fascinating. How did he see this category behaving? Surely this category would contain everything! After chatting, it became clear we had a problem with our main categories because he felt the need for this extra miscellaneous catch-all category. The ability to ask why during a face-to-face card sort makes them particularly valuable.

Record Double Placements

We guarantee that within the first five minutes someone will say "this lives here and here; I want to put it in both places!" The problem is they can't because they only have one card. However, the fact that they feel it should be in two places is valuable to note because some-thing online can live in multiple locations. Make sure you keep a note of these double placements and design them into your IA.

Think About Your Observers

If your clients, colleagues, or project stakeholders want to view the card sorts as they happen, you'll need to work out how best to make them feel part of the process. A typical solution is to mount a camera onto the ceiling of a lab (see Figure 15-9), which works well as long as it is not obscured—by you or the participants during the card-sorting exercise.

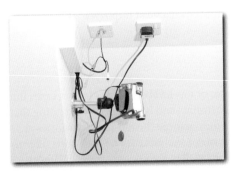

Figure 15-9: A ceiling mounted camera is useful for recording card sorting in action

Talk through the viewing requirements with your client beforehand to see what they need and test everything thoroughly beforehand to prevent any last-minute technical issues.

Keep Them Talking

You will find that participants often enjoy taking part in card sorts. They often get so immersed in trying to solve the puzzle that you have put before them that they stop explaining what they are doing and why they are doing it that way. You need to keep them talking throughout the process to uncover their thinking processes, so be prepared with lots of open questions, such as "Why did you put that there?" and "Tell me more about what you would expect this category to contain."

Often, if you remind participants at the beginning that there is no right answer to the card sort, you can help to reign in the competitive ones who try to crack the puzzle in record time. This can help to slow them all down and to keep them talking.

Add Explanations to Cards

A simple label on the cards is often not enough to give people the information they need to be able to sort them into the most appropriate categories. You will often need to add sentences to the card to explain what that card represents as illustrated in Figure 15-10.

Figure 15-10: Add explanations to give your participants a clear idea of what the card represents

Pull Together Your Results

One crucial point to remember when planning a card sort is to not expect it to give you a perfect solution. Your users will inevitably contradict one another to some extent. Make sure you plan in enough time to make sense of the results.

Card sorting is far from an exact science. It enables you to involve users in the design process and reveals how they think about the domain, but don't expect the perfect IA to drop out at the end of the process. The final decisions about what will make the best IA will still be a matter for you as the designer to decide upon given your knowledge of the users and the project objectives.

Design for Your Users' Tasks

Having studied the personas (see Chapter 14 on how to create great personas), you will hopefully have a good understanding of the types of people who use the product that you are designing. It is critical to also have a good idea of the sorts of things that they will want to do when they use the IA you are designing.

The process of breaking down these tasks into their individual components is called *task analysis* or *task modeling* and you can read about how to do it in Chapter 12.

Once you have mapped out your users' tasks you will have a good idea of both what people want to do and also in what order they want to do it in. You will also have an idea of which tasks are more important than others. This knowledge is fundamental to the design decisions you make during the IA process, particularly when you come to design the sitemap and the wireframes. Figure 15-11 shows an example of a task analysis that illustrates the individual tasks that are typically involved when buying new shoes.

You can also gain a detailed view of how your users experience particular products or services by creating customer experience maps (see Chapter 13). These maps can be created instead of or in conjunction with your task analysis to give you a good overall picture of user behavior and preferences when it comes to doing what they want to do.

If the product you are designing involves a specific process or order in which the users will want to use it, such as in the case of a transactional website, you need to design process flows (see Figure 15-12). These process flows allow you to think about and document the order in which users perform particular activities. They can be useful when planning long forms as they help you determine the most logical order to ask questions and also determine any dependencies between one set of data and another.

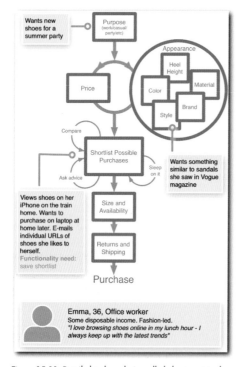

Figure 15-11: Detailed task analysis really helps to get to the detail of what is happening within an individual task or set of tasks

DOCUMENTING YOUR IA IN A SITEMAP

The sitemap is a deliverable that documents the IA of the product you are designing. It is a critical document because it defines the shape of the product in terms of the amount of top-level sections and levels within the hierarchy, as well as defining the labels for your navigation.

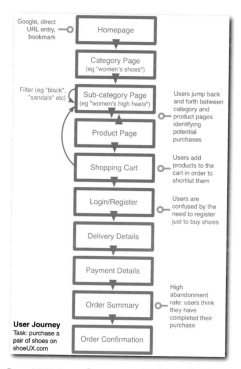

Figure 15-12: Process flows are typical IA deliverables when you need to determine how a user will move through a process

The sitemap is the first formal view your project team can have on the core structure of the product that is being designed. In this format it can be commented upon by stakeholders and amended based on feedback from the whole team, whereas before it was likely to have just been a picture you have been carrying in your head. Your big idea is now on paper and is ready to be pulled apart so you better be ready to give the rationale behind your design decisions.

The process of putting a sitemap together forces you to think carefully about who will be using your product and how they will want to move through it. Sitemaps force you to consider whether it all fits together logically and whether you have labeled its component parts in a way that will make sense to people.

You will quickly be faced with the challenge of how to label the different groups of information; this is both tricky and critical because it will ultimately become your navigation. Before you get too stuck here, check out Chapter 19 on navigation UX to get a feel for how your design will ultimately be presented on the page.

Once you have made any necessary amends following client feedback, get your sitemap signed off. Your signed-off sitemap is then used to work out the scale of the wireframing task you have before you. Ideally, you should quote your time for all tasks up until the sitemap is finished and then use the sitemap to base your quote for wireframing and prototyping. This may not always be possible as you'll be pushed to quote for the whole job, but by splitting the quote into a scoping (up until sitemap) and a production (wireframing and beyond) phases, you will stand a good chance of keeping the work at a manageable volume and pace.

Different Types of Sitemaps

There are many ways of documenting sitemaps and the correct approach is the one that suits your budget and project constraints as well as the client's house style. The following sections discuss a few examples of the different approaches that we have used in the past.

Outline View

Outline view is available in common software applications such as Word, as shown in Figure 15-13.

Figure 15-13: An example of an outline view type of sitemap

Advantages to Outline view include:

- Quick to create and to amend
- The indented levels communicate the hierarchy nicely
- Clients can edit the source files (although this isn't always a good thing)

Disadvantages to Outline view include:

- Big sites will lead to long unwieldy documents
- It doesn't bring ideas to life; it's a difficult format to get excited about
- It's harder to clearly annotate the individual components

Spreadsheets

Spreadsheets can be a more attractive option than outline view because you can take advantage of being able to create wider documents for deep site hierarchies, than word processing software programs allow. See Figure 15-14.

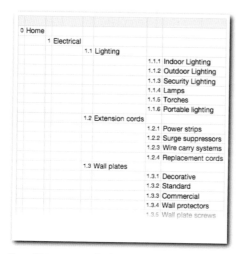

Figure 15-14: An example of a spreadsheet type of sitemap

Advantages of using spreadsheets include:

- Relatively quick to create and amend
- Formatting options offer the opportunity to make them more attractive than outline view
- Easy to open; almost everyone has Excel

Disadvantages of using spreadsheets include:

- It's a difficult format to make look visually attractive
- There are fewer templates available to reuse
- Annotation isn't going to be as clear as with a classic sitemap

Classic Sitemaps

The majority of sitemaps are created with some sort of drawing tool such as OmniGraffle, Visio, or Illustrator, as shown in Figure 15-15.

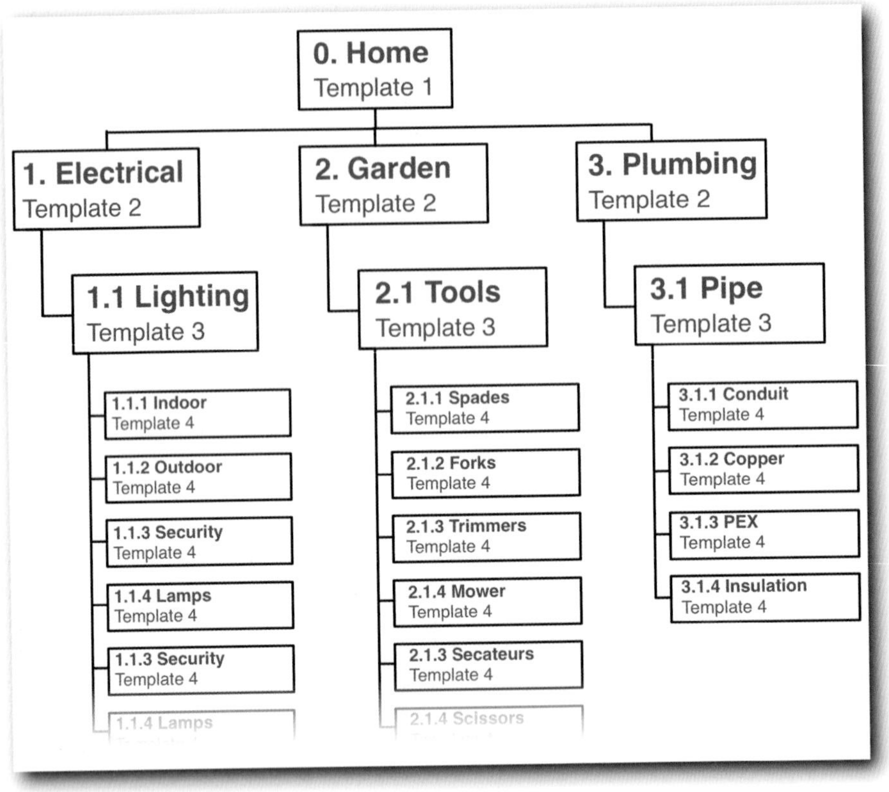

Figure 15-15: An example of a classic type of sitemap created using OmniGraffle

Advantages of classic sitemaps:

- They can be made to look fantastic
- There are loads of templates available online that you can reuse
- You can come up with your own annotation styles

Disadvantages of classic sitemaps:

- They can take ages to amend following client feedback
- They can become fiddly if you are trying to fit a large amount of information onto a fixed page size
- You will spend ages on tasks like aligning boxes and making them look great

Annotate Your Sitemaps

Each component of your sitemap should have a label that describes the name of the page or section it represents and a unique ID so it can be referenced elsewhere. If you are designing a template-driven site, you can also add the ID of the template that will be used on each page.

You can then make sure that you have a template for each different page type that your site contains.

You may also want to identify pages differently depending upon whether they are static or dynamically driven and whether they represent single of multiple stacks of pages.

You can also use a sitemap to identify areas of a site that are only available to logged in users and also areas that will be deployed in later releases that are beyond the scope of the project you are working on.

BRINGING IT ALL TO LIFE WITH SKETCHES AND WIREFRAMES

Once you have a signed-off sitemap, you are ready to bring the individual components to life. It's tempting to get stuck into your favorite wireframing software tool straight away but I've found it can be beneficial to sketch out your ideas on paper first.

Pencils Before Pixels

By sketching things out first, you can iterate more quickly than you can on your computer. You can create and throw away initial ideas without feeling you have invested loads of time creating them. You can easily share them with colleagues to get feedback and your focus will be on the ideas as opposed to lining up boxes and beautifying.

When creating rough sketches of all of your key interfaces, you can get a massive psychological boost because you will feel that you have at least some ideas for the major components of the job in hand. Stick these on the wall and walk people through them. Let people scribble on them and add their own ideas. This is one of the most exciting parts of the process, when the ideas start flowing and come to life on paper, as shown in Figure 15-16.

Figure 15-16: Sketching is quick and, most importantly, fun!

We love sketching. It has totally changed the way that approach designing new interfaces. It's so important that we've dedicated Chapter 16 to covering how to get the best from sketching.

Wireframing

Once you have worked out roughly how your interfaces will fit together, you need to define them in detail in your wireframes. There are many opinions on what wireframes should and shouldn't be in terms of defining layout and how closely graphic designers should follow them. A general rule of thumb is to talk to your graphic designer and decide between yourselves how far you want to define layout and pixel perfection in the wireframes. At cxpartners, we generally produce high-fidelity wireframes and expect the final live work to be very similar to what we design at this point in the process.

To learn more about how we go about wireframing, turn to Chapter 17 for an in-depth look at this technique, which in itself is an essential skill for all user experience practitioners to master.

Prototyping

Over the last few years prototyping has become more and more popular within UX circles because the tools have improved such that you can quickly mock up your ideas into working prototypes. Tools such as Axure are so good that we sometimes wireframe straight into them, which saves us a job when we want to create a prototype to put in front of users in usability testing.

Prototyping is great because it allows you to bring things to life. In addition to users, clients can use the prototypes, which gives them a clear idea of what is being designed. I often wonder whether clients actually fully understand wireframes, as they can be easily misunderstood. A prototype solves this problem and allows you to get great feedback from all parties.

We've dedicated Chapter 18 to prototyping. One word of warning—it's addictive so prepared to spend more time than you should bringing your ideas to life!

TESTING YOUR INTERFACES

You should test your sketches, wireframes, and/or prototypes as early as possible to see whether they work as you intended them to. By testing early, or ideally iteratively, you can iron out the big issues before more time is spent developing them. We describe the process of usability testing in-depth in Chapter 5.

GUIDING YOUR IA THROUGH THE DESIGN AND DEVELOPMENT PROCESS

There is nothing more frustrating than waving your IA work goodbye and then seeing it go live many weeks or months later in a stage that bears no resemblance to your efforts. An excuse of "it was great when I handed it over" doesn't really cut the mustard for potential new clients and employers.

So how can you ensure that you vision, insight, and usable IA makes its way to the live site? If you work with a full service agency, this should be easier because you can make it your business to keep an eye on it as it progresses through the development process. You may be asked to make decisions on problems that come to light during that process, which enables you to maintain the experience you originally designed.

If you work as a freelancer or for a specialist UX agency, you will find it harder to keep an eye on things. It's well worth offering to spend a few days in total over the development process to be on hand to answer questions and to keep the IA on the right path.

POST LAUNCH JOBS TO KEEP AN IA BUSY

The work of an IA doesn't finish when the project goes live. In many cases, this is just the beginning. As a site or product changes in terms of features and functionality, commercial objectives, and strategy, there will be work to do to keep it all in order despite changing underlying goals and objectives.

The approach you can take to keep your IA in good working order is a subset of what we have described. You can pick and choose depending on the nature of the changes and the time and budget you have available to do the work. By conducting regular user research, you can learn how user requirements are changing and then determine how you will modify your IA to meet these needs.

RESOURCES

Information Architecture: Blueprints for the Web by Christina Wodtke

Information Architecture for the World Wide Web by Louis Rosenfeld and Peter Morville

Information Architects by Richard Saul Wurman

16

USING SKETCHING TO GENERATE AND COMMUNICATE IDEAS

SKETCHES ARE A great way to generate ideas and share them early. Sketching allows you to test designs without committing lots of time to detailed wireframes or graphic designs. You do not need to be good at drawing to produce useful sketches—they help you think and collaborate and aren't an end in themselves.

WHEN TO SKETCH

Sketching is an excellent starting point for any design work. If you need to generate ideas rapidly, visually test an approach, or gather immediate feedback from clients, sketching can play an important role. Sketching is used at some point in every design project we work on.

SKETCH TO GENERATE IDEAS QUICKLY

At the beginning of a project, you need to come up with lots of ideas. The more ideas you have to choose from, the more likely there's a good one in there!

The section called "How to Sketch" later in this chapter outlines a rapid sketching exercise that can be run with or without clients. The aim is to widen the design options available to you by generating lots of ideas rapidly. Then you narrow the field by discussing the ideas and selecting those to move on with. In this situation, crazy ideas are easy to weed out: if they are impossible to draw, they will certainly be impossible to code.

Even if you don't have a team around you or clients to collaborate with, it makes sense to sketch out potential design solutions at the beginning of a project. Pushing yourself to come up with lots of ideas rapidly can generate possibilities that might otherwise remain untapped.

SKETCH TO SHARE IDEAS EARLY

Sketches are wonderful communication tools. They are useful at the beginning of a project when you are exploring a wide variety of design routes and later on when you are finessing specific interactions.

Try explaining an interaction widget over the phone to a client—it's not easy. They say a picture is worth a thousand words and here sketching comes into its own. In five minutes you can draw your idea, photograph it, and e-mail it anywhere in the world.

Another useful aspect of sketching is that you can work through the implications of design choices throughout the user journey. Imagine your client wants to add some sort of "quick-buy" functionality to their online shop. This would allow logged-in users to make a purchase without having to fill in delivery and payment details. A quick sketching session would help identify key decisions, such as whether the Quick Buy button belongs on the product page or the shopping cart page. Figure 16-1 shows two annotated user journey options for the addition of a "quick-buy" functionality to an online shop. This sketch can help the decision-making process by showing stakeholders the pros and cons of each option.

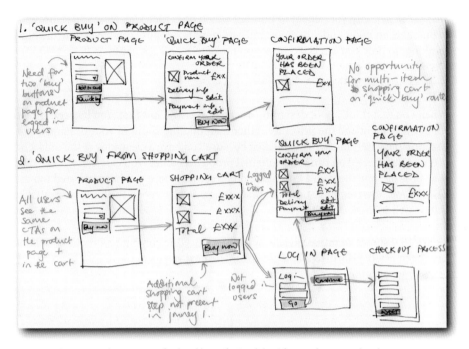

Figure 16-1: Two annotated user journeys for the addition of a "quick-buy" functionality to an online shop

The low-fidelity nature of sketches may seem like a disadvantage, but can actually be extremely useful. Imagine you need to get a client to tell you if your designs are heading in the right direction, or to choose between two possible design routes. Developing a number of different wireframes is time-consuming. Presenting finished-looking ideas can lead people to get caught up in irrelevant details. Have you ever presented an early design to show intent, and found yourself explaining again and again that, no, that isn't real headline copy and yes, you understand that this product isn't really made of 100% polyester? When presented with high-fidelity wireframes, some clients can't help but sweat the details. A low-fidelity sketch conveys enough information to elicit a decision. A sketch expresses enough to gain client buy-in. You will not have spent too much time working up your designs, and no one will mistake the ideas for a finished product.

The low-fidelity nature of a sketch helps to convey the big picture idea without having the client treat them as some form of finished product.

Share sketches with your client to find out which ones they like. Now you know which route to pursue with higher fidelity wireframes or graphic designs. You have done the big-picture thinking, so now you can concentrate on the details and aesthetics.

SKETCH TO GENERATE WIREFRAMES

When you first think about designing a screen, sketch it out first. You'll spend time thinking about the content and the priorities rather than fiddling about in your design tool of choice. Creating the wireframe will be quicker, because you have a clear idea at the outset of what needs to go where. You can spot potential problems earlier. You can share your sketch with your boss or your client and thus agree on direction before you have invested too much design time. You can move onto the finer design details safe in the knowledge that your time will be well spent.

Figure 16-2 shows an initial sketch for a wireframe. The content and required interactions have been listed, prioritized, and grouped. The next step is to move into Visio or OmniGraffle or other wireframing tool of choice.

Figure 16-2: An initial sketch for a wireframe

Don't forget to photograph the results of your whiteboard sketching session.

If you are working as part of a team on a project, this sketching can be conducted collaboratively, on a whiteboard. Whiteboard sketching is great because it is so easy to remove an unwanted feature and replace it with something else. Figure 16-3 shows a collaborative wireframing session using a whiteboard.

Figure 16-3: A collaborative wireframing session using a whiteboard

LOW-COST UX WITH SKETCHING

Have you ever been asked to solve a client's million-and-one UX problems with no time on a tiny budget? The next time this happens, sketching may be able to help you provide an on-budget solution.

As a UX professional, it is often your knowledge and problem-solving skills that are more important than polished deliverables. Instead of worrying that you can't possibly come up with the 20 wireframes necessary to redesign your client's website in the three days your budget allows for, consider running a sketching workshop with their development team. If you can help them come up with the ideas and the ground rules, they may well be able to work out the details themselves.

Another option for low-cost UX is to identify and communicate *quick-wins*—improvements that are easy to fix and produce a tangible usability benefit without the need for a complete redesign. Sketching is incredibly useful for communicating quick-wins. You can draw directly onto printouts of the relevant screens. You can project the screens onto a whiteboard and draw possible solutions on top. If you are identifying quick-wins as a collaborative exercise, this is a fast, flexible, and easily re-drawn approach. Photographs of the amended screens are easy to share and discuss further. Figure 16-4 shows some quick-wins drawn on a whiteboard.

Figure 16-4: The results of a quick-wins exercise with a projector and whiteboard

WHY IS SKETCHING IMPORTANT?

Sketching is important because it is all about thinking and collaborating, rather than the more solitary pursuit of designing. Sketch because:

- **It is fast and low fidelity**—You can test out ideas without investing too much time on them. You can generate lots of ideas from which to narrow down.
- **Everyone can get involved**—No need to be a designer, or even be good at drawing. You can examine ideas on a level playing field; the CEO's sketch is not any more important than anyone else's.

HOW TO SKETCH

Sketching is all about expressing your thoughts and getting information across to others, so how you go about it is entirely up to you. However, here are some tips if you are not sure where to start.

DON'T BE SCARED

People who don't regularly draw are often apprehensive about putting pen to paper. Perhaps they decided that they couldn't draw when they were at school and are worried that they will be judged harshly. However, the sketching described here is intended as a way of quickly and easily communicating ideas—there is no good or bad.

EQUIPMENT

All you really need to get started is a pen and some paper, but there are some simple ways to enhance your sketches to really make them come alive.

- Use a pen of a suitable thickness. For small sketches, a simple ballpoint is perfect. For bigger drawings, something like a fine Sharpie is more appropriate. Figure 16-5 shows a set of six rapid sketches drawn with a writing pen and a bigger sketch drawn with a fine Sharpie.
- Add a sense of depth with a fatter, medium-gray pen.
- Use a bright color to add emphasis and highlight key features, such as calls-to-action. Figure 16-6 shows a product page sketched with a Sharpie, with gray used to add depth and weight, and a bright emphasis added to the Buy Now button.
- Plain paper is fine, but squared or dotted paper will help to draw straight lines without a ruler.
- If you want to get really fancy, there are plenty of UX sketching templates on the Internet to buy or download. There are browser templates, device templates (such as paper iPhones with blank screens to draw on), and stencils offering common user interface elements. We sometimes use browser templates for collaborative sketching exercises, but none of these things is imperative for getting ideas across.

Take a look at others' sketches for inspiration. For example, Eva-Lotta Lamm's sketchnotes typically use a black pen and single highlight color (see www.evalotta.net). Despite the restricted palette, they are vibrant and communicative.

Figure 16-5: Small sketches drawn with a writing pen and a larger sketch drawn with a Sharpie.

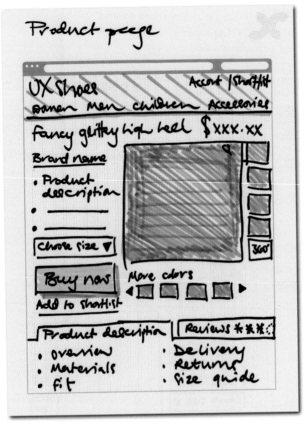

Figure 16-6: Depth and emphasis can be added with gray and a bright highlight

RAPID SKETCHING EXERCISE

Chapter 11 on ideation workshops describes a rapid sketching exercise to conduct with clients, based on Leah Buley's sketching methods. This approach allows all key stakeholders to contribute ideas to the project and encourage honest feedback. All clients present will have a strong sense of ownership of the chosen ideas. A collaborative sketching session like this is something we run whenever the project allows.

We also conduct similar sessions when no clients are present in order to generate ideas. In this case, all designers working on the project will get together for a couple of hours to sketch and discuss. We also ask others in the office who are not working on the project to join in, if they have time available.

Rapid Sketching with Colleagues

To run a rapid sketching exercise with colleagues, we use the six-up sketching exercise described in Chapter 11. Everyone present is given a piece of US Letter paper, divided into six small rectangles. A timer is set and everyone is given around 20 minutes to fill each rectangle with an idea for a screen from the project. When the 20 minutes is over, we each describe what we've drawn. Participants then choose and discuss their favorite ideas. They are free to pick their own ideas or others. This phase of the exercise generates lots of discussion and opinions on the relative merits of the ideas. Each participant then chooses one design to progress further. We spend another 20 minutes sketching those designs at a larger size—a single screen on a sheet of US Letter-size paper. Once the sketching is finished, we again describe our work for the group. Again, we discuss the relative merits of each idea.

At the end of this exercise, the designer responsible for the project will have a stack of ideas that have been discussed, evaluated, and explored further. They should have a really good idea of next steps for the project.

RESOURCES

Sketching User Experiences: Getting the Design Right and the Right Design by Bill Buxton

Understanding Comics: The Invisible Art by Scott McCloud

Sketching User Experiences: The Workbook by Saul Greenberg, Sheelagh Carpendale, Nicolai Marquardt, and Bill Buxton (2011)

Amy McGuinness discusses sketching as part of the UX process on the cxpartners blog: www.cxpartners.co.uk/cxblog/3_ways_with_sketches_ideation_problem_solving_persuasion

Sketchnote Army website (good for inspiration): sketchnotearmy.com

Eva-Lotta Lamm's website, including a portfolio of sketchnotes: www.evalotta.net

Leah Buley and Brandon Schauer's Good Design Faster slides: www.slideshare.net/whati discover/good-design-faster

17

DESIGNING GREAT WIREFRAMES

WIREFRAMES ARE DIAGRAMS that represent the framework of a website or application. They are a step on the journey between information architecture and the finished product. They allow you to explore content, navigation, and interactions separately from visual design elements such as colors and fonts.

Generally a wireframe deck will not cover every single screen from a digital product, but showcases key templates, from which the remainder of the site can be extrapolated.

The aim of wireframes is to be shared, scrutinized, and collaborated on. They are design tools that allow you to make mistakes and to test, learn, and improve. This happens early in the project, when changes are relatively inexpensive.

WHY ARE WIREFRAMES IMPORTANT?

What exactly is a wireframe? The common analogy is that a *wireframe* represents a finished website or application in the same way as architect's drawings represent a finished building. They are important because they allow you to explore, test, and iterate design ideas. Wireframes vary widely depending on designer, project, and purpose. However, they are generally images representing the digital product in grayscale, showing navigation structures, representative or dummy content, calls to action, imagery (and other media requirements), form elements, and advert placement. Graphic design in the form of final imagery, font use, and overall look and feel are missing. However, page layout and visual weighting are addressed. Wireframes are often annotated, for example with functional descriptions or content requirements.

TEST EARLY

You should develop wireframes and interactive prototypes (see Chapter 18) in order to test your ideas early. Whether that assessment is via user testing, team walkthroughs, sharing with clients, or sanity checking with your family, wireframes help you to decide what's working and what isn't.

Wireframes are particularly useful for gathering early feedback via user testing (see Chapter 5). It is possible to get great results from user testing even low-fidelity wireframes, perhaps still on paper rather than onscreen. In user testing wireframes, you learn whether participants understand the navigation and calls to action and if they are interested in the content. As a designer, you might hope to have to change only a few words as a result of user testing, but outcomes can be anything from giving a content block more prominence, to changing the wording on a button, from adding notes on image styles, to reworking the information architecture. For early stage concepts, you may learn that you have to go away and start again. When you start again, you will start with much more information about what the product needs to be.

Discovering at the wireframe stage that the idea failed is much more cost effective than having a fully designed and developed product fail.

SHARE WITH CLIENTS

A wireframe is quick and easy to edit. Clients can review wireframes and make observations about navigation, interactions, and content without getting caught up in the details of the graphic design. A wireframe does not feel like a finished artifact—stakeholders are able to comment without feeling that the design is too far along to change.

Wireframes can communicate a great deal about the finished product. They are a useful conversation piece for team members as disparate as project managers, product managers, business analysts, developers, graphic designers, content specialists, SEO specialists, sales and marketing, and more.

As a UX practitioner, it is often easy to get caught up in the user needs, when any commercial product has both business and user requirements. Sharing wireframes with clients allows them to evaluate how well the design will meet their business needs.

BRIEF THE DESIGN AND DEVELOPMENT TEAM

In some cases, a wireframe deck is the most formal specification document a project will get. It will be the wireframes that are passed onto visual designers as their brief. In turn, the wireframes and visual designs are passed to the developers to form their brief.

It is important to establish a strong working relationship with visual designers. Wireframes allow you to explore content and layout ideas without worrying about the visual design. This provides freedom for both the UX practitioner and the graphic designer to concentrate on their own specialty. It is important that visual designers feel liberated rather than constrained by wireframes. This can be achieved by involving visual designers in the wireframe iteration process, so they have ownership and don't feel that they are simply expected to "color in" the wireframes.

It is equally important to have a good relationship with the development team. They need to understand the reasoning behind the wireframes in order to allow the project to flex and grow as development progresses, even if you are no longer there. Again, involving developers in the wireframe design process will provide this engagement with the wireframes.

Involving content specialists in the wireframe iteration process will allow them to begin their work at an early stage. They can collaborate on content needs and begin to draw up content requirements. Again, ownership of the designs is important—if the team understands the reasoning behind any design decisions, they will be able to make intelligent choices as the build progresses, even if you are no longer there. There's more on working with different disciplines in Chapter 2.

WHEN TO CREATE WIREFRAMES

We create wireframes in some form every time we work on a design project. Sometimes they are sketches (see Chapter 16) that never get produced digitally. Sometimes they might be better described as *prototypes* (see Chapter 18), as they are in some way interactive. Techniques such as creating wireframes directly into HTML may be blurring the lines between sketching, wireframes, prototypes, and live websites, but there will always be a need to test content and interaction ideas cheaply and early, and wireframes are well suited to that task.

HOW TO DESIGN WIREFRAMES

How you go about designing wireframes is of course a personal process. Over long years of doing this ourselves, we have learned plenty of lessons about the best approach for us. Here's how we do it. We hope it helps you discover the best way for you.

BEFORE YOU START

Before you begin wireframing, it helps to gather some information. Try starting with the following:

- A clear picture of your product's users and their goals. Task models, user journeys (see Chapter 12), customer experience maps (see Chapter 13), and personas (see Chapter 14) are useful for this.

- A clear understanding of the business goals for the project. Stakeholder interviews (see Chapter 3) and requirements workshops (see Chapter 4) are useful for this.

- An information architecture (see Chapter 15). You really need an IA before you can start wireframing as it has a direct correlation to a website's navigation system.

- Design ideas, whether generated in an ideation workshop (see Chapter 11) or perhaps during a sketching session (see Chapter 16).

Figure 17-1 shows some sketches and a sitemap for the fictional shoe retailer, ShoeUX.com.

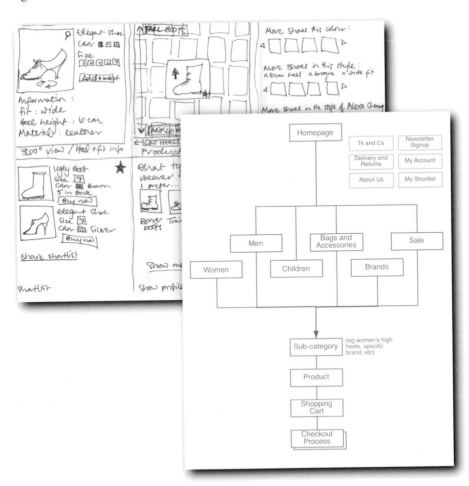

Figure 17-1: Sitemap and sketches for a fictional shoe website

FIRST STEPS

Before you make any marks on paper or screen, there are certain things it helps to consider.

Screen Goals and Entry and Exit Points

For the particular screen you are working on, think about the entry and exit points. What is your user coming here for? Where have they been previously? You certainly can't guarantee that they've followed your ideal user journeys, but considering whether they might have clicked a link on the homepage or come via Google, a social networking site, or other means can help produce design ideas.

What do your users want to do on this screen? Where do users want to go next? Where does your client want them to go next? What are the business goals for the project and for the specific screen you are considering?

In a very broad sense, you'll be designing content and layout to meet your users' needs, and calls to action to meet the business needs. Listing these items in advance really helps clarify the work your screen needs to do in order to be successful. Figure 17-2 shows example entry points and goals for the fictitious ShoeUX.com homepage.

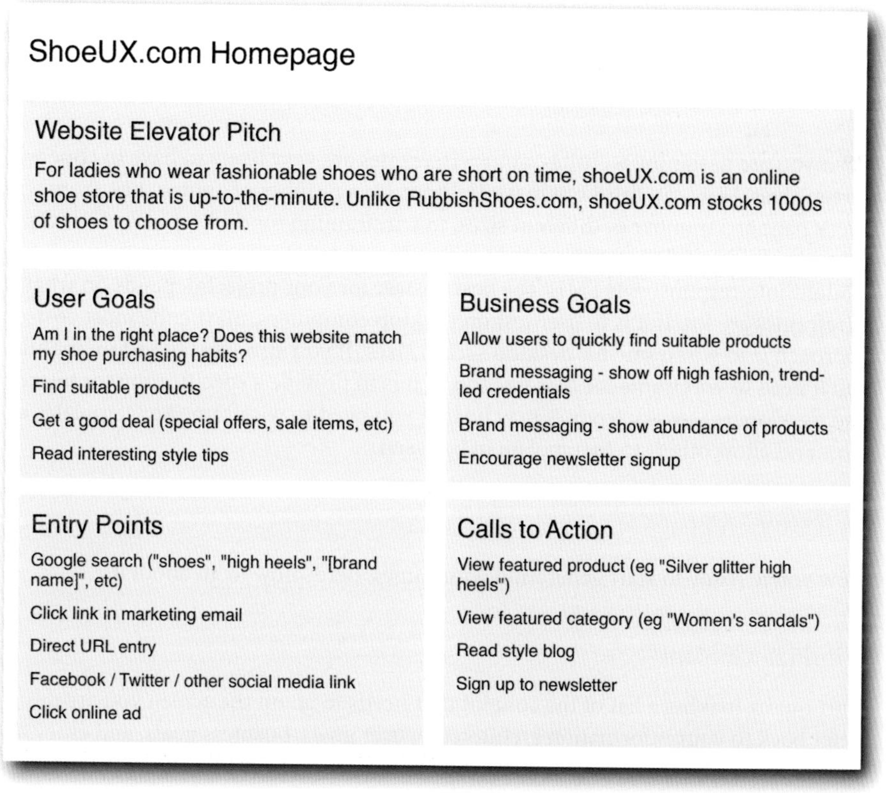

ShoeUX.com Homepage

Website Elevator Pitch

For ladies who wear fashionable shoes who are short on time, shoeUX.com is an online shoe store that is up-to-the-minute. Unlike RubbishShoes.com, shoeUX.com stocks 1000s of shoes to choose from.

User Goals

Am I in the right place? Does this website match my shoe purchasing habits?

Find suitable products

Get a good deal (special offers, sale items, etc)

Read interesting style tips

Business Goals

Allow users to quickly find suitable products

Brand messaging - show off high fashion, trend-led credentials

Brand messaging - show abundance of products

Encourage newsletter signup

Entry Points

Google search ("shoes", "high heels", "[brand name]", etc)

Click link in marketing email

Direct URL entry

Facebook / Twitter / other social media link

Click online ad

Calls to Action

View featured product (eg "Silver glitter high heels")

View featured category (eg "Women's sandals")

Read style blog

Sign up to newsletter

Figure 17-2: List of entry points, page goals and calls to action (CTAs) for the example shoe website

Your Wireframes' Users

Who are you handing your wireframes to and what do they need from them? Thinking a little about this in advance will help your wireframes to be more usable. Perhaps a product manager needs them to get signoff for their project. For this they probably don't want too much distracting detail. Alternatively, it may be that your wireframes are the only specification this project is going to get, and you need to make sure that the developers know exactly how every interaction works. Graphic designers need to know that you are not treading on their toes and that they have plenty of freedom to do more than just "color in" your wireframes. Content specialists may need strong copy direction, or may prefer to produce their own content guidelines. Other UX practitioners may want to run user tests or edit the wireframes later in the project. Marketing managers may want to know any new innovations so they can plan their ad campaigns. Legal teams may need to review copy and interactions to ensure they comply with local laws. The list goes on. Essentially, each project is different, but if you understand who your wireframe users will be before you start, you can try to meet their needs. There's more on working with clients in Chapters 2 and 30.

Your Product's Context of Use

Gone are the days when you could design a website and expect it to be used only on a desktop machine with a monitor of a minimum size. Before you start wireframing, you need to think about which screen sizes to optimize your designs for. This can be rather outfacing: screen sizes currently vary from cinema display TVs, to desktop monitors, to tablets and mobiles (at portrait or landscape orientation). The list is ever growing and it is reasonable to expect that there will be popular new devices available within the lifetime of your product.

So, if you are designing websites, your wireframes are very likely to have to cope with multiple screen sizes. How can this be achieved? There are a number of approaches, from wireframing every page at a number of different sizes, to wireframing for desktop screens and providing prioritized content lists for the developers to translate into smaller screens or wireframing straight into responsive HTML. The best answer for your project depends on what the wireframes are for. If it is to user test on desktop computers, maybe the most cost-effective approach is to wireframe for desktop screen sizes. If you also need to test on mobile sizes, you'll need to wireframe for that size too. If it is to provide a specification for visual designers and developers to work from, it may be that you need to wireframe key templates at different sizes and allow others to extrapolate in between.

WIREFRAMING

Now you're ready to start generating wireframes, here's how to go about it.

Prioritize Content

Start out by making a list of the content that needs to go on the screen you are designing. Refer back to your information architecture, user goals, business goals, and entry and exit points. Make sure there is navigation and content in your list to support these goals and journeys.

Once you have your content list, you need to prioritize it. Review each item on your content list against the screen goals and number them in priority order. Chapter 11 on ideation workshops describes a content prioritization exercise to run with clients. For the fictional ShoeUX.com website homepage, you might end up with something like this:

1. Header and footer area, including logo, navigation, and company phone number (to help users find suitable products and instill trust in the business)

2. Seasonal and trend-led messaging and associated products (to help surface relevant products in addition to main navigation routes and reinforce the "high fashion" brand message, to help users understand if this website meets their needs)

3. Free delivery and returns messaging (really important to encourage new users to shop for shoes online as product fit is so important and difficult to predict)

4. Featured products and categories (important to get products on the home page to allow users to quickly find suitable products and show abundance)

5. Style blog or other fashion credentials (to show off the brand's high-fashion credentials; to help users understand if this website meets their needs)

6. Newsletter sign-up (to meet key business goal)

This prioritized content list is incredibly useful. If you are designing for cell phone screen sizes, you may well have already done the majority of the work: you have an order for the blocks of content on the screen. Passing this list on to visual designers will help them give visual priority to the correct place. Passing this list on to developers will help them produce code that presents content in the right order whatever the viewing device. It may also help them prioritize the development of tricky functionality—if a low-priority feature will take a long time to develop, they may choose to deliver it last or push it into a second phase.

Some UX practitioners produce wireframes that are less about layout and more about an annotated list of content and functionality, with diagrams showing specific interactions.

Start Drawing

Now you know what you're doing and why, it's time to make some marks, whether by sketching on paper or by opening your favorite diagramming program. When you start drawing, you may find it doesn't make sense to stick strictly to your prioritized content list. Some items in the list may need to be grouped logically and this will disrupt the order, which is fine.

When you create a wireframe, you are trying to answer a number of questions. How does the information architecture translate into a navigation structure? How can the page design support the user's flow through the site? What is the primary call to action and how can it be made prominent? What should go at the top of the page? Will there be more than one column? The list goes on.

Don't expect to get the answers right first time. That's the point of wireframes—they are intended to be part of an iterative user-centered design process.

For each item on your prioritized content list, make a block on your wireframe.

- Represent images with gray rectangles
- Represent navigation items with accurate text
- Use representative or real headings
- Use real or dummy text for content
- Mock up forms and buttons with rectangles and other shapes

Play around with the layout and see what works. Different layouts will provide different visual weights and different ways for the eye to journey around the page.

Figure 17-3 shows a first-pass wireframe for the homepage of the fictional ShoeUX.com website. The wireframe is based on the prioritized content list discussed previously. After the main navigation, the content with the highest priority is seasonal and trend-led messaging, so this has been given the "hero" area at the top of the screen. Free delivery and returns is given high prominence, alongside a featured product area. Example copy is used for headings, but actual content is replaced by faux-Latin text to indicate layout and approximate word count before real copy is developed. The newsletter sign-up form is represented with a rectangle for a text input field and a rectangle with rounded corners for the button. The footer area is simply represented by a gray rectangle—the details will be filled in on a later iteration of the wireframe.

The "Lorem Ipsum" Debate

Lorem ipsum is the dummy text used to replace real content in wireframes and visual designs. It is nonsense Latin, derived from an original passage by Cicero, but with words altered, added, and removed. It is designed to move people's focus away from copy and onto other interface elements when final copy is not available.

There has been impassioned debate on the use of lorem ipsum within the UX community recently. The use of placeholder text is under fire because it does not represent real content, and this is problematic in an industry where content is hugely important. It is difficult for a design to support the meaning of content if the content is not there.

However, there are times, especially early in the design process, when realistic copy is not yet available, and dummy text is a useful tool. Decisions on how appropriate it is to use lorem ipsum must be made on a project-by-project basis. Here are some guidelines for sensible use of dummy text:

- Use real content where available.
- Always use actual copy for navigation items.
- Always use actual or indicative copy for headings and sub-headings.
- When real content is not available, use dummy text, but begin with an introduction to the type of content required. You can always add real content if it becomes available later.

- Always use examples of real content for data tables and similar—you need to be sure that your layout can cope with genuine data formats.
- Ensure you involve the content-creation team in the wireframing process. They should be encouraged to produce copy to fit user and business needs, rather than simply to fit the wireframe template.

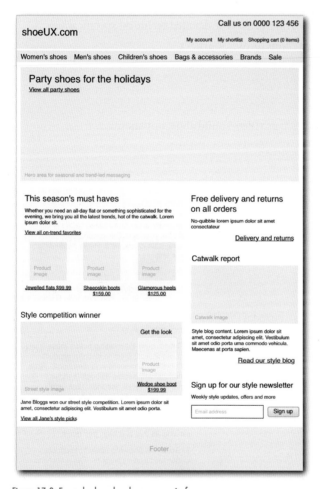

Figure 17-3: Example shoe shop homepage wireframe

There are plenty of lorem ipsum generators available on the Internet if you feel it would be useful to your project.

Annotations to Wireframes

There are many types of notes that you can add to wireframes. What's best for your project will generally depend on who will be using the wireframes and why. Notes are there to help others work on the design and development in your absence. Make sure your name and contact details are somewhere on the wireframes so people can ask you questions later.

Figure 17-4 shows annotations to the imaginary ShoeUX.com homepage wireframe. Here are some annotations to consider for your wireframes:

- User goals for the screen
- Business goals for the screen
- Likely entry and exit points
- Functional descriptions of interactions or detailed technical specifications
- Storyboards of key interactions or user journeys
- Rationale for design decisions
- Copy direction
- Image direction
- Other media direction (such as video, sound clips, or panoramas)

Figure 17-4: Example shoe shop homepage wireframe annotations

Share, Test, Iterate, and Improve

When you have wireframes you are happy with, it's time to test them out. Share them with your colleagues and your clients. Do they understand what each screen is for? Is the wording intuitive? Can they flow through the product in the way you envisaged? Are the calls to action clear and inviting? Is the visual weighting conveying the right message?

One effective method for examining wireframes is a team walkthrough. View the wireframes together. At every stage, walk through what the user is doing and thinking. What do they know? What do they need to know? How are they feeling? Do the designs meet their needs?

There are plenty of team members you should consider sharing your wireframes with: visual designers, developers, content and copy teams, SEO experts, analytics experts, accessibility specialists, and product specialists. Each of these specialists will have a different priority for the designs and consulting them will help get the balance right.

The most robust method for validating wireframes is to test them with real users. User testing provides genuine evidence on which to base your design. It can be particularly helpful if there are conflicting requirements from different members of the client team.

We generally run one-to-one testing sessions on wireframes using a *think-aloud protocol*. This means asking users to imagine they are using a real product and to tell us what they are thinking as they progress. This is a great way of eliciting answers to the same types of questions as outlined previously. Can they find what they want? Do they know where to go next? How do they feel about the process? There's much more on this in Chapter 5 on usability testing.

Clients are sometimes surprised that it's possible to test wireframes, as they don't look "real." However, our experience is that test participants are extremely able to suspend disbelief and become engaged with extremely early stage concepts, even sketches. However, we have found that it is extremely important to create a realistic user flow by ensuring that data is consistent from screen to screen. Taking the shoe website example, ask the participant to imagine purchasing a specific pair of shoes. Refer to the same shoes throughout the journey, ensure that the price is consistent across screens, and make sure that the numbers in the shopping cart add up.

Test participants can suspend disbelief and become engaged with wireframes. However, you must ensure that their journey through the product is consistent. Keep naming the same, ensure that pricing is consistent across screens, and make sure that the numbers in the shopping cart add up.

When you have elicited feedback on your wireframes, it's time to decide how to address it. Don't take negative comments personally—remember that you wireframe in order to question and improve designs at the earliest stage possible. Do you need to change wording? Change emphasis? Provide extra content? Remove content? Provide stronger calls to action? Figure 17-5 shows the example shoe shop homepage with amends made after client feedback. More emphasis is placed on surfacing products and product categories in the main column.

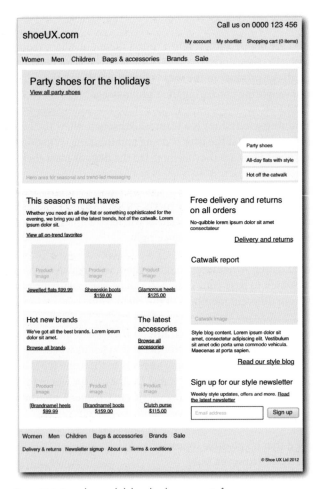

Figure 17-5: Example amended shoe shop homepage wireframe

WIREFRAMING IN PRACTICE

It's best to start wireframing by sketching on paper, as it's a quick way of getting going. There's no option to procrastinate by setting up grids, layers, and the like in a drawing tool.

Once you have a sketch on paper, it's time to open a drawing tool. If you need a new tool for creating wireframes in, what should you choose? If you are a Mac user, OmniGraffle is a great diagramming tool. For Windows users, Visio is popular. Balsamiq is available on Macs, Windows, Linux, and online. Axure is available for both Macs and PCs and is particularly useful for creating clickable prototypes (there's more on prototyping in Chapter 18). However, any program in which you can accurately place shapes, lines, and copy will work. PowerPoint, Keynote, Illustrator, Photoshop, and even Excel are all options. Some people wireframe directly into HTML. There are also a growing number of online wireframing tools, as well as apps for tablets and cell phones.

Professional diagramming tools like OmniGraffle and Visio add extra functionality that is useful if you'll be wireframing a lot, such as support for multiple pages, layers, items that will repeat over several templates (good for navigation structures that appear on every page), and pixel-perfect guides and grids.

WIREFRAMING TOP TIPS

For detailed instructions on creating wireframes in OmniGraffle, Axure, and PowerPoint, see the excellent *Communicating the User Experience* by our colleagues Richard Caddick and Steve Cable. In the mean time, here are some practical tips to get you started.

Set Up a Template

A few basic set-up tasks will ensure your wireframe deck is consistent and clear to others.

Where your software allows, work in actual pixel dimensions and use realistic font sizes. This will make for easier user testing and a clear understanding of what will be visible to users without scrolling.

Use guides and grids to set up a column-based layout. This will keep your wireframes aligned and well structured. Graphic designers and developers often work to this type of grid: ask your team if there is a particular grid they like to use and if possible, work to that.

Figure 17-6 shows the example ShoeUX.com homepage wireframe, with the underlying five-column grid exposed. Pixel measurements are shown next to the wireframe to give an indication of in-browser display.

Once you have settled on a layout grid and other styles, try to stick to them throughout your deck—doing so will provide consistency and a strong framework to base your design work on.

Housekeeping

Pagination and page titles may be the last thing on your mind when you're in the middle of a creative flow, but they are invaluable when taking feedback from others (especially if this feedback is delivered over the phone or via e-mail).

Keeping track of revisions is also important. When discussing a wireframe deck that has been through several rounds of amends, it really helps to know that everyone's looking at the latest version. Do this via sensible filenaming and including the filename or version number on every wireframe in the deck. Consider including a change log so everyone can see what revisions were made when.

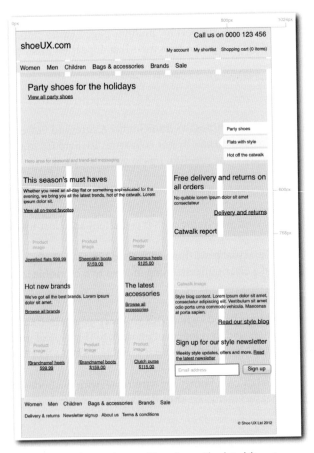

Figure 17-6: A wireframe with exposed five-column grid and pixel dimensions

Stencils, Libraries, and Patterns

There are some great wireframing resources available on the Internet. Explore and find the ones that work best for you.

Wireframe templates for different drawing tools get you off to a good start. Stencil and icon libraries provide ready-made UX shapes to use in your wireframes. Try cxpartners.com/resources for the templates and stencils produced for *Communicating the User Experience* by Richard Caddick and Steve Cable. Konigi also has an excellent OmniGraffle UX template at konigi.com/tools. Yahoo! provides a comprehensive stencil library for a wide range of applications at developer.yahoo.com/ypatterns/about/stencils.

Design pattern libraries document common user interface design patterns—these are tried and tested solutions to common interaction design problems. Again, Yahoo! has a comprehensive library at developer.yahoo.com/ypatterns, and there are plenty more, including ui-patterns.com and welie.com.

RESOURCES

Communicating the User Experience (2011) by Richard Caddick and Steve Cable

A Project Guide to UX Design by Russ Unger and Carolyn Chandler

Yahoo! Developer Network Stencil Kits:
http://developer.yahoo.com/ypatterns/about/stencils/

Yahoo! Design Pattern Library:
http://developer.yahoo.com/ypatterns/

cxpartners UX Resources:
http://cxpartners.com/ux-resources/

UI Patterns User Interface Design Pattern Library:
www.ui-patterns.com

Welie.com Patterns in Interaction Design:
www.welie.com

100 Things Every Designer Needs to Know About People: What Makes Them Tick? (2011) by Susan Weinschenk

Seductive Interaction Design: Creating Playful, Fun, and Effective User Experiences (2011) by Stephen P. Anderson

The Design of Everyday Things (2002) by Donald A. Norman

18

USING PROTOTYPES TO BRING YOUR IDEAS TO LIFE

PROTOTYPING HAS ALWAYS been an important part of the design process in both digital and physical product design. It is inevitable that at some point designers will need to visualize their ideas. Prototyping provides an ideal method of doing this to share our vision with colleagues and client audiences and of course with users.

The recent boom in the UX market has seen a growth in the production of software aimed at UX designers. There are now numerous prototyping tools that are available for the non-technical UX designer to build and share high-fidelity prototypes with project stakeholders. This growth in tools reinforces the fact that prototyping has never been more important given the interactive nature of the products and services we design.

This chapter explores the pros and cons of prototyping and shows you the different types of prototypes that you can create to suit your own projects.

WHAT ARE PROTOTYPES?

Prototypes represent the first building blocks of a digital product. They can take many forms, from basic paper mock-ups to more complicated prototypes that can be used on their intended device. They give you the chance as the designer to explore your ideas and to bring them to life quickly and cheaply. They allow you to make mistakes early and learn what you need to do to create an acceptable final product.

In the physical product world, prototyping is a critical process. It allows people to understand the form factor of an object for the first time to see if it will fulfill its intended purpose. It allows people to understand a concept and provide feedback on it. Once something takes shape, it is so much easier to understand and develop. Prototypes, such as the one shown in Figure 18-1, present the ideal format for designers to share their ideas and vision with a wider audience.

Figure 18-1: Architects make models of buildings to share their vision with stakeholders

In digital product design, the purpose of the prototype is identical. Arguably something as rough as a sketched wireframe could be considered a prototype as it is the first incarnation of a product. Within UX projects, prototypes will vary in completeness (or fidelity), from simple paper prototypes to clickable prototypes that can be shared online.

If you want to learn more about how to create great wireframes, see Chapter 17.

WHEN SHOULD YOU CREATE PROTOTYPES?

The case for creating prototypes will vary depending upon the outputs of your design projects. If you are designing simple templates for a CMS-driven site, you are less likely to need to produce prototypes than if you are designing a mobile app that uses a novel interaction design.

The beauty of prototyping tools such as Axure (www.Axure.com) is that you can create simple prototypes very easily without any coding knowledge. This makes it so easy to create a simple prototype that you might as well create it and take it into testing instead of using static, unlinked pages to make the experience more realistic for your test participants.

A recent project we worked on included a novel idea for the way users navigated around the website. This idea had come from a creative agency and the client was keen to see if it would work with users. We were skeptical to say the least. In this type of situation, you should always create some sort of a prototype. If it works in usability testing, it justifies the development cost of building it. If it fails, the team won't waste time and money bringing a flawed idea to life.

Tip: Most design projects that we work on have at least one round of user research built into them. Given we know we are going to be testing with users, it justifies producing a prototype. We know it will give us what we need for testing. We know that if we are designing something with a complex form for instance, we will make sure we produce our wireframes in a tool such as Axure that will also give us a prototype at the same time, which saves us time in the long run.

THE PROS AND CONS OF PROTOTYPING

Prototyping has become a very popular technique among UX professionals because it can be a cheap, fast, and fun way to bring ideas to life. It also produces a perfect output for usability testing that can be as simple or as complex as your project constraints allow. It is not a perfect technique though so let's examine, in detail, the pros and cons of prototyping.

We love prototyping; here are some of the benefits of the technique.

PROTOTYPES ARE QUICK AND EASY

Techniques like paper prototyping give you a quick and easy way to explore, discard, develop, and communicate your ideas. You can try things out with materials that everyone can get hold of. Users will be happy to offer suggestions for improvements because they can see it's just work in progress and they won't hurt your feelings.

PROTOTYPES GIVE YOU SOMETHING TO PUT IN FRONT OF USERS

One of the founding principles of UX design is to fail first and to fail early. This means you should involve users as early (and frequently) as possible during the design process to help you to learn what works for them. Prototyping ideas and putting them in front of users is a great way of doing this (see Figure 18-2). It

One of the founding principles of UX design is to fail first and to fail early.

forces you to think through your ideas fully, to visualize them, and then to work out how they respond to user inputs.

Prototyping tools will allow you to get good feedback on interactive elements of digital products such as forms. Despite the form only being at a prototype state, the user is still able to interact with it as if it were the final form. They still have to interpret the questions and input their responses. You can also mock up some form validation to give a feel for how this is planned to work.

Figure 18-2: A mobile app prototype being tested in a real usage environment

This gives valuable feedback that you would never get from "flat" or JPG versions of static interfaces because users cannot fill out these forms so will not fully consider the obstacles they present.

Users are very good at understanding the limitations of a prototype but still responding to it as if it were a finished product. The result of this is excellent user feedback that you can use to improve the actual final result.

CLIENTS KNOW WHAT THEY ARE GETTING WITH PROTOTYPES

A prototype may take many forms, from a low-fi (basic) to a hi-fi (more fully featured) final result. The beauty of a prototype is that it is unambiguous—you can see what it is and likewise a client has a good idea of what they will be getting. When using techniques such as wireframing to visualize ideas, conversely, you can't always be sure that they have successfully communicated your vision to a client.

A prototype is more tangible; it can be used and played with. It provides a deliverable that clients and stakeholders can easily understand and provide feedback on, whether it is what they want/need or not.

A functioning prototype can also present a clearer deliverable for a client to understand. A prototype that contains different interface states that are hidden until requested is simpler than a huge pile of wireframes that repeats very similar wireframes with only subtle "state change" differences.

THE NATURE OF A PROTOTYPE ENCOURAGES USEFUL FEEDBACK

The rough and unfinished nature of a prototype can also help with the quality of feedback that you get from users. Because people can see that something is work in progress, they are happy to criticize it. They can see that you haven't put too much work into it and feel they won't hurt your feelings if they pull it apart (see Figure 18-3). Sometimes it is sensible to deliberately make prototypes look a bit rough for exactly this reason.

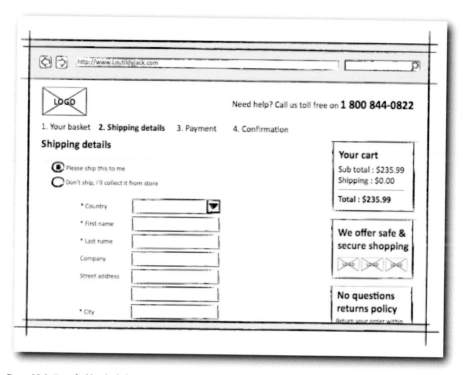

Figure 18-3: Users feel less bad about criticizing rough-looking prototypes so we often give them this appearance

PROTOTYPES GIVE YOU FAITH THAT SOMETHING WILL WORK

Prototypes are often essential. We worked on an interface that used a completely novel interaction style. It was a new interface that users hadn't seen before. In this situation it was vital that we prototyped and tested it so we could be sure that it was going to be understood by users.

PROTOTYPING REVEALS DESIGN PROBLEMS

By building a prototype, you are forced to work through design problems you never considered. It is this challenge that makes the process so enjoyable.

PROTOTYPES ARE ESSENTIAL FOR DESIGNING DYNAMIC INTERFACES

Modern interfaces dictate that the experience that is delivered to the user is so much more than what content is displayed and how it is presented in the page. Modern interfaces move and respond to interactions in ways that are deliberately designed to enhance the experience. These must be prototyped first to ensure they work in harmony with the overall experience of using the product.

Static wireframes cannot deliver this and can lead to the designer missing significant parts of the experience that need to be considered and designed. The result is often an incomplete product that doesn't flow and may not have been fully though out. Generally these "design bugs" will be picked up by developers, who will question how something is supposed to work as they may not have seen a design solution for it. This is fine if the designer is available to address the issue. However, a designer might not be available within the required timeframe (such as when using a waterfall process, for example).

Prototyping more dynamic interactions such as the way a drag-and-drop feature works or the way that a menu panel appears and disappears may require skills with software such as Flash to bring them to life. For more established interactions you may not need to mock it up because project stakeholders will know what you mean. You can also show your project team examples of existing interactions that you may wish to recreate from existing products or from libraries such as http://query.com. Don't feel you need to prototype everything, save time where you can because you will always need it elsewhere!

TOOLS LIKE AXURE GIVE YOU WIREFRAMES AND A PROTOTYPE "FOR FREE"

Tools like Axure allow you to create functionally rich prototypes without needing to go to the time and expense of bringing a front-end developer into your prototyping phase. This means you can create and amend them faster, which gives you more time to get user input.

MANY PROTOYPE TEMPLATES ARE AVAILABLE TO REUSE

The boom in prototyping has made many templates and widgets for common interface elements available online, which you can download for free. If you need a working calendar for Axure for example you can just download one. You don't need to spend ages building your own. This allows you to spend your time concentrating on getting the overall experience as good as you can, without wasting time on elements that may well fail (and be discarded) following usability testing.

If you are considering prototyping, you should bear the following drawbacks in mind before you start.

PROTOYPES CAN BE TIME CONSUMING TO BUILD

If you need to produce a hi-fidelity prototype for your project you need to be realistic when quoting for how long you think it will take to produce. If you are used to creating static wireframes, you will be surprised just how long it will take to add interaction and different page states to your prototype.

To help with your design time quotes, make sure you have a sitemap of what you are designing first and identify the pages or interfaces that will be the most complex. Give yourself more time to do these. You should also prioritize the key pages within a journey, such as the checkout process within an e-commerce site. Your estimate will depend upon your familiarity with the tool you use, but by identifying the scope of work in this way you will be more likely to end up with a realistic and achievable quote.

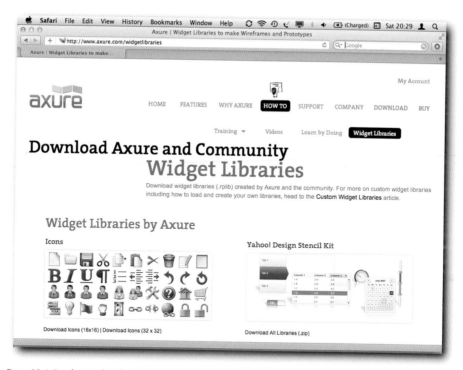

Figure 18-4: Templates such as these are easy to find and download online

SOURCE: Reproduced with permission from Axure Software Solutions, Inc © 2012

You also need to be careful not to spend time recreating particular features and functionality just because you can! It doesn't make sense to spend three hours building the perfect calendar picker if you only have a day to build the whole page! Many of these common interface elements are available to download for free. Build your own libraries of these they will save you hours of time and effort.

PROTOTYPES CAN BE TIME CONSUMING TO AMEND

Once you get the hang of prototyping, particularly with tools that allow you to create quite complex prototypes, you will see how easy it is to get carried away with essentially recreating an entire website or app. This is all well and good until you come to amend it following user or client feedback.

You can guarantee that the thing you need to change is hidden within multiple dynamic panels on Axure or within some devious smoke and mirrors piece of functionality that is time consuming to unpick and rebuild. The power of these tools can also be their downfall.

You need to recognize how far you should develop your prototype. As you get more user and client and feedback you can justifiably increase its scope. Start small and build up over time. Don't build more than you need to be sure the approach will work.

QUOTING DESIGN AND BUILD TIME FROM PROTOTYPES CAN BE DIFFICULT FOR OTHER TEAM MEMBERS

Prototypes as a deliverable are great. They contain all of the features and functionality of a website or app in a nice tidy package that a client can play with and check over. The same deliverable as static wireframes would end up as a huge pile of individual screens, which become unwieldy and hard to interpret.

You may then find that developers and designers will find it hard to quote from viewing the prototype as there will be many hidden panel, layers, and interfaces that will only be shown if certain things happen. One way to help to alleviate this is to add a comprehensive clickable index at the beginning of an HTML prototype, which makes the scope of the prototype clear to all involved.

A pile of static wireframes works well in this situation, as it presents a clear picture of the scope of the project that is being developed.

PROTOTYPES WON'T ALWAYS LOOK PRETTY

If you take particular pride in making your static wireframes look beautiful, you might struggle to make your prototypes look as good as you can with tools like OmniGraffle. Prototyping tools can be used to get the same visual effect but they correctly focus on function as opposed to form.

This really isn't a problem, as it will help you to focus on getting the fundamentals of your interface right first. This also makes sure you don't spend valuable time making something look beautiful that might fail in its first round of testing. You will rarely have the luxury of time so this keeps you working efficiently within the constraints of your project.

HOW TO CREATE PROTOYPES

The beauty of prototyping is that you can use the technique to some extent regardless of the time and budgetary constraints of your project. At the early stages or when time is tight, use paper. If time allows and the project suits it, create a fully blown Axure masterpiece! If you can code, just go ahead and do your thing!

There are many types of prototypes that you can create. Let's examine a few in more detail.

PAPER PROTOTYPING

It may seem like a strange idea to construct a prototype for a digital product out of physical materials such as paper, but it can really work well due to its obvious widespread availability and low cost.

Sketching (see Figure 18-5) is arguably a form of paper prototyping and as a technique has seen a huge recent resurgence in popularity, as it allows people to quickly generate and share ideas.

Paper prototypes are commonly used early in design projects to explore different ideas and concepts for interface designs and also for features, content, and functionality that they may end up containing. Typically in usability testing with paper prototypes users are asked to tap on objects within the prototypes to simulate a click for desktop interfaces. Of course for prototypes aimed at users of mobile devices paper will still allow users to tap and swipe to mimic real use.

Figure 18-5: Sketches provide perfect low-fidelity paper prototypes

Once users have interacted with a paper prototype, the next screen is shown by a new piece of paper being passed to the user. You can make interactions with paper prototypes slightly more realistic by getting creative with common device templates such as templates of common iOS and Android interfaces.

LOW-FIDELITY DIGITAL PROTOTYPING

Tools like Balsamiq (http://www.balsamiq.com/) enable you to generate quick prototypes that can be used for early stage concept testing or even to explore more complex interface design ideas.

You can also use tools like PowerPoint and Keynote to produce perfectly acceptable low-fidelity prototypes. These tools allow you to build links between pages so the resulting prototypes can offer some realistic interaction for users. The downside of these tools is that they are not specifically designed for this purpose, so may lack dedicated features for UX designers and a large user community to provide templates and support.

HIGH-FIDELITY DIGITAL PROTOTYPING

Tools such as Axure (see Figure 18-6) allow you build advanced prototypes that can provide a very similar experience for users of a digital product to that of the final release. Of course the majority of the interactions that are built within these tools are largely smoke and mirrors in that they are not generally plugged into any live data feeds. They allow you to produce detailed and realistic interfaces that provide really good candidates for user testing.

The success of tools like Axure means that their user base is ever growing. It is easy to seek help and advice from fellow users as well as from the prototyping tool developers (Axure's customer service via Twitter is fantastic).

Figure 18-6: An prototype generated from Axure in use during usability testing

The other benefit of its widespread use is that the UX community happily shares the widgets they make. There really is no need to try to recreate common elements such as date pickers, carousels, form elements, device-specific interface elements, and icons to name but a few. This will save you hours and also help you to create great looking prototypes in a relatively short period of time.

High-fidelity prototypes do have their problems. It is easy to get carried away with them and build an entire website or app just because you can. They can be really time consuming to change and amend following user and client feedback and some can be expensive to buy in the first place.

Don't ignore them for these reasons though. We've found it so liberating to be able to use these tools to bring my ideas to life, where previously I've had to rely on technical colleagues to do just that. Give them a try; you will love them!

PROTOTYPING FOR MOBILE

You may find yourself needing to design a prototype for a website or application that needs to work across multiple devices. Due to the significant growth in these platforms, there has been a resultant growth in tools to prototype for mobile platforms.

You can use tools such as Proto.io (http://proto.io/; see Figure 18-7) to prototype for the iPhone and iPad. Proto.io is an online tool, so you'll need a good connection to use it. It offers an easy-to-use interface and all the common interface elements that you'll likely need.

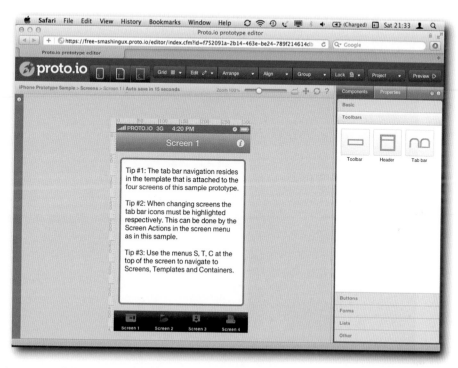

Figure 18-7: Tools like Proto.io make prototyping for mobile really quick and easy

SOURCE: Reproduced with permission from Cyberopsis Webdata Limited © 2012

If you favor an offline approach, you can use tools such as Keynote to produce perfectly acceptable prototypes for mobile. Various stencils are available (check out Mockapp and keynotopia.com) which also give you all the interface elements you need. The "transitions" and "builds" options in the inspector can be used to mimic interface behaviors.

A really cool tool that you can use to display your prototypes on mobile devices is LiveView (http://www.zambetti.com/projects/liveview/). This tool allows you to broadcast a prototype to a mobile device across a wireless network. This enables you to test prototypes on mobile devices from any design tool, be it Axure, OmniGraffle, Keynote, or anything else that you choose to use.

PROTOTYPING WITH CODE

For those who can, prototyping with code presents a sensible approach because you are producing something that you might be able to use later in the front-end build phase of the project.

It also makes sense to prototype with code because you don't need to spend ages trying to recreate the effect of a piece of code in a tool like Axure; you can just make it work "for real." See Figure 18-8.

This method is probably the hardest to do if you are a rookie coder and in reality you are more likely to turn to a bespoke drawing tool to help you. Of course, if you are a competent coder this is likely to be the obvious choice for you.

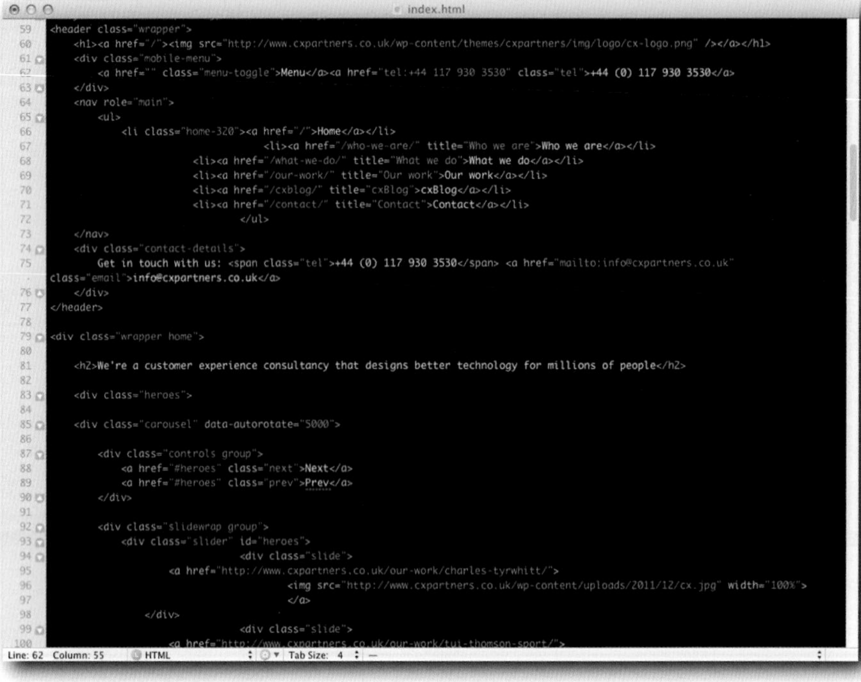

Figure 18-8: Those who can code, will code!

RESOURCES

Measuring the User Experience by Tom Tullis and Bill Albert

Interaction Design: Beyond Human-Computer Interaction by Helen Sharp, Yvonne Rogers and Jenny Preece

Communicating the User Experience by Richard Caddick and Steve Cable

PART

IV

UX COMPONENTS DECONSTRUCTED

CHAPTER

19

NAVIGATION UX DECONSTRUCTED

NAVIGATION IS FUNDAMENTAL to everything that UX designers create. Good navigation helps people to find things, to understand what options they have available to them, and to orientate themselves.

Users notice navigation when it doesn't work so well, such as when they can't find what they want or don't understand the options they are being presented with. Good navigation is invisible to the user's experience. They use it without thinking when it offers them what they need when and where they need it in terminology that makes sense to them.

The purpose of navigation is to link related objects to one another. As a UX designer, it is your job to understand what is related to what and why, and to present and organize information in a way that is intuitive for the task in hand.

Navigation is about signposting, directing, orientation, and organizing. Many navigation conventions exist which UX designers must be aware of so that they can reuse them in order to make navigating as easy as possible within the products that they design.

KEY USER TASKS AND QUESTIONS

Users simply want to get on with the task at hand. Users will use navigation:

- To work out how they can find something specific
- To be shown things they didn't know about
- To show them where they are and where they can go from there
- To make it clear what their options are and to understand the scope and offering of a website
- To demonstrate what content, features, and functionality something offers
- To allow them to progress with their tasks
- To find things similar to what they are looking at
- To understand how a set of information has been organized
- To get a feel for the character and personality of a brand or service

This list illustrates just some of the different roles that navigation plays within the user experiences that you'll design. Navigation is not simply there to help move users around; it forms the very foundation of user experiences and is critical to successful products and services.

TYPICAL BUSINESS GOALS

Businesses want navigation to work well so users can navigate as quickly and simply as possible through their digital products. Businesses will use want navigation to:

- Guide users through a process or set of information while making them aware of other related products and services along the way.
- Guide users through a process such as a checkout or registration process as quickly as possible.
- Rank well with search engines by using popular search terms as navigation.
- Make the user experience as enjoyable and as efficient as possible.
- Prioritize key (and profitable) information, products, and services through navigation, labeling, and prioritized calls to action.
- Raise money through referral deals such as the way affiliates get paid for directing traffic to other websites.
- Make things hard to find, such as links to unsubscribe or contact information when they want to encourage to stop people leaving a service or to reduce customer help desk costs.

It is interesting to consider that final point. Sometimes your clients may not want you to make things easy to find within the navigation you design. This seems counterintuitive (from a UX perspective), but is relatively commonplace, so be prepared for it to crop up with commercial clients. You will often be asked to prioritize commercial needs before user needs.

In the majority of cases, commercial objectives for navigation are around factors such as efficiency, as they will want users to complete their tasks as easily as possible. This aspect of UX design is rarely contentious since the objectives of the UX designer and the client are identical.

EXAMPLE NAVIGATION WIREFRAME

Figure 19-1 illustrates some different types of navigation that are typically seen on a homepage.

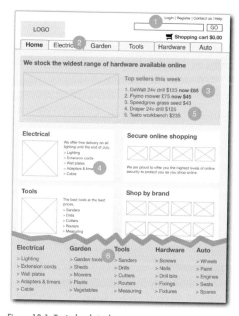

Figure 19-1: Typical website homepage navigation

1. **Site tool navigation:** Site tool navigation identifies commonly used website features such as register, login, contact us and help. These are links that will be required by users across the site and are as such, available from every page.

2. **Global navigation:** The global navigation represents the main sections of the website and is typically available from every page. When displayed horizontally such as this, be careful of character limits of labels, as you may quickly run out of space. Global navigation is also sometimes shown down the side of the page but when displayed this way it can take up valuable screen estate.

3. **Navigation as promotion:** Navigation is used to push products that are available on promotion to increase traffic and therefore sales of these items.

4. **Sub-navigation:** The sub-sections of the global navigation element Electrical are in this example made available from the feature block. This makes it quicker for users to skip down multiple levels within the website hierarchy to the specific section they need.

5. **In-page navigation:** In this example the name of the product is clickable which will link through to the product page (see Figure 19-2). Product images are often also clickable, users expect to be able to click on product images to find out more about that particular product.

6. **Footer navigation:** A recent trend has seen the expansion of footer areas to show more of the website's navigation. This is partly due to increasing the search ranking of pages by showing navigation keywords and also to help navigation when reading long pages. This area typically contains links to top-level sections as well as key utility navigation tools, such as links to contact details and sitemaps.

Figure 19-2 illustrates some key areas of navigation on a typical product page.

1. **Breadcrumb navigation:** Breadcrumb navigation gets its name from the *Hansel and Gretel* story, where they leave breadcrumbs as a trail to help them to find their way out of the woods. They are used in Figure 19-2 to denote the location of the page within the hierarchy of the site. They also allow users to quickly skip to different levels of the website and can be useful to orientate users, particularly when they have arrived via search engines.

2. **Call to action navigation:** Call to action navigation is deliberately distinctive within a page because it represents the key component of the page that the site owners want users to click. They are often connected with how the site makes money. Call to action navigation is typically represented as buttons; they are visually stronger than simple text links.

   When choosing whether to use a text link or a buttons for navigation, I always return to the adage "links take you somewhere while buttons do something." It's a pretty reliable guide to helping you decide which is the most appropriate for your interface.

3. **Tabbed navigation:** You will often see tabs used to organize and compartmentalize large sets of information that would otherwise lead to very long scrolling pages. As a designer, it feels right to tuck everything away in tabs but you'll notice from usability testing that people don't always see them. Use them with caution!

4. **Contextual navigation:** Contextual navigation takes users to content that's relevant to the information they are viewing at any one time. The motive for doing this may be to offer help, to promote a higher value item, or simply to promote other content on the website.

5. **Zeitgeist navigation:** Zeitgeist navigation is used to convey to the user what content is popular at that point in time. It is used to convey that a site is active and being used as well as to promote what other people are finding useful and interesting. This often manifests itself in lists such as Top 10s, Most Read, Bestsellers, or Most Shared. These are either automatically generated or manually maintained by website editors.

6. **Category navigation:** When showing items that belong to larger categories of products or information, it is useful to provide a link to the parent category, which allows users to broaden their search. This can be particularly useful when users arrive at a product page from a search engine and want to broaden their search to see more related choices.

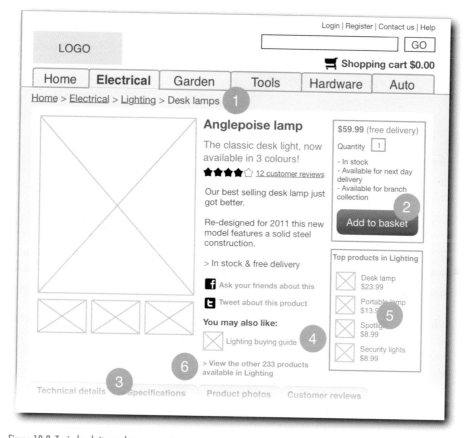

Figure 19-2: Typical website product page navigation

TOP NAVIGATION TIPS

Consider the issues covered in the following sections when designing your navigation.

INVOLVE USERS WHEN YOU DESIGN YOUR NAVIGATION

By involving users you can verify if your navigation design makes any sense to them. Can they move around the site as they need to? Are crosslinks and calls to action in the right places? You can also check users' expectations around the location of navigation elements and test the language you have used to label your navigation. Card sorting, shown in Figure 19-3, is one way to involve users early in navigation design decisions.

To learn more about card sorting, see Chapter 15 for an in-depth look at this technique.

Figure 19-3: Card sorting is a great way of involving users in the design of your navigation

CHECK YOUR COMPETITORS FOR PATTERNS

Within certain domains such as e-commerce or travel there may be well-established ways of categorizing and labeling navigation. Consider the way that the software on your computer shares the positioning and labeling of common navigation such as File, Save, and Print.

Why would you design software that doesn't reuse these conventions? When conventions such as these exist, be sure to reuse them. Don't make users learn a new way of doing things when they visit your site.

USE FREQUENTLY SEARCHED FOR NAVIGATION LABELS

Labeling navigation can be challenging. You are often faced with issues such needing to choose labels that are brief to save space on the interface, but are also suitably descriptive. There may be conventions within a certain marketplace that you should consider. Tools such as thesauruses can be useful for choosing suitable synonyms if you find yourself stuck.

> Tip: Given the importance of keywords when searching, you should Google the terms you are considering to see what results they return. You can also use tools such as the Google Adwords Keyword tool (www.adwords.google.com) to check the volumes of searches for certain keywords. You can find out how unique or how commonly used they are on the web via the Competition column. It doesn't matter how easy the site is to navigate if users can't find it on the Internet in the first place.

DESIGN FOR MUTUAL EXCLUSIVITY

Your navigation must contain categories that are sufficiently different from one another to prevent a user from thinking, "It could be in there, or it could also be in there."

PLAN FOR EVERY NAVIGATION SCENARIO

Once you have designed your sitemap (see Chapter 15 to find out how), you need to design every level of subsequent navigation to ensure that you have considered every navigation scenario.

Common questions to ask during this process include the following:

- How many levels of navigation do I have?
- How will I show each level within the interface?
- Which levels will always be displayed?
- Will I show "parent" categories as well as "sibling" categories?
- Do I have enough space on the page to show the most complicated navigation scenario?

USE NAVIGATION TO DRIVE THE PRIMARY GOALS OF WHAT YOU ARE DESIGNING

It is likely that whatever you are designing has some primary goals that it is trying to achieve. Navigation plays a critical part in achieving these goals. If the goal is to encourage users to sign up for something or download something, your navigation has to drive people to these elements.

MAKE NAVIGATION LOOK LIKE NAVIGATION

The navigational links must be clear to users. They don't have to be blue and underlined but make sure your users know that they are clickable.

DOES YOUR NAVIGATION PASS THE TEST?

Take a look at something you are designing or pick a finished interface. Ask yourself the following questions:

- Is it clear where you are in the website?
- Is it clear how to move on from where you are?
- Can you easily get to popular sections such as search, contact, and help?
- Is it clear what is and what isn't navigation?
- Can you get back to the homepage?
- Is it clear where the website wants you to go next?

If the answer to any of these questions is no, there may well be an issue with the navigation. This is a great way to identify problems with existing interfaces as well as using it as a checklist to ensure you don't miss anything when designing new ones.

COMMON MISTAKES

Make sure you avoid the following common mistakes when designing your navigation.

USING BRAND-BASED NAVIGATION LABELING

Companies often like the navigation labeling to reflect their brand. This can cause problems for users because the terms they use mean nothing to them. One example springs to mind that used terms such as "Think," "Believe," "Adapt," and "Try" as main navigation headings. Users had absolutely no idea what they meant of what information they would find in those sections.

It's usually a safer bet to convey these brand attributes within the graphic design, content, and photography and keep the labeling of navigation in the clearest possible language.

NAVIGATION THAT DOESN'T TELL YOU WHERE YOU ARE GOING

The classic example of this is the infamous Click Here link. If you read links in isolation (as screen readers will) you can quickly ascertain whether they are well written. Click Here fails immediately. Where is it taking me? Will something start downloading? What if it takes me somewhere I don't want to go? Keep your links as descriptive as possible to clearly convey what will happen when people select them.

NOT INVOLVING USERS IN THE DESIGN PROCESS

When users are not involved with testing navigation, the result typically has at least one if not all of these common mistakes! If time is tight, just run some quick tests with colleagues to see whether they understand the navigation solution that you are proposing. You will always learn something that will improve your design.

NOT FOLLOWING NAVIGATION CONVENTIONS

Within environments such as design agencies, designers are often under pressure from clients to make their work "different," "innovative," and "award winning." Sometimes the focus of this attention can fall upon navigation. This can be because it is a common component of interfaces and people feel that if they can make a common component different, they will make the final design more memorable. They will often end up making the product memorable for all the wrong reasons!

Mess with navigation at your peril. Make sure that you trade off any "innovative" navigation solutions with rigorous usability testing. You may just be gambling with one of your client's most important assets.

CHECK HOW LINKS WILL BE MANAGED

I was once reviewing a website for a large government organization. It quickly dawned on me that there were no links in the body content of the page. Instead, they were all listed instead within a Related Links feature block on the right side.

Users were given no contextual links in the places where they needed them. I was told that links were kept separately to prevent broken links when linked to pages were removed. A content management consideration was trumping a critical user experience requirement. The tail was wagging the dog. Thankfully, we found a technical workaround and in-page text links were made available to content editors.

CATCH-ALL NAVIGATION LABELING

Information architecture can be hard! Sometimes you get in a situation when designing navigation structures where you just want to design a big bucket and label it Miscellaneous!

This problem can occur when the information architecture hasn't been designed to scale over time. Either new content is added that has no natural home or there is no space for new navigation within the interface design.

What often happens is that top-level navigation sections are added with ambiguous labels such as Miscellaneous, Resources, and More Info, which then become large amorphous dumping grounds for content. Users avoid them because they are too vague to be useful and as thus the content receives little navigation traffic.

Tools and Techniques for Creating the Best Navigation UX

Chapter 15, on information architecture, helps you to define the navigation of your product. Chapter 5, on usability testing, helps you test its effectiveness with users. Chapter 17, on wireframing, helps you learn how to lay out navigation within the interface that you are designing.

RESOURCES

Designing Web Navigation by James Kalbach

Information Architecture: Blueprints for the Web by Christina Wodtke

Information Architecture for the World Wide Web by Louis Rosenfeld and Peter Morville

Ambient Findability: What We Find Changes Who We Become by Peter Morville

CHAPTER

20

HOMEPAGE UX
DECONSTRUCTED

HOMEPAGES ACT AS signposts for the rest of the digital product. They should—among other things—convey the proposition of the product to the users as well as route the users through to useful content and functionality.

Homepages are often poorly designed. This is sometimes due to them being overdesigned, which means they are seen as so important to the success of the product that they are overloaded with content and functionality. In reality, many

users never see product homepages, because they often arrive at other key pages such as product pages direct from sources such as search and links in social media.

This chapter identifies the key user and business goals that a homepage should address, together with some common mistakes when designing them. It also lists some top tips for you to refer to. Use this chapter as a checklist the next time you need to design a killer homepage.

KEY USER TASKS AND QUESTIONS

Users will arrive on a homepage for lots of different reasons, depending on the context of their visit. The homepage you are working on will have its own unique user tasks to support so use this list to make sure you've considered these generic common homepage user tasks.

I KNOW WHAT I'M LOOKING FOR; DO YOU PROVIDE IT?

Navigation categories, featured products, and proposition messaging will all help to address this question as well as a search function.

I'M A RETURNING CUSTOMER, HELP!

Returning customers may be looking for login details or aftersales sections to help them to chase up orders or to report problems.

LET ME GET IN CONTACT WITH YOU

You can't force users to transact with you online if they would rather call you.

I'M LOST, HELP!

Users will often backtrack to a homepage after being dropped deep into a site via a Google search. Homepages should help to orientate users and help them navigate to where they need to go.

WHO ARE YOU AND WHAT DO YOU DO?

The most common homepage mistake is to not clearly communicate to the user what the site or digital product is and what they can do there. Fail to convey this quickly and you will lose users to your competitors.

DO I TRUST THIS PLACE?

Users will decide whether they trust the site in a matter of seconds based on their first impressions of the professionalism of the site. Give the users reasons to trust the site.

I HAVE COME TO DO SOMETHING SPECIFIC, JUST LET ME DO IT!

A homepage should support the most frequent and most important user tasks. The Google homepage prioritizes search. An online bank prioritizes login. Identify your key user tasks and make sure they are prioritized on the page.

SHOW ME THE LATEST CONTENT THAT IS PERSONALIZED TO ME!

Logged in and logged out states of homepages are very different. If you are designing a homepage, you might need to design two different states to support this. These different states will have different objectives, content, user goals, and business goals.

Flickr is a great example of a site that offers two very different homepages depending on whether you are logged in.

WHAT IS THE LATEST INFORMATION?

Consider Twitter. Your Twitter homepage is an ever-changing stream of updates. Users will visit to read the latest from the people they follow. A homepage should highlight the new and recently updated content to highlight potentially interesting content to users.

INSPIRE ME AND SHOW ME WHAT IS POPULAR

Sometimes users will want to be entertained. A homepage should provide suggestions and ideas for content that may be of interest to users. A homepage can also highlight what others are viewing or buying. This reflection of popular content helps users find content that may also be of interest to them.

TYPICAL HOMEPAGE BUSINESS GOALS

Your client will be very interested in what appears on their homepage. It is your job to make sure that the homepage supports the key business goals of the site. Specific goals will vary but typical business goals for homepages include the following.

PROMOTE NEW PRODUCTS, SERVICES, AND CAMPAIGN INFORMATION

The homepage is considered key real estate. It is often used as a key signposting page to highlight new products and services to users to increase awareness of them. The homepage must also reflect any campaign activity so that users who visit after seeing current campaigns see continuity across different offline and online platforms.

PROVIDE MANY ROUTES TO CONTENT VIA NAVIGATION, SEARCH, AND FOOTER LINKS

It is in the best interest of the business to provide as many routes to content as possible. This is a great example of a business goal that maps perfectly to the user's goal. This direct mapping of shared goals is often quite rare!

DISPLAY ADVERTISING

The homepage represents a key advertising space and placements on this page can command high prices. The advertising requirements of homepages are critically important to understand fully before embarking on sketching homepage layout ideas. You will need to balance the needs of the advertisers with the overall user experience.

DISPLAY TARGETED INFORMATION TO LOGGED-IN USERS

Logged-in users will have profiles that should be used to inform what is displayed to that user. A more targeted and personalized homepage for a logged-in user will yield higher financial returns on an e-commerce site than a generic set of content and functionality.

SUPPORT THE BUSINESS MODEL OF THE SITE

If the product for which you're designing the homepage gets revenue from selling products, be sure to prioritize products on the homepage. If it makes revenue from subscriptions make it easy for users to sign up.

MAKE A GREAT FIRST IMPRESSION

You have only one chance to make a first impression. In a competitive online marketplace, it is easy for potential customers to go elsewhere. Test different design routes to identify which result in the most positive user reaction and make sure the homepage is continually optimized once the site is launched.

MAKE IT SIMPLE FOR USERS TO COMPLETE THEIR TASKS

Users will appreciate a digital product that is easy to use. They will return to your product if they enjoy using it. A business goal should always be to meet the needs of the users; it just makes good business sense!

COMMUNICATE THE PROPOSITION AND WHY IT IS UNIQUE

Visiting users who don't know the brand won't spend a long time trying to understand what it offers them. Some homepages use video to convey this information; others can communicate it clearly with good photography. Others may manage it with a short tagline. This is critical; get it wrong at your peril!

DEMONSTRATE THAT THE SITE IS REGULARLY USED AND MAINTAINED

A homepage should communicate that the site is regularly updated and is being used by a broad and active user base. This may be communicated subtlety to users by adding features such as dates to news stories and conveying popularity via Facebook Likes. A homepage should demonstrate to users that it is alive and well!

GIVE USERS REASONS TO TRUST YOU

Users will look for reasons why they should trust you. If the business is well established, tell the user how long it has been around. If the site has a huge user base, convey that to the user. If the business is a member of recognized trade bodies and associations, make that obvious too. If the business has some great testimonials and user feedback, that information can also be used to engender user trust.

SUPPORT THE FUNDAMENTAL TASK

If you are designing a site for a multinational company, the first page the user often sees (almost a pre-homepage homepage) is a language selector. Consider whether you need to support a fundamentally important task such as this before you get stuck into your homepage design.

GIVE USERS WAYS OF PROMOTING YOU IN THEIR OWN NETWORKS

Social sharing facilitates the promotion of businesses by the digital equivalent of word of mouth. If appropriate you might find that displaying social sharing links to sites such as Facebook and Twitter an effective way of encouraging this user behavior.

EXAMPLE HOMEPAGE WIREFRAME

Figure 20-1 shows an example homepage wireframe and the following text explains it in detail.

1. **Communicate a clear proposition:** A customer should be able to quickly grasp who you are and what you do from a homepage. This will be conveyed by elements on the page such as tag lines, photography, navigation, and brands that are visible on the page.

2. **Promote the best sellers:** Features such as best sellers work well because they also convey the behavior of others. Because these will change frequently they convey to the user that the site is being used and may indicate bargains that could save them money.

3. **Maintain easy access to the main site categories**: It is critical to offer users as many routes to content as possible. You need to support users who want to browse the main site categories and also users who want to search for known items.

4. **Provide reasons to trust**: Users may not have heard of particular sites before and will make up their minds very quickly regarding whether they trust them. They may look for concrete reasons to trust such as heritage, customer feedback, and awards as well as more indirect indicators such as professionalism of design and quality of content.

5. **Conventional location of site tools**: Generally it's a good idea to innovate with content and proposition and imitate in terms of design patterns and conventions. Don't just relocate the search to be different for the sake of it.

6. **Make it easy to drill down to lower levels**: You should use the homepage to bring low-level content to the surface and not force users to click through endless category and sub-category menu pages.

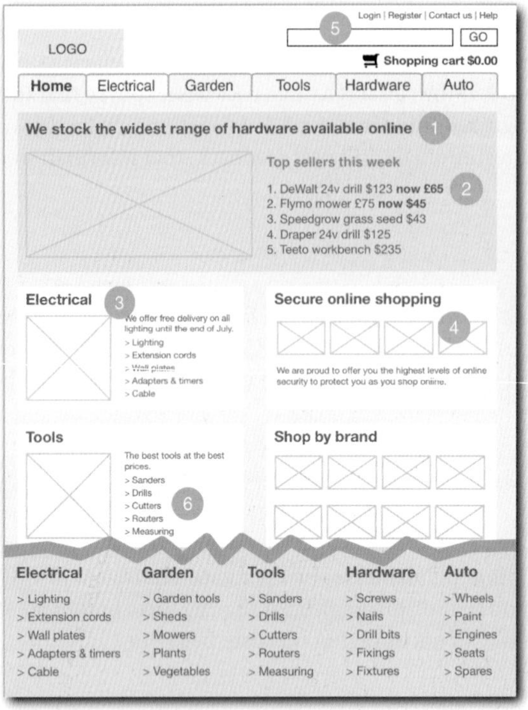

Figure 20-1: An example of a homepage wireframe

TOP HOMEPAGE TIPS

You should consider the following tips when designing homepages.

MAKE SURE YOU HAVE A SIGNED-OFF LIST OF REQUIREMENTS FOR THE PAGE

Without a list of user and business requirements, how do you know what you need to include on the page? Ideally you should have a prioritized list so you'll know which elements get top billing.

THINK ABOUT WHAT YOU HAVE ALREADY DONE THAT CAN INFORM THIS TASK

Think back to what has already been produced within your design project and question whether you can use it to help to design your homepage. Are there results from the competitor research you can use? What did you learn from the benchmark usability testing? There is little point in doing these activities if you don't then use them in your final design work.

SKETCH OUT IDEAS BEFORE TURNING TO YOUR COMPUTER

Once you have a good grasp of the requirements for the page, challenge yourself to sketch out three or four variations of possible homepage layouts. Try to do this quickly. You'll be able to rapidly iterate and throw away bad ideas before you get a chance to invest too much time in them.

FREQUENTLY REFER TO YOUR USER AND BUSINESS GOALS

As your homepage develops refer to your list of business and user goals. Interrogate the design with a goal of spotting areas that can be improved. A good design must support these goals, otherwise it cannot fulfill its intended purpose.

AVOID USING LOREM IPSUM

Although you are a UX designer and not a copywriter, you should still try to use real copy where you can to add context to your homepage wireframes. This makes it easier for project stakeholders to understand them and it makes them more meaningful when usability testing.

TEST AS YOU GO

Once you have a first draft of a wireframe, put it in front of colleagues and ask them if they understand what the proposition is and whether the page offers them options they would find useful. This early feedback can be a useful way to spot issues at a stage where they can be easily fixed.

STRIP OUT AS MUCH AS YOU CAN

During the design process you should always challenge the inclusion of every element. If there isn't a case to keep it, take it out. Simple is always better.

COMMON HOMEPAGE MISTAKES

You should be careful to avoid these common mistakes when designing homepages.

THINKING THAT THE HOMEPAGE IS THE MOST IMPORTANT PAGE ON THE SITE

In many UX design projects, the homepage commands a disproportionate amount of attention. It is often the first page to be wireframed and commands the greatest client focus. In reality, key areas to focus might instead include product pages and buying funnels.

FORGETTING ABOUT LOGGED-IN USERS

Logged-in users may require a completely different homepage to suit their specific set of needs. In reality you will need to design two separate homepages when there is a use case that involves a returning journey while logged in.

IGNORING THE NEEDS OF THE USER

If you have had little time or budget to research user needs, it is likely that your work will be focused entirely on the business requirements for the homepage. As a UX designer you should champion the users and their needs. Make sure you consider what the users needs might be and make sure the homepage caters to them.

NOT MAKING IT CLEAR WHAT THE PROPOSITION IS

Show your wireframe to colleagues and ask them if they can determine the proposition of the digital product from it. If users cannot grasp the proposition of a site, why would they stay to try and find out?

CRAMMING TOO MUCH STUFF IN

A wireframe, although clearly not a final indication of layout and positioning, will convey a sense of whether you are trying to cram too much into one page. Challenge the inclusion of every element to keep your homepages as simple as possible.

NOT BUILDING FLEXIBILITY INTO DESIGNS

Some homepages need various states. Consider how a news homepage changes when a massive story breaks. If you have a comprehensive set of requirements you will know you need to consider these different situations.

FAILURE TO COMMUNICATE NEW, POPULAR, AND IMPORTANT CONTENT

Your wireframes should contain features and content ideas that will convey to users that the site is frequently updated and is being used by an active community of users. Does your homepage wireframe convey this to users? How can you improve it to make this more visible?

Tools and Techniques to Use to Create the Best Homepage UX

By creating task models (see Chapter 12) and customer journey maps (see Chapter 13), you will have a good idea of what tasks the users will want to perform from the homepage.

By creating personas (see Chapter 14), you will have a good reference to check your homepage wireframes against. Which specific key tasks and behaviors will your homepage need to support for your key personas?

Sketching (see Chapter 16) is a great way to generate lots of ideas for your homepage. Challenge yourself to come up with lots of different ideas and then focus your attention on the best ones.

Usability testing (see Chapter 5) will also uncover some useful user tasks and behaviors that you can use to inform the design of your homepage. You can also use this technique to evaluate the early versions of the homepages that you produce.

RESOURCES

Homepage Usability: 50 Websites Deconstructed by Jakob Nielsen and Marie Tahir

Information Architecture for the World Wide Web (2nd Edition) by Louis Rosenfeld and Peter Morville

21

CATEGORY PAGE UX DECONSTRUCTED

A CATEGORY PAGE is a staging post on your user's journey. It is the term used to describe the page that a user sees when they click on a top-level navigation link, such as clicking the Women link on Gap.com. The purpose of a category page is *signposting*; it should provide all the information required for the users to make a choice and continue. In some situations, this page provides links to content or groups of products, in other situations it may be a product listing, or perhaps a hybrid of the two.

KEY USER TASKS AND QUESTIONS

Consider the journey your users are on when they visit your category page. Where have they been and where are they hoping to go? Answer their questions and support their tasks and you will help them move on.

- Be sure readers can determine whether the organization provides the products or services they require
- Filter or sort products in order to narrow choices and make a selection from a range
- Understand the differences between products or services in order to make a selection

These user concerns all center on understanding product offerings in order to choose one or more to explore further. The information required to make that decision will vary greatly as the products or services differ, but the underlying function of the page remains the same. Think about the key information required to make a decision and ensure it is provided here.

TYPICAL BUSINESS GOALS OF THE CATEGORY PAGE

A category page is one of the shop windows of an online business. It should allow users to get a quick overview of the products or services available on the website. Businesses will want to showcase their offerings and to efficiently move users on to more detailed information and, hopefully, to purchase.

- Show abundance of products or services
- Allow users to narrow their choices
- Group products or services in order to allow users to understand them more fully
- Provide enough information for the users to make a choice and move on to purchase (or other desired outcome)

These goals can be met with intuitive grouping and filtration options. These groupings should use user-centric language and not simply reflect internal business structures.

EXAMPLE CATEGORY PAGE WIREFRAMES

Category pages can be seen to fall into two distinct types, illustrated in Figures 21-1 and 21-2.

SIGNPOSTING CATEGORY PAGE

Figure 21-1 shows a homepage-like, signposting category page, providing links to content or groups of products.

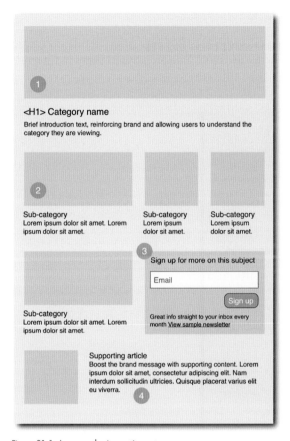

Figure 21-1: An example signposting category page

1. **Homepage-like template:** A signposting category page is very much like a homepage. It is the homepage for that category. Thus, on a full-size monitor, it can be image-rich. Prominent "hero" area copy and images should enforce the brand and illustrate the selected category.

2. **In-page navigation:** Users find in-page navigation easy to scan. It allows them to understand quickly and easily the options available to them. The space available for imagery and a sentence or two of copy provides a strong and memorable indication of the usefulness of links. This approach pairs well with the use of rollover menus for the main navigation.

3. **Newsletter sign-up:** When you know which aspect of your offering a user is interested in, it may be appropriate to offer them additional information tailored to their needs. If you provide an e-mail newsletter that can be customized to address the specific category they are currently viewing, this is a great way of capturing their information while supporting their needs.

4. **Supporting content:** Articles and blogs can be used to underpin brand expertise and add variety to the page. However, low-quality, filler content should be avoided, as it may undermine the user's trust.

PRODUCT LISTING CATEGORY PAGE

Figure 21-2 shows a product listing category page. This page is very similar to a search results page, in that it is a list of relevant items. See more on search results pages in Chapter 22, "Search UX Deconstructed."

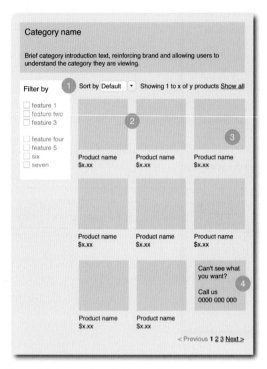

Figure 21-2: An example product listing category page

1. **Sorting and filtration:** Some users like to "view all." Others don't. Design to allow both types of behavior. Some types of products lend themselves to user controlled filtration and sort options. If relevant, provide these filters. They are powerful tools for users to reduce abundance and find their perfect product. Usability testing (Chapter 5) can identify which are the most important facets users may need to filter by.

2. **Odd numbers of products can be easier to scan:** Users are more likely to be able to make a choice from a selection if the row contains an odd number of items. It would seem that this is a manifestation of the "rule of odds" in image composition, which suggests that an odd number of subjects is more interesting than an even number of objects. Odd numbers of items cannot be paired or grouped easily, which keeps the eye moving across the composition. In web design practice, this generally means designing for three or five products per row on a category or product listing page.

3. **Provide the right level of information to make a choice:** Users need to understand enough about any particular product or service to decide whether to click to find out more. They don't want to spend too much time jumping between a category page and unwanted product pages. Provide too little information on a category page and users must visit the product page to decide if they are interested. This may require an image,

name, price, star rating, specification, or more. However, it's a delicate balancing act between enough information and a too-busy page that's impossible to scan. Again, usability testing can be used to identify this key information.

4. **Provide alternatives for users who haven't found what they want:** Links to similar categories or information about how to access custom products ensures that users can continue their journey even if they haven't found a product of interest to them.

TOP TIPS FOR DESIGNING CATEGORY PAGES

When designing category pages, consider the following key issues.

TASK MODELS ARE INVALUABLE

Task models (see Chapter 12) and customer experience maps (see Chapter 13) are incredibly useful for designing category pages. If you understand your users' decision-making process, you can provide exactly the right information for them at this point in their journey. Trying to sell electrical goods? Price and specification are important here. Televisions, for example, mostly look alike, but are differentiated by the description, the price, and other attributes like screen size. Ladies shoes? The picture is of primary importance—your user will know if she likes them from the photo and will then consider size, price, and other variables.

Design your interface to allow your users to sort and narrow products in a way that's meaningful to them. Sorting ladies blouses by physical dimensions is about as useful as sorting a sea of black or silver televisions by color.

USER-CENTRIC LANGUAGE

Use language that reflects your user's world, not your client's internal structures or business-facing terminology. One common manifestation of this is the inclusion of "video" as a navigation item. In most cases, this is simply a reflection of the fact that video is produced and owned by specific people within the business. Users generally come to websites for information on a specific subject and will be looking for that subject, rather than at the media that delivers the message.

COMMON MISTAKES WITH CATEGORY PAGES

It's not unusual for us to see the following issues within category pages.

INAPPROPRIATE ADVERTISING

For transactional websites attempting to make a sale, third-party advertising on product listing pages can cause issues with trust and credibility. Users are not open to advertising at this point in their journey—they are interested in the displayed products and do not want to be distracted. They may question the quality of the products if the business feels the need to dilute them with additional advertising.

Smashing UX Tools and Techniques for Creating the Best Category Pages

Usability testing (see Chapter 5) and expert reviews (see Chapter 10) will provide clear insights into your user's needs for a category page. Usability testing will also help you to determine the terminology your users employ to describe and group the products on display. Developing a task model (see Chapter 12) is a key method for determining the types of information that users need to see on a category page in order to make a decision and move on.

POOR FUNCTIONALITY

Poorly implemented sort or filter functionality—whether it's a confusing design or a troublesome technical implementation—can really floor users. They will rapidly lose interest and seek what they require elsewhere.

RESOURCES

Art Composition Rules: Rule of Odds from About.com: http://painting.about.com/od/composition/ss/art-composition-rules_2.htm

22

SEARCH UX DECONSTRUCTED

SEARCH is one of the most common user tasks when using digital products. Good search tools are a combination of great technology and sound UI design. Search within UX design projects is often considered a technical issue, but as a UX designer you can do a lot to influence the final user experience of the chosen search solution.

This chapter identifies the common user tasks and business goals for search and shares some top tips for designing search. It also identifies some common search UX design mistakes that we often see when usability testing search interfaces.

Use this chapter as a checklist when designing and evaluating search interfaces to help you to optimize the user experience on your own products.

KEY USER TASKS AND QUESTIONS

Users will have high expectations of search due to their inevitable familiarity with tools like Google. They will expect your site search to work as well as, and the same as, the big search engines.

When designing a search UI consider how it will address the following typical user tasks and questions.

HELP USERS TO FIND WHAT THEY'RE LOOKING FOR

This may seem like a task that is totally reliant on the technical aspects of the search but the UI design is critical to helping the users get to the result they need. The presentation and layout of search results together with the features that allow the users to manipulate the results they get are all vital elements of the search UX.

HELP USERS IF YOU DON'T HAVE WHAT THEY NEED

Searches will not always yield results. You will need to consider this eventuality and consider what to tell users in this instance. Good "no results" pages link to search help, offer tips on why their search may have yielded no results, and some even suggest related searches that will actually yield results.

SHOW USERS HOW TO SPELL SOMETHING

Users don't always use search engines to find things. People have discovered that they can use search engines to do all sorts of things like check spellings, do mathematical calculations, and translate words. These are edge cases but illustrate how tools are often used for purposes that differ from their intended purpose.

DO THE WORK FOR THEM

Users have learned that they don't need to know how to spell to be able to use search. Search tools support users by being flexible enough to understand what they mean and to still present relevant results.

Consider how your search UX will offer this flexibility to your users and how it can take effort away from people. Features like auto fill can be really useful as they save users from needing to spell searches correctly as well as saving them from typing their searches in full.

HELP USERS FILTER THROUGH A LONG LIST OF SEARCH RESULTS

A good search results page will allow users to get to a highly specific short list of results very quickly by offering relevant filters and sorting options. Users should be told how many results sit within a filter and should be able to easily apply and remove filters. Users should immediately be made aware of the impact of filters on their final result listing and should be warned when over-filtering will lead to no results being displayed.

INDICATE HOW MUCH CONTENT YOU HAVE RELATING TO A SPECIFIC TOPIC

Once a search has been executed, it should be clear how many results have been returned. This should be updated when filters are applied or when the user chooses to search within results.

HELP USERS CHOOSE WHICH SEARCH RESULT IS THE BEST

A useful search result has a clearly worded title that acts as a link to that content. It also contains a short summary of that content and conveys its format and size (if relevant). The source of the information is also important (particularly when results come from multiple sources). If the content has a rating or any other indication of quality, this should also be shown (such as a hotel's star rating). The date that the content was published can also be useful, particularly if the search results are displaying news content.

The specific contents of a search result will depend upon the context within which the search result is displayed. For example, a search result for an auction site will need to show the latest bid amount, time remaining, and an option to bid on that item. A search result on a shopping site may offer the option to add to a "compare" feature in addition to price, availability, and delivery information. Consider what the most critical information is to display within the context of your project.

HELP USERS UNDERSTAND THE CONTEXT OF WHAT THEY'RE LOOKING FOR

A good search engine will convey the context of a search by presenting related searches as well as picking up where that search related to in the taxonomy of the site. This helps to convey to the users which category their search results belong to so they can move to parent categories if they wish to broaden the scope of their search.

USERS WANT TO DO SOME ADVANCED SEARCHING

This is the task that the ubiquitous Advanced Search link assumes but of course is rarely what the user is actually thinking. Advanced search typically takes users to a separate page or expanded set of elements. Make sure you consider how this will work and what functionality it will offer.

TYPICAL BUSINESS GOALS OF A SEARCH UX

Search presents a unique opportunity from a business or commercial perspective because the users tell you specifically what they are looking for as opposed to less specific user activity such as browsing. A business will typically have the following goals from search and the design of pages such as the search results interface.

GIVE PRIORITY LISTINGS TO PROMOTED/REVENUE GENERATING CONTENT

For any search term there are likely to be results that have a greater commercial incentive to prioritize than others. On an e-commerce site this may mean that certain results are prioritized over others as they may yield bigger financial returns if sold. Other websites may prioritize search results that relate to current campaigns that are trying to promote certain products and services.

PROMOTE RELATED CONTENT

Some search results pages will feature content that is indirectly related to the main search term. Using an e-commerce example to illustrate this, consider that a search for torches/flashlights may also yield results for batteries to maximize the sales of products related to the original search term.

PROMOTE SPECIFIC LANDING PAGES

Campaign activity such as TV ads will be likely to increase search traffic around particular keywords. These searches will often need to be routed to the most appropriate landing pages that have been optimized to suit that particular campaign. Search results pages often flag these promoted results in the form of Best Bets or Featured links, which are designed to collect this traffic and send it to the most appropriate destination.

PROVIDE RESULTS AS FAST AS POSSIBLE

Search engines like to tell their users how fast they managed to generate a list of results. The specific speed is irrelevant. The message they want to convey is that they found what you wanted really quickly and thus provided a good service.

COMPENSATE FOR USER ERROR

Good technology should ensure that human error doesn't prevent the user from getting what they need. It is in the interests of the business to deliver regardless of user error, as this provides an opportunity for them to exceed user expectations. An example of this is accepting a spelling error and displaying results for the correctly spelled query.

DISPLAY RELATED ADVERTISING

It is likely that a commercial client will want to display advertising on a search results page that relates to the user's search query, given that this targeting may make it more effective than a "normal" placement on another page.

SHOW WHAT PEOPLE WHO SEARCHED FOR "X" ENDED UP BUYING

This is a clever feature because it infers to the users that they can save the effort of coming to the inevitable conclusion of starting with one product and buying a superior alternative option. In effect it is a contextualized cross/up sell and can work very effectively (although this may be more effective from product pages as they offer more space to do this properly—See Chapter 23 for more tips on designing product pages).

ALLOW USERS TO COMPARE FUNCTIONS FROM PRODUCT LISTINGS

Users will often want to create a short list from a long list of product search results. Provided the results are comparable and have a shared data set this is relatively simple to do by offering a compare option against each result. This often then generates a table containing the selected products that makes it easy to compare one directly with another.

SHOW THE USER SOMETHING USEFUL THEY DIDN'T KNOW

A well-designed search experience will uncover content that is useful and related to a users search that the user may not know exists. This may end up selling you the product you have never heard of or uncovering a great article about your favorite sport star. Great search experiences are all about serendipity and discovering useful content you never knew existed!

EXAMPLE SEARCH RESULTS WIREFRAME

Figure 22-1 illustrates an example search results wireframe.

1. **Reminder of search term:** It's a smart idea to remind the users of what they searched for within the page as it make them aware of any typos they may have made. By locating the search term within the results page, you also add context to the results.

2. **Clear indication of amount of results:** If the user sees that the search has returned a large amount of results, they are likely to realize that they need to be more specific with their search terms. Sometimes a reflection of volume from a search can also be reassuring on e-commerce sites as a reflection of breadth and depth of stock coverage.

3. **Options to sort results:** Websites will often default to what they want you to see, such as "our favorites" or "best sellers," which is often a sneaky way of trying to shift surplus stock. Users will typically want to switch to View By Price: Low To High.

4. **Numerous filter options with totals:** Filters allow users to quickly customize a set of results to suit their own specific requirements. By displaying the amount of results within a filter, you also communicate the impact of selecting a filter before it has been selected. This can help to prevent over-filtering, whereby users are left with zero results.

5. **Useful individual search results:** A useful search result tells the users whether they want to investigate it further. In this example, it is useful to see a photo, a price, the name of the product, customer reviews, and stock and delivery info. Consider what they key information set for your search results in the context of your own projects should be.

6. **Simple and uncluttered interface:** A purpose of a search results page is to let you find what is available and to let you access it as easily as possible. This page is a route to content and as such isn't somewhere where users should need to spend a large amount of time. Keep your search interfaces as simple as possible to facilitate this behavior.

7. **Options to change layout:** For some search results, an option to change the layout of results can be useful. When searching for products a grid layout may make it easier to view products for example. Also when searching for images users want to see multiple thumbnails per row to help them to scan as many as possible without scrolling.

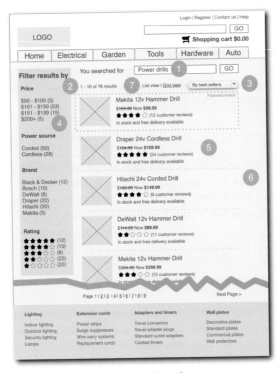

Figure 22-1: An example of a search results wireframe

TOP SEARCH UX TIPS

You should consider the following top tips when designing search interfaces.

WORK WITH YOUR DEVELOPERS TO MAKE SURE THEY CAN DELIVER WHAT YOU DESIGN

Good search is clearly heavily dependent on the technology doing its job well. Involve your developers during the design process to ensure you design something that is technically feasible. Furthermore, functionality like post-search filtering can have various implications for the data and it may require significant attention before it is interface-ready.

TEST ANY SOLUTION YOU COME UP WITH

Elements of search that need particular care and attention include the applying and removing of filters, especially when there are complex sets of filters available. Make sure you test your designs with users before the developers start coding to ensure that your filtering works the way that users expect.

MAKE SURE USERS CAN SIMPLY REMOVE ANY FILTERS TO START AGAIN

Filters are really useful but you need to help users avoid the situation where they over-filter and end up with no results. Make sure it is easy to remove any filter selections and that the users are aware of the impact of applying each filter before they select it.

PEOPLE WILL EXPECT PERFORMANCE LIKE GOOGLE—MANAGE THEIR EXPECTATIONS

Designing search can be difficult because user expectations are so high based on their experiences with tools like Google. Learn from these tools and reuse the design patterns they use to display results. You may not be able to offer the same performance as Google, but you can reuse the patterns, which are some of the most well recognized ones in use across the web.

Make sure you keep in close contact with the technical team that's building the search to ensure that you don't end up designing something they can't build within the constraints of the project.

PROVIDE LIST AND GRID DISPLAY OPTIONS WHEN APPROPRIATE

A traditional list view isn't always the most appropriate way of displaying results. You may also want to consider whether a grid view would be more useful. This can work really well when displaying results with images such as Facebook friends or LinkedIn contacts where users just want to scan people's faces. If appropriate, offer both and set the most appropriate as a default.

GUIDE USERS TO THE BEST RESULTS

Hotel aggregator sites show star ratings next to each result to allow users to judge the appropriateness of each result to their needs. News sites display the amount of comments against lists of articles to convey which are being discussed the most. Consider how you can add value to search results in the context of your own project to help to guide users to the most appropriate results.

COMMON SEARCH UX MISTAKES

You should be careful to avoid these common mistakes when designing your search interfaces.

NOT HELPING TO PREVENT OVER-FILTERING

It is so frustrating when results pages offer the options to filter to exactly what users need but then generate no results. Users must be made aware of how many results sit within each filter.

NOT PROVIDING USEFUL "NO RESULTS" PAGES

When a search returns no results, users should be offered guidance on how they should adjust their query to find relevant information and also general tips on searching. If they don't think they can find what they need, they will simply go elsewhere.

FAILING TO MEET COMMON SEARCH EXPERIENCE EXPECTATIONS (AUTO FILL)

The proposed search tool for you project may be nowhere near as advanced as Google but you can go someway to provide the typical search UI that users expect. User expectations around search are often unrealistically high. This means you should dedicate extra time to designing search and test it thoroughly with users to get it right.

NOT TELLING USERS HOW MANY RESULTS THEIR SEARCH HAS FOUND

This is such a simple one, but is commonly left out. By telling the user how many results they have, you give them a sense of whether they need to be more specific and also whether this is the right place to try and find that item.

LACK OF TIME SPENT CUSTOMIZING OUT-OF-THE-BOX SEARCH SOLUTIONS

Large design projects often require that a technology choice be made, which can mean that the search solution decision is made for you. The solution is often a default offering, which can provide a less than perfect user experience. Work with your developers to see what can be done to customize the out-of-the-box solution to get it to do what you need.

SEARCH RESULTS LACK USEFUL INFORMATION

Many search results offer little to allow users to pick the relevant result for them. Consider what the key user questions will be when deciding which search result offers them the best option. What information will users need to answer these questions? What are the conventions set by competitor sites? Test various results formats to see which offer the best solution to meet user needs.

RESULTS NOT DEFAULTING TO RELEVANCE RANKING

In most cases, users expect results to be prioritized by relevance. Some sites will change this to rank by best sellers or a similar moniker, which is often a way of shifting surplus stock. Make sure it is easy for users to switch among sorting options such as relevance, price, A-Z, date, and popularity.

MAKING IT DIFFICULT TO VIEW ALL RESULTS ON ONE PAGE

Despite the common preoccupation with the fold, we commonly see users in user test sessions happily scrolling up and down long pages of results scanning for options that take their eye. They often prefer this over clicking between pages, as they think it's much easier to find what they need. For this reason, always add a View All option when the amount of results can be realistically shown in one long page.

Tools and Techniques to Use to Create the Best Search UX

User and business requirements are absolutely critical to giving you the solid foundations for your search UI design. Learn how to gather client requirements in Chapter 4 and user requirements through techniques such as usability testing in Chapter 5.

Search is often designed to match common search design patterns. Turn to Chapter 6 on competitor benchmarking to understand more about how to learn from and evaluate your ideas against competitor's offerings.

By considering the key user tasks and questions, you will be able to design a search UI that meets these needs. Check out Chapter 13 on customer experience mapping and Chapter 12 on task modeling to see how you can identify and document these user needs.

RESOURCES

Information Architecture: Blueprints for the Web by Christina Wodtke

Information Architecture for the World Wide Web by Louis Rosenfeld and Peter Morville

Search Patterns by Peter Morville and Jeffery Callender

Designing Search by Greg Nudelman

23

PRODUCT PAGE UX DECONSTRUCTED

EFFECTIVE PRODUCT PAGES are critical from a user and a business perspective. You will have noticed during your design projects how much attention they receive as they represent such as critical stage within the purchasing user experience.

Product page design is made difficult by the amount of competing requirements that often

exist for these pages. When designing them, you will be faced with that classic UX design challenge of meeting user needs while still meeting the commercial objectives of the page.

Use this chapter as a checklist when designing and evaluating product pages and learn from the classic product page design mistakes that we see time and time again in our user research.

KEY USER TASKS AND QUESTIONS

If you fail to give potential customers what they need from a product page, they can very easily click to a competitor site instead.

The specific nature of the product ultimately determines how many of the following user tasks and questions you need to answer, but use this section as a checklist to get you started with your page sketches.

IS THIS THE ONE THEY WANT/NEED?

Your users might not know whether the product you are showing them is the one they need. Your product page must communicate this to them as quickly as possible before they go elsewhere to buy it.

HOW MUCH IS IT? ARE USERS GETTING A GOOD DEAL?

Online shoppers are a very price sensitive bunch. Pricing information must be very clearly available on the page and customers will be keen to understand what savings they are making when buying from you.

IS IT IN STOCK?

There are few things more frustrating than finding the perfect product at the perfect price to then find that it is out of stock. Reassure customers that items are in stock and—if you can—reflect how much stock of something you have.

HOW MUCH IS DELIVERY?

We have all been caught by the promise of cheap product costs only to be burnt by expensive delivery costs, particularly when shopping on online auction sites. Delivery of products causes huge levels of user anxiety, so reassure your users by providing simple delivery information.

ALLOW USERS TO GET A GOOD LOOK AT THE PRODUCT

You need to compensate for customers not being able to study a product in their hands. Use photos and video to bring the products to life. Consider how you can offer the customer the next best thing to having the product in their hands.

SHOW USERS HOW IT IS USED AND WHY THEY MIGHT NEED IT

It is not clear how all products work and what their benefits are. The job of a product page must be to communicate to the users what a product does and why it might be useful.

DO USERS NEED TO BUY ANYTHING ELSE TO MAKE IT WORK?

If the product needs any accompanying accessories to make it function properly, make sure that the user knows at this point. This prevents them from receiving a product they cannot use immediately and the resulting wait for essential accessories to arrive.

IS THIS A SAFE PLACE TO BUY FROM?

You may not be designing a product page for a well-known brand that users already trust. Consider how you can use content such as site security information, brand heritage messages, customer reviews, and parent company information to reassure your customers.

IS IT GOOD QUALITY?

The price of a product may indicate quality but you can let customers decide for themselves by providing good quality photos and detailed customer reviews.

CAN THEY GET IT IN DIFFERENT COLORS? IS IT AVAILABLE IN THEIR SIZE?

Online customers have specific requirements that they need to meet. They may be flexible on color for a new shirt but of course it absolutely has to fit properly. Consider what this fundamental information might be and make sure you've got it covered.

WHAT IS THE RETURN POLICY?

Online shoppers are often worried about what happens when they need to return something bought online. You can address this anxiety simply by carefully spelling out the return policy.

USERS WANT TO BUY IT

Regardless of the cost of the item the single most important thing a product page must do is to facilitate the purchase of that product. You must make this the easiest and most well-designed aspect of the product page.

WHAT DO OTHER PEOPLE THINK ABOUT IT?

Customers are particularly influenced by the opinions of others when it comes to purchasing goods, particularly when they are buying lifestyle products and high-value goods. Customers will expect to see the opinions of others to help to inform their purchasing decision.

PEOPLE WHO VIEWED THIS ENDED UP BUYING

Online customers are getting used to information gleaned from other customers' behavior. This can be useful because the customer feels they are benefitting from the work done by others. Chat with your developers and identify whether you can offer any of this behavioral marketing functionality.

LET USERS BROWSE TO SIMILAR PRODUCTS

It is important to offer online customers a sense of place within the product catalogue so they can browse to similar products. Your page navigation should facilitate this behavior by allowing customers to move up, down, and sideways to other products within the catalogue.

WHAT PAYMENT OPTIONS DO USERS HAVE?

Online customers will expect to be able to use all of the common methods of payment when shopping online, particularly some that offer fraud protection. Ensure that it is easy to find out how they can pay before they are let down in the checkout.

HELP!

Buying some products can be difficult and customers will often need help. Make sure help is available at all times. This will reassure users even if they don't end up using it.

TYPICAL BUSINESS GOALS

The product page is critically important to the commercial objectives of a digital product.

When designing a product page, you need to consider how it will help to deliver the following business goals.

MAKE IT EASY TO BUY

If you get this one wrong, don't bother reading the rest!

MAKE THE PRODUCT LOOK AS GOOD AS POSSIBLE

Whether this is achieved by content such as photos, video, reviews, or customer comments, this will be a very important requirement to fulfill.

DEMONSTRATE THE BENEFITS

The benefits of the product and also the benefits of buying from this particular site are important to convey to the online customers. The key selling points and benefits of the product should be clear. The page must act as the salesperson.

MAKE THE CUSTOMERS FEEL THEY ARE GETTING A GOOD PRICE

Online shoppers are often on the lookout for a deal and they will be happy to shop around to get the best price. It is critical to convey offers clearly to customers in a way that they can understand. The best offers show a saving and are time bound to trigger action.

USE THE OPINIONS OF OTHERS TO HELP INFLUENCE THE CUSTOMERS

The nature of the product will determine whether the opinion of an expert or other shoppers will be the most appropriate means of influencing the customer to purchase. Consider how the customer should be encouraged to leave a review once they have purchased their goods.

UPSELL ACCESSORIES OR HIGHER-VALUE ALTERNATIVES

Sales of accessories are often where retailers make their profits, particularly when selling highly competitive consumer goods such as digital cameras, mobile phones, and computers. Retailers will sell some products at a loss and make profits from accessory sales. This traffic must be capitalized on to return profit, which is where sales of accessories become paramount.

ADD VALUE BY DIFFERENTIATION

When selling products that are available from many places, retailers have to differentiate themselves. Typical ways that retailers try to add value to their proposition include offering expert advice, long no-questions-asked return policies, money-back guarantees, sharing stories of their expertise and experience, access to exclusive products, and by stocking vast product ranges.

ENCOURAGE EASY AND FAST ONLINE SHOPPING

This is a great (and possibly rare) requirement because it is one that the customer and the business share! The business wants to make sure the customer feels that buying from them is as easy as possible. This way, customers will endorse the site via word of mouth and return to purchase again.

USE SCARCITY TO ENCOURAGE SALES

Retailers will often attempt to trigger customers to buy by making it clear that there is a limited stock of particular items that are often discounted to clear them. This information is often prioritized on product pages to ensure that customers realize how scarce that product is.

USE TIME-LIMITED OFFERS TO PROMOTE SALES

By limiting the time available to buy, retailers try to encourage purchasing and reduce procrastination. This can be seen on online auction sites. As the clock ticks down, bidders often engage in frenzied bidding, which often leads to them spending more than they anticipated just to secure a successful purchase.

REMOVE REASONS NOT TO BUY

The single most important aspect of the product page is that it makes the products easy to buy.

A good product page should acknowledge and address every common anxiety around buying a particular product. If you sell clothing, be sure to reassure customers that they can return items that do not fit. If you are selling large, heavy items, make it clear how much delivery costs.

EXAMPLE PRODUCT PAGE WIREFRAME

Figure 23-1 illustrates an example product page wireframes.

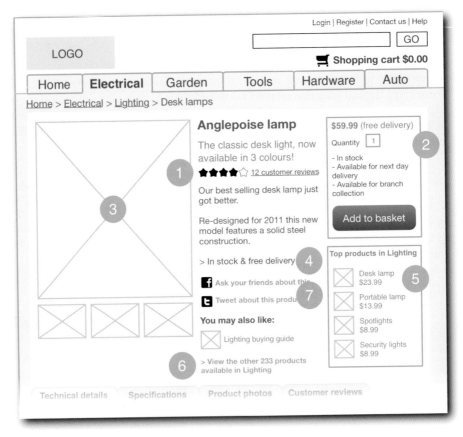

Figure 23-1: Example product page wireframe

1. **Customer ratings:** Users can see what other people thought of the product. The number of reviews is important; star ratings based on a few customer reviews will count for less than a score based on a high number of reviews.

2. **Prominent pricing and call to action:** The call to action to buy should be one of the most prominent and clear components on the page. It is critical to check that this is still as prominent within the final visual design.

3. **Large photo and multiple other views**: Users want to be able to examine the detail of a product before they buy it, much as they would in a shop. They may also want to check it is the one they need so options such as alternative views and zoom functions can be really useful.

4. **Stock and delivery information**: Users need to be reassured that if they need a product by a certain time, it can be delivered to them on time.

5. **Alternative suggestions based on customer behavior**: Customers will value the decisions made by others and will benefit from knowing what people ended up buying.

6. **Options to move within the catalog**: A customer may wish to broaden their search if this specific product isn't right for them. The breadcrumb-style catalog navigation allows users to jump to different levels within the product hierarchy.

7. **Options to promote via social networks**: Retailers know how important an opinion from a friend can be when making purchases. This function allows users to consult their peers for advice.

TOP TIPS FOR A GREAT PRODUCT PAGE UX

You should consider the following top tips when designing product pages.

LIST THE USER AND BUSINESS NEEDS BEFORE YOU SKETCH

This seems obvious, but designers are often too quick to try and solve the design challenge before they understand it fully. You have to be fully aware of what the page is trying to achieve for the stakeholders involved. Once you have finished your sketches, strip anything out that isn't meeting a user or a business need.

DESIGN FOR THE WORSE CASE SCENARIO

If your design can cope with the most complicated product in the range, it can cope with any product in the range. Don't choose the simplest or the most popular products to make your wireframes look beautiful. If appropriate, design a solution for the most complicated product, a product with medium complexity, and then do the most simple one last.

TEST EARLY

We designed a product page that needed to sell a mobile phone as well as a line rental contract. The complexity of the information involved led to a design solution that differed from the norm. We tested an early prototype with users to reassure us that our approach was going to work.

Without validating early you can spend hours finessing something that is fundamentally unusable and without testing early you will never find out before it is too late to fix it.

CONSIDER THE PRODUCT BEFORE YOU LAY OUT THE PAGE

The problem with designing templates for content management systems is that by their very nature they assume that all products are the same. Consider how a department store would approach selling a sofa in-store compared to selling expensive perfume. The selling approach is customized to the product.

You must consider the nature of the product you are selling with regards to its price and its purpose to determine the most appropriate way of selling it online.

CONSIDER BUYER ANXIETIES AND ADDRESS THEM

When you consider your own experiences of purchasing online, you will be able to recollect the anxieties you had that stalled your decision to purchase. Usability testing will uncover the most common anxieties that you can then address within the final design.

We recently observed in usability testing how expectant parents were failing to buy strollers online because they couldn't be sure they would fit into the trunk of their cars. Sites that showed photos of a folded stroller fitting into a typical trunk reassured customers and helped to mitigate the number of returns.

COMMON MISTAKES

Be careful to not make these common mistakes when designing your product pages.

PROVIDING EXPERT-LEVEL CONTENT FOR MAINSTREAM AUDIENCES

We frequently watch users struggle during user research when they are confronted with reams of technical information. This often happens when users research and buy products like computers, TVs, and mobile phones online. Information for experts should be available but supersede the mainstreamer information.

UNCLEAR CALLS TO ACTION

A product page must make priority calls to action clear and obvious to the users. If the dominant call to action to buy is lost within the noise of the page, the page will fail.

PHOTOS THAT ARE NOT USEFUL (SMALL, DON'T SHOW USE, NO ZOOM)

Simply providing photos of the product is not enough. They must be large enough to make them easy to view, detailed enough to demonstrate their content, and shot in a way that shows the product in its best light. Photos should also demonstrate a product in use and provide useful functions such as zoom and slideshows to allow customers to examine them in more detail. Read more about what makes a great photo UX in Chapter 26.

LACK OF CLEAR PRODUCT KEY FEATURES

A customer shouldn't have to work to determine the benefits of a particular product. If a customer cannot determine the benefits quickly and easily, the page isn't doing its job.

LACK OF VIDEO WHEN IT'S REALLY NEEDED

Video isn't always appropriate but can provide a useful addition to product pages. Consider whether video will address a user or a business need and if it does investigate the likelihood of it becoming available before you add it to your wireframes. Video does a great job of conveying a lifestyle that a product may fit into as well as demonstrating a product in use.

LACK OF CLARITY AROUND SOURCE OF REVIEWS

Customers expect reviews to be impartial and to be from people who are like them. We conducted some research with mothers who were reading reviews about baby equipment. The reviews failed to state that they were from other mothers. As a result, the study participants didn't trust the reviews because they thought the retailer wrote them. People became skeptical and lost trust in the retailer and shopped elsewhere as a result.

NO STOCK OR DELIVERY INFORMATION

Lack of stock availability and inflexible delivery are two of the biggest customer frustrations when shopping online. If the product page is the first place a customer discovers that something is not in stock, this indicates a problem elsewhere on the site. Reassure your customers of delivery options on a product page to remove reasons to not buy from your site.

NO REASON TO TRUST THE RETAILER

Online shopping still causes customer anxiety. From our international research we have seen how trust in buying online varies hugely based on cultural differences. Websites must give their customers reasons why shopping with them is safe.

LACK OF BASIC INFORMATION SUCH AS SIZE, COLOR, AND WEIGHT

Every product has attributes that are fundamentally important for the users. Determine the fundamental information for the products you are designing and ensure they are prominently displayed.

Tools and Techniques for Creating the Best Product Page UX

A thorough requirements-gathering process is critical to designing successful product pages. Turn to Chapter 4 to learn more about gathering business requirements and to Chapters 6 and 7 to learn how to gather customer requirements by usability testing and contextual research.

Once you have gathered all of the necessary requirements check out Chapter 16, which introduces how you can use sketching to bring your ideas to life.

Many users enjoy researching products when they are on the move. To learn tips and tricks for designing for mobile, please turn to Chapter 33.

RESOURCES

Information Architecture for the World Wide Web by Louis Rosenfeld and Peter Morville

100 Things Every Designer Needs to Know About People by Susan Weinschenk

Submit Now by Andrew Chak

24

SHOPPING CART AND CHECKOUT UX DECONSTRUCTED

FOR TRANSACTIONAL WEBSITES and apps, getting the shopping cart and checkout process right is imperative. No matter how interested users are in a product or service, if they cannot complete payment, their patronage is lost. Users feel more secure about entering confidential payment information when a trustworthy process is used.

KEY USER TASKS AND QUESTIONS

What do users need from your shopping cart and checkout process? Consider this list as a good start in addressing user needs:

- Make final purchase decisions
- Understand how much they will pay for the products or services they are buying
- Understand and feel comfortable with any additional charges, such as delivery costs, taxes, or gift wrapping
- Arrange affordable delivery at a convenient time
- Trust that their payment details are in safe hands
- Enter required information quickly and easily
- Avoid entering too much information
- Understand why non-standard information is required
- Avoid signing up for spam
- Feel reassured that their order has been placed
- Understand when to expect delivery or other next steps
- Understand what to do if they have a question or problem with their order
- Feel confident that they've ordered the right thing from the right vendor

TYPICAL BUSINESS GOALS

The basket and payment system is the workhorse of any transactional website or application. It must be smooth, error-free, and trustworthy. Checkout pages should:

- Take payment for goods or services
- Engender trust
- Reduce cart abandonment rates
- Increase average cart value: encourage users to spend as much as possible without putting them off with heavy up-sell
- Gain permission to gather and store user data
- Encourage registration/sign-up
- Encourage take up of marketing opt-ins (such as for e-mail newsletters, paper catalogs, or third-party affiliates)
- Encourage choice of most business-friendly delivery options
- Inspire return visits
- Reduce customer services contacts (such as phone sales or queries and complaints)

EXAMPLE SHOPPING CART WIREFRAME

Figure 24-1 illustrates some key shopping cart UX considerations.

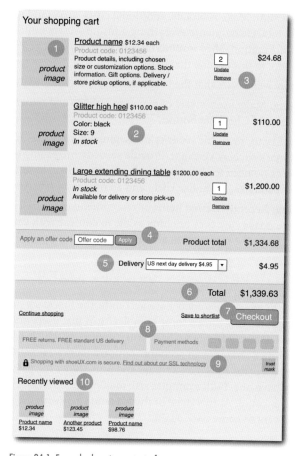

Figure 24-1: Example shopping cart wireframe

1. **Clickable product image and name:** Users often use the shopping cart as an informal shortlist. They may add many items to their cart, and then compare and decide which to buy. Be sure users can see what is in their cart and can click back to the relevant product pages.

2. **Helpful product details:** Include relevant details about any product in the shopping cart. Where size or other options have been chosen, reassure the users they have made the right selection. A product code is useful if the user needs to get in touch. If gift services are available on a per-item basis, make a note of that here. If there are different delivery options for different items, they can be conveyed here. Stock information is particularly useful to enable carts to cope with users returning after a period away. Newly unavailable items can be conveyed and alternatives can be offered.

3. **Editable cart contents:** Allow users to easily remove items or change amounts.

4. **Offer codes:** Don't make too much of discount code entry—users with a code need to find it, but you don't want to alienate those without one. Make sure any applied offers clearly show savings in the cart total.

5. **Delivery costs are important:** Provide delivery costs at the earliest available opportunity (even if it starts as an indication of the lowest delivery cost).

6. **All figures should work as a sum**: Make subtotals, additional costs, taxes, and delivery charges clear. Make the final total clear. Ensure everything adds up—users notice discrepancies and unclear information. They want to be sure they can trust you with their money, and dodgy math is sure to undermine that trust.

7. **Provide a clear call to action**: Make sure that the users can easily find how to proceed.

8. **Checkout-specific messaging**: Make users aware of payment options and returns policy without distracting from the main Checkout button.

9. **Own the security message**: Try to "own" the security messaging for your site—don't leave all the work to a trust mark such as VeriSign. Provide security messaging that is subtle and trustworthy. There's no need to shout too loud, as long as the relevant cues are there—HTTPS and browser padlocks, a familiar URL, and an otherwise trustworthy site.

10. **Encourage further shopping**: Recently viewed items or recommendations based on cart contents are appropriate here. Make sure they are impossible to confuse with cart contents and do not distract from the main call to action.

EXAMPLE CHECKOUT PROCESS WIREFRAMES

If you are designing for a website in which customers have accounts, the first stage of checkout should be to allow them to sign in. This causes some complexity in that users must choose whether they should log in or not. Figure 24-2 shows one design approach, which asks users to choose between the "new customer" and "got an account" options. Figure 24-3 shows another approach, which asks all users for an e-mail address and only shows the password field to users who state that they have one. Both examples risk making new users feel that they'll be forced into creating an account. At this stage in their relationship with the supplier, most users won't know if they'll want to come back again.

Figure 24-2: Example login option, with user selection

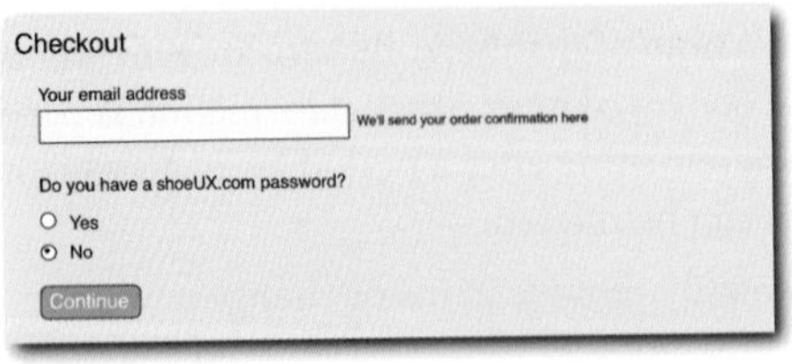

Checkout

Your email address

We'll send your order confirmation here

Do you have a shoeUX.com password?

○ Yes
⊙ No

Continue

Figure 24-3: Example login option, with progressive disclosure of password field

Be sure to also provide a checkout process indicator. Ideally, this will not consist of too many steps (although it should not be misleading). Strip down any website navigation to a home-page link (to reduce clicks away from the checkout process). Make sure customer service contact details are visible. Most users will not need them, but many will be reassured by their presence. Figure 24-4 shows an example header area.

Figure 24-4: Example header area

Figure 24-5 shows an example delivery page during the checkout process.

1. **Chunk information:** Group form fields into logical chunks, so users can scan them easily. Smaller chunks make the form feel less intimidating. Some websites use progressive disclosure here, and display only the section of the form that the user is working on.

2. **Summary of shopping cart:** Reassure users that they are buying the right thing, by showing a persistent shopping cart summary. This summary should include all items for purchase and the total price.

3. **Retain any information you already have:** If you have already acquired information such as an e-mail address, make sure it is auto-filled here. If the user has logged in, this form could be entirely pre-filled. Alternatively, logged-in users could be presented with a purchase summary, rather than a form to check.

4. **Minimal information:** Don't ask for any more information than is absolutely necessary. If you need to ask for information that users are not used to providing for online transactions, explain why you need it and consider making the form field optional.

5. **Delivery options:** Show clear delivery options, defaulting to the cheapest, or to any selections made at the cart stage. If possible, include actual delivery date estimates.

6. **Strong call to action:** The Continue or Next button should be the clearest thing on the page. The last thing you want is for your users to fill in all their information and then fail to submit it. The placement and naming of this call to action should be consistent throughout the checkout process.

7. **Forms best practice:** Over many years of user testing forms, we have found that lining form fields up on a vertical axis is the most usable way of laying them out. Users can easily scan the page and see what they need to complete. The Continue button should also be on this axis, as this is where the user's eye will be drawn. There's more on forms in Chapter 28.

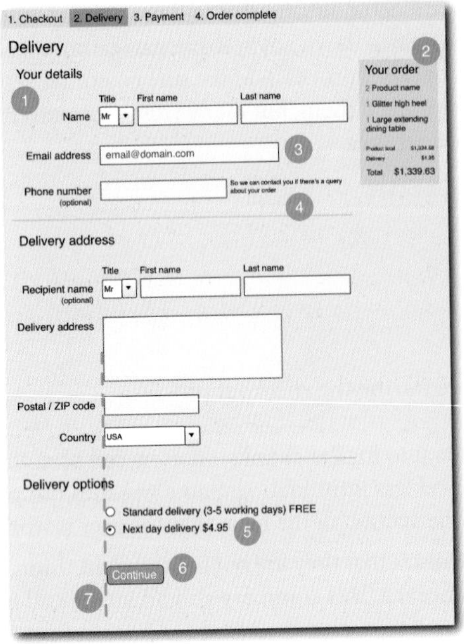

Figure 24-5: Example delivery page during the checkout process

Figure 24-6 shows an example payment stage of the checkout process. Clearly, payment laws and options differ across countries. Simple options are shown here.

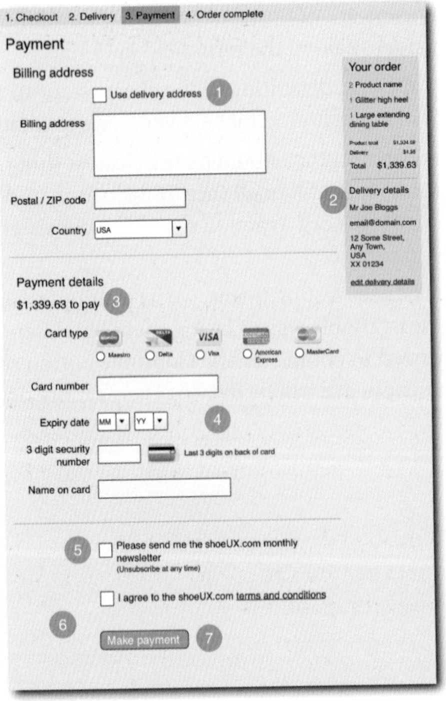

Figure 24-6: Example payment stage of the checkout process

1. **Delivery address:** Provide an option to use the delivery address as the billing address.
2. **Repeat delivery details:** Reassure the users that they've entered the right delivery details, and allow them to go back to edit them if they spot a mistake.
3. **Show amount payable:** Show the amount that the users will be charged when they make payment. This helps breed trust.
4. **Payment fields:** If possible, only display form fields relevant to the selected payment method. For example, some cards require a Start Date field and others don't.

   Cards typically represent expiry dates with numbers only (such as 10/12 not October 2012). Try to reflect the wording on the card in the form fields. Don't make users do a mental translation from one to the other.

   The location of the security number for American Express is different than other cards.
5. **Marketing opt-ins:** This is the last place you want to erode your users' trust: they are just about to pay for their goods or services. As such, it is important to viewed as trustworthy, and not as if you are trying to trick your users into accidentally signing up for unwanted things.

   To achieve this, here are a couple of simple guidelines:

   - The number of marketing opt-ins should be kept to a minimum. In testing over the years, we have seen users become particularly annoyed with websites asking for permission to share their details with third parties.
   - Wording should be clear and straightforward (no double-negatives).
   - Opt-ins should never be pre-ticked. Users need to feel they are in control of what they are signing up for.
6. **Offer to save details for next time:** If your website can save user details to an account, here is a good place to ask them to provide a password. They've just spent some time entering all the other account details. All they need to add is a password and the work is done.
7. **Call to action:** The call to action should be prominent. When payment is about to be taken, it is appropriate to change the wording to reflect this.

EXAMPLE CONFIRMATION WIREFRAME

An order confirmation page is essential to reassure users that their order has been placed. Figure 24-7 illustrates some key confirmation page UX considerations.

1. **Order number:** Provide a unique order number on the confirmation page. It will provide reassurance and be useful if the users need to get in touch regarding the order.
2. **Print:** Make sure that the screen prints nicely—some users will want to keep a hard copy for their records.
3. **Delivery and payment details:** Remind users of the delivery and payment information they have provided. For payment details, simply provide enough information for the users to identify the payment method, not full card details.

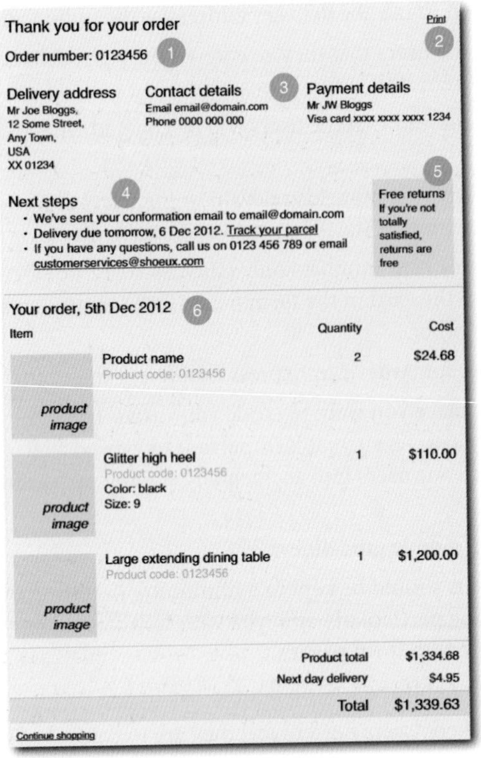

Figure 24-7: Example confirmation wireframe

4. **Next steps:** Outline what will happen next. This should include any confirmation e-mails, delivery dates, and tracking information. Provide contact information, should the users have a query or problem. Other key information might include a map of the venue's location if the user has bought tickets, or instructions for how to complete digital downloads. Think about any anxieties your users may have about their order and try to allay those fears.

5. **Returns information:** For physical goods, it makes sense to display returns information here. It shows confidence in the product and reassures the users that they have purchased from a reputable seller.

6. **Order summary:** Summarize the completed order, including product names, thumbnails, quantities, and costs.

TOP TIPS FOR SHOPPING CART AND CHECKOUT PAGES

Consider the following issues when designing your shopping cart and checkout process.

BE TRUSTWORTHY

If your users trust your product, they will happily enter confidential information such as payment details. If they do not trust your product, they will not.

Trust is earned in many ways, but here are some pointers:

- **Be bug-free.** A slow or error-prone product implies a careless attitude. Users will be less likely to trust the business with their credit card details.
- **Provide real-world contact information.** We've seen lots of people look for this in user tests. A typical comment is "I'm looking for a phone number—it proves they really exist." This is clearly extremely important for smaller retailers that users may not have come across before.
- **Enable product reviews from real people.** Even the odd negative review will merely reinforce the credibility of the reviews.
- **Provide clear pricing, both for products and any additional costs such as extras, taxes, and delivery.** No one likes to be surprised by the final bill.
- **Use simple copy with no jargon or legalese.** Users particularly hate feeling as if they are being tricked into signing up for things they don't want.

SHOPPING CARTS ARE USED AS SHORTLISTS

Lots of people use their online shopping cart as an informal shortlist. They browse and add all the items they are considering, and then compare them and make a final decision within the cart.

Design the cart to support this behavior: provide product image thumbnails, details of any chosen size or customization, and links back to product information.

If possible, do not force the shopping cart to expire—a user may come back later and decide on a purchase. Consider allowing the users to save their shopping carts, for example to a shortlist. This could encourage repeat visits and higher engagement with the site. Clearly these approaches require a level of messaging around stock availability: returning users may find that items have become out of stock in their absence and should be notified of this at the earliest opportunity.

KEEP IT SIMPLE

Your users are likely to be distracted—at work, minding the kids, watching TV—make sure they don't have to concentrate too hard to complete checkout. Provide clear calls to action, remove distractions, avoid jargon and legalese, use simple language, and don't ask users to provide unnecessary information.

USE FORMS BEST PRACTICE

See Chapter 28 for a detailed examination of forms best practice. Top tips include:

- Vertical alignment of form fields makes for easy scanning.
- Explain why you need any information that may not seem directly related to purchase.

- Provide contextual (in-line) help for potentially tricky fields.
- Error messages shouldn't make the users feel small or stupid. In fact, calling them "errors" is a huge no-no. Highlight any invalid form fields and provide information to the users to help them complete them—don't just repeat the field name.

COMMON MISTAKES WITH THE CHECKOUT PAGE

What should you avoid when designing shopping carts and checkout processes?

INSTILLING FEAR

Most users know that they should worry about online payment security, but most will know very little about how the technology works. Reminding users of potential security issues with large Trustmark logos and liberal use of the word "secure" may have the opposite of the desired effect. They suddenly think "oh! I need to worry about security!" but they don't know enough about the subject to be reassured with regards to your product.

In our experience of user testing websites over many years, we have hardly ever seen users actively looking for a Trustmark logo (such as VeriSign or Internet Shopping is Safe—a logo representing a company that guarantees the website's payment safety). We have tested an awful lot of transactional websites, so what's going on? Of course, it may be because users are not parting with their own money in a user test. However, test participants often comment on other aspects of trust and security, so this is unlikely to be the only reason. It is probable that users are looking for other measures of trust, including browser security indicators (such as HTTPS or a padlock symbol), brand dependability, clarity, and lack of duplicity. A Trustmark has its place alongside other measures of trust, but do not rely on it as the only one.

ASSUMPTION OF CONTEXT OF USE

Users browse and purchase across all types of Internet-connected devices. It may be an edge case that a user wants to purchase a large-ticket item on their cell phone, but it's not impossible, and is becoming more and more common.

Additionally, multi-channel user journeys are increasing in prevalence. Customers may browse products on their cell phones on the train on their commutes home, view options with their spouse on their tablet at home, and finally make a purchase from their desktop computer at work. Designing to support these behaviors is imperative for retaining customers in an increasingly connected world. Think about:

- The display of your website across a range of devices. When possible, provide full functionality for mobile devices. How often have you been frustrated with the mobile version of a website and scrolled down to the bottom of the page in the hopes of finding a link to the full site?
- Functionality such as user accounts, shortlists, and sharing options to allow users to travel seamlessly from one device to the next.

Smashing UX Tools and Techniques to Use to Create the Best Cart and Checkout Pages

User testing (see Chapter 5) your checkout process will help you understand if you have got the design right. It will help you make tweaks and improvements to streamline the process.

Task models (see Chapter 12) will help you understand the information your users need from your product.

Stakeholder interviews (see Chapter 3) and requirements workshops (see Chapter 4) allow you to understand the business logic behind the checkout process requirements.

RESOURCES

Forms that Work: Designing Web Forms for Usability (2008) by Caroline Jarrett and Gerry Gaffney

Web Form Design: Filling in the Blanks (2008) by Luke Wroblewski

Form design guidelines crib sheet from Joe Leech at cxpartners: www.cxpartners.co.uk/ cxblog/form_design_guidelines_crib_sheet_free

Mobile form design strategies from Chui Chui Tan at cxpartners: www.cxpartners.co.uk/ cxblog/mobile_form_design_strategies

E-commerce trustmarks: do they matter, from Econsultancy: www.econsultancy.com/uk/ blog/5303-e-commerce-trustmarks-do-they-matter

The $300 Million Button by Jared M. Spool at User Interface Engineering www.uie.com/ articles/three_hund_million_button

25

ARTICLE AND CONTENT PAGE UX DECONSTRUCTED

THE HUMBLE ARTICLE or content page is easy to overlook during the design process, but it may be your user's primary reason for interacting with your product. It may be the primary reason for the existence of your product.

A content page can describe many different entities: news articles, blog posts, information pieces, and editorial—the list is long. The subject matter will vary as widely as the human imagination. However, there is some commonality: they are all pages that are designed to be read. Your primary goal as the creator of such pages is to facilitate reading. Secondary goals may include printing, sharing, saving, commenting, and discovering more. Key business goals will be around driving revenue, improving brand awareness, and meeting performance indicators. For example, by serving ads, by improving brand awareness, or by increasing the amount of time spent on the site.

KEY USER TASKS AND QUESTIONS

What will your users want to do on an article page? Remember to provide ways for them to complete these key tasks and your article page will meet their needs.

- Read the information provided
- Save the article
- Share the article with others
- Find out more on this subject—on your website or elsewhere
- Decide if they can trust the information provided
- Comment on the article or upload their own content

Design for readability with clean typography and plenty of whitespace. Make it easy for your users to go away and come back again, for example, by providing saving or sharing options. Trust can be earned by providing relevant content and allowing open discussion. Consider the key tasks or questions the users of your specific article page will have and design to meet them.

TYPICAL BUSINESS GOALS

It is important to remember that there is a business driver for every page on a website. In the case of article and content pages, this is not always as easy to discern as for clear money-generators, like product pages. Unless you are working on a pure content site, such as a news site or blog, a key business goal for content pages is likely to be to sell advertising space. This is sometimes seen as conflicting with user goals, but we have found ads to be generally accepted by most participants in usability testing.

- Sell advertising space
- Increase amount of time spent on the website
- Increase the number of page impressions
- Encourage engagement with the brand
- Promote a product or event
- Interest the users in related products or services
- Generate user comments or feedback
- Be seen as an expert in the field
- Encourage users to contribute content or otherwise get involved
- Drive social sharing and other user promotion

Make sure you understand your client's goals for the page before you design it. Designing to include advertising from the outset will allow the layout to meet both business and user needs. Influence your user's next steps by designing the business goals into the page.

EXAMPLE ARTICLE PAGE WIREFRAME

Article pages can differ wildly—the content could be anything from a blog about knitting to a national newspaper story. They can be permanent or transient, ad-funded or ad-free. However, Figure 25-1 is an attempt to distill the major considerations into an example wireframe.

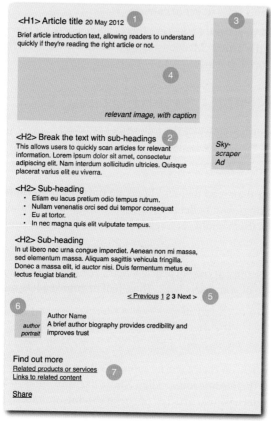

Figure 25-1: Example article page wireframe

1. **Title and introduction:** Allow users to find out quickly and easily if they are in the right place. Provide unambiguous titles and brief intro copy describing the article's contents. A date can help establish relevance.

2. **Headings and sub-headings:** Use headings, sub-headings, and lists to break the text into easily digestible chunks. Allow users to understand the gist of the article from skim reading.

3. **Advertising:** Many websites that provide written content earn revenue from advertising. Balancing the business need for advertising against potential usability and trust issues can be tricky, but in our experience, users are accepting of considered ads.

4. **Images:** Images are great at illustrating a point or providing extra information. However, if there is no natural image to accompany the text, don't fill in with obvious stock photography. We've seen people get angry in usability tests when faced with stereotypical imagery that clearly has nothing to do with the information being presented.

5. **Pagination:** There are often arguments in UX circles as to whether to use pagination or not. Users viewing an article on a desktop computer in a well connected home are happy to scroll to read a long article. A user on a mobile phone may prefer their information in smaller chunks. One of your client's main goals may be to drive page impressions and to serve ads—paginated articles increase these metrics.

6. **Byline:** Establish trust by attributing authorship to a real person. Provide a short biography and perhaps their image, plus ways to get in contact.

7. **Related information and calls to action:** Make sure there's somewhere for users to go when they've finished reading the article. Meet business goals with links to further reading, related products, or social sharing.

TOP TIPS FOR DESIGNING CONTENT PAGES

When designing article or content pages, consider the following key issues.

WRITE FOR ON-SCREEN READING

Users tend to scan web pages rather than read them, so break up the content to support this. Use descriptive headings, sub-headings, and bullet points. Users need to understand quickly if the content is relevant to them. The user should get a sense of the article from scanning the headings.

Use short, uncomplicated sentences and cut overall article length. For generalist content, assume that the average reading age of your users is 12. Thus, half of your readers may have a poorer reading standard.

PROVIDE SOMEWHERE TO GO AT THE END OF THE ARTICLE

Your users have just read a great article on their favorite subject. Where should they go now? Don't leave them wondering—give them some ideas. Align "more like this" links to key business goals such as related products, similar articles, or social sharing options.

DESIGN FOR SAVING AND SHARING

Users may want to save an interesting article for later, or they may want to share it with specific individuals. Make the article printer-friendly, using CSS. Make it easy to e-mail the article to themselves or others and consider whether connecting with social networks is important here. Make it easy for users to save the page to their favorites. Remember that users may be using several different devices to access your article.

COMMON MISTAKES

If users are interested in the content of your article page, they will put up with plenty of poor design decisions. But why make your users suffer? Usability tests repeatedly show the following issues.

POOR ADVERTISING CHOICES

A poor choice of advertising partner can seriously erode trust. Does your great article really deserve to be forever linked with an ad for a dodgy loans company? Should a news article about a drowning be accompanied by an automatic ad for a pool? What does that say about your client's brand? Conversely, relevant advertising is often seen as supporting content. For example, an article for home improvement accompanied by an ad for a trusted DIY shop is seen as helpful and builds credibility.

Users are typically happy with ads from reputable businesses. If the ad is for something clearly associated with the article content, it may even boost credibility.

Poor placement of advertising can be thoroughly distracting. Trust is another issue here— users may start to question the credibility of the information provider if the page is peppered with intrusive adverts.

POOR SUPPORT FOR COMMENTING AND USER GENERATED CONTENT

Perhaps your users are so fired up by the article that they'd like to comment on it. A thriving user community is something that many businesses crave. However uncommented articles or spam-filled comments are a sorry sight. Be honest about likely numbers of comments or user uploads and availability of moderation and design accordingly. Social sharing tools (such as Facebook, Twitter, and the like) may be a more appropriate option for many businesses.

Smashing UX Tools and Techniques for Creating the Best Content Pages

Use stakeholder interviews (see Chapter 3) or requirements workshops (see Chapter 4) to understand your client's goals for the page.

Usability testing (see Chapter 5) prior to design work will provide invaluable insights into user needs from your article page. Wireframes (see Chapter 17) will help to work through design choices with your client. Further usability testing (see Chapter 5) will allow you to validate and refine your designs and ensure that your article page is both readable and likely to be read.

RESOURCES

Letting Go of the Words: Writing Web Content that Works by Janice (Ginny) Redish

The Elements of Style by William Strunk Jr and E. B. White

26

PHOTO UX DECONSTRUCTED

PHOTOS ARE CRITICAL to the success of digital products, but are seldom discussed by UX designers. This is strange because of the huge impact that photo selection has on the final user experience. In all of our user research, we see just how much users rely on good photos to help them to make choices and decisions. We know how important photos are to users, so why don't user experience designers pay them more attention during the design process?

There is a lack of guidelines around photo selection from a user experience perspective. This chapter identifies some of the qualities that a photo needs to improve the user experience as well as the commercial benefits of good photo selection.

KEY USER TASKS AND QUESTIONS

A good photo can answer all manner of user questions in a split second. Users often have key questions they need to answer when performing tasks using digital products. Photos that improve the user experience are ones that have been selected with user tasks in mind. Good photos address these questions and lead to products and services that typically perform extremely well in user research.

The following sections cover typical user tasks and questions commonly associated with photos.

WHAT DOES IT COME WITH?

Photos are a great way of illustrating products and their accessories. They enable users to ascertain whether they are getting value for their money.

WHAT DOES IT DO AND WHAT ARE THE BENEFITS?

A good photo can clearly demonstrate what a product does and its benefits, which means users need not read paragraphs of explanatory text.

DO I WANT IT AND DOES IT LOOK GOOD?

The motivation behind a purchase is often how we will look and be perceived by others if we own a particular product. A good photo allows potential customers to answer this question almost instantly.

IS IT WORTH PAYING MORE FOR?

Users may wonder what added benefit they will get if they pay a few dollars more. A good photo can give them all they need to justify spending more.

IS IT THE RIGHT ONE AND WILL IT FIT?

One of the downsides of buying online is a lack of perception of scale and—as returning goods is a hassle—it's important that photos communicate scale.

HOW DO I USE IT?

A photo that illustrates how something is used can help people understand how it might be of use to them.

User tasks and questions around photos will vary, of course, but what is consistent is how important photos can be assisting users with their tasks and for helping answer users questions.

TYPICAL BUSINESS GOALS

The typical commercial goals of a photo are to help to sell a product or service. A photographer will often be briefed to shoot a scene or object in such a way to meet the following requirements.

SHOW THE PRODUCT IN THE BEST WAY POSSIBLE

In order to be successful the photo must present a flawless representation of the product.

SELL A LIFESTYLE

Users are often not buying a product as much as a lifestyle that they aspire to. The photo should reflect the lifestyle that the users see as being associated with the ownership of that particular product.

SHOW WHICH ACCESSORIES GO WITH IT AND HOW THEY ENHANCE IT

Users will buy more accessories if they understand how they complement the main product.

HELP THE VIEWER TO IMAGINE OWNING/ EXPERIENCING IT

Photos that demonstrate something being used help people to see how it can fit into their own lives.

SHOW THE KEY SELLING POINTS

A photo that successfully communicates the key selling points of a product prevents the users from having to do any more work to understand your proposition.

SHOW QUALITY AND VALUE

Conveying intangible benefits such as brand heritage, experience, trust, and quality can be difficult in words. Users will often interpret a huge amount from photos that they use to reinforce their decision to purchase.

From a business perspective photos play a hugely important role in selling products and adding interest to content, particularly online. Photos are typically commissioned based on business goals and not user goals because user goals are not always fully understood. There is a role for the UX designer during this commissioning process to ensure key user goals are considered when planning the kind of photos required.

EXAMPLES OF GREAT PHOTO UX

Figures 26-1 through 26-4 show some examples where photos have been used to improve the user experience.

The photo shown in Figure 26-1 is useful because it highlights the benefits of the product. The photo helps the users imagine how the product could be of use to them.

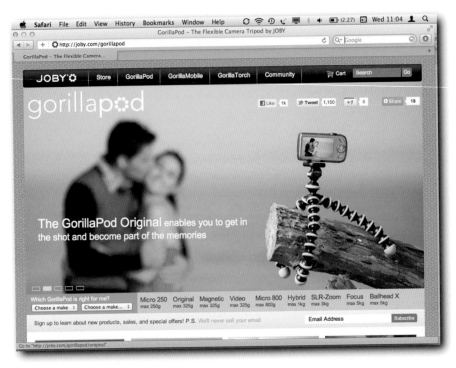

Figure 26-1: Great photos demonstrate how a product works

SOURCE: Reproduced with permission of JOBY, Inc © 2012.

When users are trying to follow instructions, great photos can be the difference between success and failure. The photos shown in Figure 26-2 are helpful because they help to answer potential user questions such as "what is it supposed to look like?". Good photos provide an instant confirmation that you are on the right track, which encourages people to continue with their tasks.

Figure 26-2: Photos really help when we try to follow instructions

SOURCE: Reproduced with permission of Elizabeth Benker, author and photographer, www.TheFoodieMethod.com
© Lizzard Design LLC 2012

Photos can be used to address user anxieties about using products and services. Elderly customers of this frozen meal delivery service were worried that bad weather might stop deliveries from reaching them. Photos such as the one shown in Figure 26-3 led to user comments in usability testing such as "the drivers will deliver whatever the weather," which gave them the confidence to use the service.

How can you communicate more conceptual selling points of a product such as heritage and craftsmanship in a snapshot? Photos such as the one shown in Figure 26-4 are excellent examples of how craftsmanship can be instantly communicated without any text or lengthy descriptions. These types of photos stick in the viewer's minds and act as reference points to justify future purchases.

Figure 26-3: This photo addressed a key user anxiety that poor weather would lead to customers not getting their food

SOURCE: Reproduced with permission of Wiltshire Farm Foods ©2012

Figure 26-4: This photo instantly conveys craftsmanship and quality

SOURCE: Reproduced with permission of the Morgan Motor Company © 2012

TOP TIPS FOR PHOTO UX

In our user research one common theme always emerges when the conversation turns to photos. Users want to see photos as big as possible. They want to examine the product's details and immerse themselves in photos. Small photos are fine for social networking avatars and signposting, but it's important that you make content photos as large as possible large (or failing that, enlargeable).

You can get early feedback to guide your photo selection in early rounds of usability testing. Show users examples of the types of images you are thinking of using and determine whether they find them appropriate and useful. This can be a great way of getting an early indication whether you are on the right track.

As a UX designer, you should start considering photos when you design the wireframes. Even though you might only indicate the placement of photos in wireframes, you should be influencing the photos that are used within the products and services you design. The wireframe shown in Figure 26-5 illustrates how you can go about doing this.

Figure 26-5: You can annotate your wireframes to influence the choice of photos

It's important that you use good photos within your UX deliverables too. One classic example is persona profiles that use stock photos that just don't look believable. It is critical that deliverables such as personas really bring users to life. Use photos of real people and you'll see how this dramatically improves your personas and makes them easier to empathize with. You can see the impact of this by checking out the personas in Chapter 14.

COMMON MISTAKES WITH PHOTO UX

One type of photo causes more swearing, disgust, and derision than any other in usability testing. The dreaded clichéd stock photo—such as the one shown in Figure 26-6—is unfortunately very common across the web due to its widespread availability and affordability. Users hate them. They look cheap, and users can't associate with the people they contain or the situations they recreate.

Figure 26-6: Clichéd stock photography is cheap and may erode user trust

Photos are often used to break up long portions of text but add no actual value to the experi-ence (see Figure 26-7). These are often called ornamental photos. Content photos are ones that add value. Content photos contribute something toward the goals of the users and the business. Make sure that ornamental photos are not being used when content photos are really what you need. Use ornamental photos if you lack any other appropriate way of breaking up text to make it easier to read.

Figure 26-7: Ornamental photos such as this might look great, but ask yourself if they are helping to meet user and business needs

Tools and Techniques for Creating the Best Photo UX

Check out the chapters in this book on usability testing (Chapter 5) and task models (Chapter 12) to better understand the information your users need from your photos and which types of photos you should use to help your users.

RESOURCES

How to use photos to sell more online: http://www.smashingmagazine.com/2010/06/25/how-to-use-photos-to-sell-more-online/, by James Chudley

How to use photos to improve the user experience: (http://www.slideshare.net/cxpartners/how-to-use-photos-to-improve-the-user-experience), by James Chudley

How to Use Images by Lindsey Marshall and Lester Meachem

CHAPTER

27

HELP AND
FAQ UX
DECONSTRUCTED

HELP AND FREQUENTLY asked questions (FAQs) are an interesting area to design, in that they are areas where it is more than possible that your users will be angry or frustrated before they get there. They can also be grouped under the title of Customer Services. In fact, Customer Services might be a better name for the content. It has a positive slant, whereas Help sounds negative and FAQ is jargon. Your users will have unanswered questions and may be anxious to find an answer. As such, it's important to be incredibly reassuring, trustworthy, and usable within your Help section.

As the Internet and its audience have matured over the years, attitudes to Help and FAQs have changed. In the past, usability practitioners recommended creating an FAQ section, as it was the accepted approach and hence met user's

expectations. As the Internet grew in popularity, we kept seeing in testing that non-expert users did not understand the term FAQ. Additionally, the FAQ section was often used to "hide" frightening information, or worse still, group important information. Neither of these approaches is right for users. Providing important information in a contextual fashion, at the point of decision-making, is far more appropriate. So, as design has matured again, with contextual help much more common, we find ourselves recommending that online customer services be an evolution of Help and FAQs. It should group all contact and FAQs into a single, reassuring area. This is increasingly extending into the social sphere, with conversations between businesses and their customers happening on Twitter, Facebook, and elsewhere.

KEY USER TASKS AND QUESTIONS

Why do users click on links labeled Help, FAQs, or Customer Service? Because they have a question that has not been answered elsewhere. The website may have failed them and they may be angry or impatient. The user may see it as an admission of defeat to even click the link—how many people do you know who refuse to read manuals or to ask for directions?

If they do click on the Help link, what do they need?

- Users need to find an answer to a question and move on. They may be thinking, "this site has really failed me; I don't want to be here; just answer my question quickly."
- Your user's question may be common or it may be unusual. They may have phrased their question in a way your system understands or they may not.

Your Help section needs to answer questions quickly in terms your users understand. It needs to provide alternative routes for users unable to answer their questions within the site or application, such as customer service contact details.

TYPICAL BUSINESS GOALS OF THE CUSTOMER SERVICE PAGE

Businesses want to project a brand-appropriate, friendly, helpful face to their users. They may also want to improve their online customer service offering in order to reduce calls or e-mails to customer support centers. Likely business goals include:

- Prevent expensive calls to their call center or e-mails to customer support by providing answers to the most common problems in a language that users understand.
- Make their users feel loved.
- Improve trust and promote a strong brand image.

Understand your users' likely questions and use user-centric language to help meet these goals. Provide clear customer service contact details for users who cannot answer their question via your system.

EXAMPLE HELP WIREFRAME

Figure 27-1 illustrates a customer services main page.

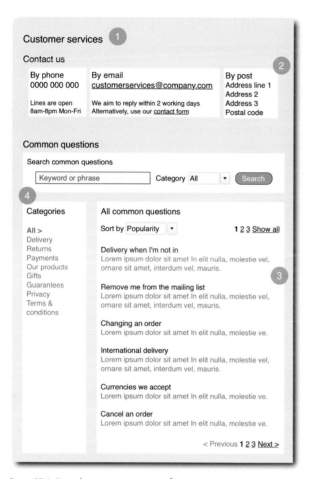

Figure 27-1: Example customer services wireframe

1. **Customer services:** The term "help" implies a crisis, and FAQ is jargon that some users may not understand. Customer services suggests helpfulness and a user focus.

2. **Contact details:** Provide information about how to contact a real person—it's impossible to second-guess all your user's queries. We find in usability testing that people are reassured by the visibility of a telephone number. They often have no intention of calling it, but simply knowing that this is an option buys user trust.

3. **Common questions:** Provide answers to common questions in a language your users will understand. Ensure that the questions are genuine and not a sales pitch. Don't forget to include content that supports both pre- and post-sale users.

4. **Search and browse:** Allow users to navigate help articles by both search (via keyword) and browse (via categories). Some users will want to use each method to find their answer.

TOP TIPS FOR THE CUSTOMER SERVICES PAGE

These top tips should help you provide a supportive and reassuring help section.

DO YOU REALLY NEED IT?

Providing important information in a contextual fashion, at the point of decision-making, is more useful than directing users to another section of your product.

Think carefully about any requirement for the Help or FAQ pages. Are they really necessary? Would users' questions be better answered via contextual information, direct links, or an improved site search?

In *The Humane Interface,* Jeff Raskin points out that when people get stressed (for example, because of an error) their locus of attention narrows. So they tend not to look around for help. Putting help in line (for example, as tool tips or other contextual help) is the solution.

TERMINOLOGY

Before you use the term FAQ, ensure that your user base understands what it means. If not, Help or Customer Services are great alternatives.

CURRENT INFORMATION

Provide up-to-date information. Anything inaccurate or outdated will badly erode trust.

Customer service staff often update and run online help centers. This is excellent for providing the latest information. Train them to write well for the web, using short sentences, scannable headings, and user-centric language.

A SOCIAL MODEL

Conversations between businesses and their customers happen in many places: on the company website, via calls or e-mails to customer services, and increasingly via social networking and dedicated apps. Social media are a great place to discover the questions your users are asking. For organizations with a large enough user base, user forums and social help can be a fantastic way of generating help content. However, they require moderation and responses from the business to be successful.

COMMON MISTAKES WITH CUSTOMER SERVICES PAGES

Avoid these common mistakes to keep your help pages easy to use.

QUESTIONS, QUESTIONS

Phrasing FAQs as questions makes them difficult to scan. This sounds counter-intuitive, but a vertical list of sentences beginning with "How," "Why," and "When," is not as useful as a list of topics such as "Delivery," "Returns," and "Warranties."

ALL PART OF THE SAME EXPERIENCE

Off-the-shelf FAQ applications can generate pages that look as if they don't belong to your website. Even if you use a bought-in package, ensure that the look and feel of your help section is the same as the rest of your site. It can seriously erode trust if your users feel there is a visual disconnect between these two aspects of the site or product.

FAQs written by customer services staff, when the rest of the website is written by others, can lead to differences in tone and naming. This can be confusing to users. Ensure that naming is consistent throughout. For example, the main part of a website may use the word "guarantee," whereas customer services uses "warranty." If the Help section of the website is the only place where the word warranty is used, users may not be sure that it is the same thing as the guarantee they were hoping to find more about. Also look out for business-centric language and jargon—always use the terminology your users are using and will understand.

Smashing UX Tools and Techniques for Creating the Best Help Pages

Call center listening (see Chapter 7) helps you understand the main questions that people call to answer. Can any of them be fielded within your product?

Usability testing (see Chapter 5) also helps you understand your users' questions. Can they find the answers in the existing product? Can they find the answers within competitor products? If so, how? Competitor benchmarking (see Chapter 6) helps establish the best practice in the field.

Search analytics (see Chapter 8) uncovers what existing users are searching for. When are they getting null results? What are the most common queries to existing help pages? What search terms are your customers using?

RESOURCES

Infrequently Asked Questions of FAQs by R. Stephen Gracey on A List Apart:
http://www.alistapart.com/articles/infrequently-asked-questions-of-faqs/

Essential Help and FAQ Usability Tips from Specky Boy Design Magazine:
http://speckyboy.com/2011/08/10/essential-help-faq-usability-tips/

FAQs about FAQs on the Internet FAQ Archives:
http://www.faqs.org/faqs/faqs/about-faqs/

The Humane Interface: New Directions For Designing Interactive Systems (2000) by Jef Raskin

28

FORMS UX DECONSTRUCTED

A FORM REPRESENTS a conversation between an organization and its customers. Good forms are quick, painless, and are a pleasant conversation between the business and their users. Poor forms result in a painful dialogue, one that a product's users will not want to repeat.

Great forms can make long interactions feel shorter. Get them wrong and interacting with your product feels like hard work.

If you put users at the heart of the design process, filling in your forms will be a breeze.

KEY USER TASKS AND QUESTIONS

Users generally don't want to be filling in a form. For most online transactions it's a necessary evil. Typically, users will want to:

- Complete the form in as little time as possible.
- Understand how to answer the questions correctly.
- Provide the bare minimum of information.
- Trust that their personal details are in safe hands.
- Complete the form in one go, without having to come back later with additional information. If they need to break to find extra information, they won't want to lose the work they've already done.

TYPICAL BUSINESS GOALS

Forms are often the transactional workhorses of an online business. A lot of effort will have gone into attracting customers and persuading them to buy (or otherwise convert). It's essential to continue that good work into the forms where the all-important user data and payment details are collected. Businesses typically want their forms to:

- Aid as many transactions as possible: show minimal dropout in the analytics.
- Gather enough user information to complete a transaction.
- Gather additional user information for marketing and business intelligence purposes.
- Gather clean information that populates their databases with non-duplicate, accurate, correctly formatted data.
- Obtain user agreement to terms and conditions relevant to the transaction.
- Encourage sign up to marketing communications such as e-mail newsletters.

There are clearly some potential conflicts between what users and businesses want from forms. It is important to get the balance right between collecting enough user data for business needs and not overwhelming users with too many requests for personal details.

EXAMPLE FORM WIREFRAMES

Figure 28-1 illustrates some forms using UX best practice methods.

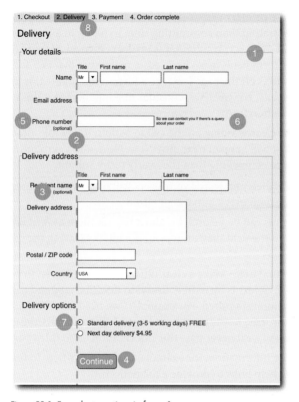

Figure 28-1: Forms best practice wireframe 1

1. **Group related information:** A long form can be pretty intimidating. Break it down into logical chunks and it will be easier to scan and much less daunting.

2. **Vertical layout:** Over many years of usability testing digital forms, we have found that a vertical layout works best. Left-align the form entry fields along a single vertical axis, so that the users can scan down and see exactly what they need to fill in. This approach works equally well for form labels to the left of the form fields (as shown here) or for form labels above the form fields.

   We believe this works best because it prevents users simply not seeing some form fields. Users often miss the right column in side-by-side layouts. Additionally, it draws the eye to the primary call to action—the Continue button—which should also be aligned on the same vertical axis.

   One exception to this rule is name input fields. As users typically write the individual components of their names (title, first name, and surname) in a horizontal line, it makes sense to mirror this with the forms input. Another exception is day, month, and year fields that go together to make a date. There are also circumstances where it makes sense to horizontally align radio buttons, for example, payment card selection options.

3. **Mark optional fields:** Be clear about which form fields are mandatory and which are optional. Technically savvy people know that an asterisk means that a form field must be completed. However, it's polite to also reassure users that a field can be left blank. This can be achieved by simply writing "optional" next to the field label.

4. **Clear call to action:** Make the primary call to action stand out. There's nothing more frustrating than committing time to filling in a form, only to find that how to submit it is unclear. Vertical alignment under the form fields helps here. Also, make sure that any secondary buttons on the page (such as address lookup) are less important visually. For websites, consider making them text links instead of buttons.

On the web, there's no need for a Cancel button. The user can navigate away if they want to, and a Cancel button may get clicked accidentally.

Use clear wording on the call to action. If possible, describe what will happen next. Buy Now, Next, and Continue are much more compelling than the overly techy Submit.

5. **Clear form labels:** Use clear labels and words your users will understand. Sentence case is easier to read that title case with every initial capitalized.

   On the web, in-field input hints can be helpful, but don't rely on them as field labels. Once the user has clicked into the field they disappear, potentially leaving the user with no idea what to type.

6. **Supporting text and contextual help:** Make a clear differentiation between form labels and supporting text. Supporting text is incredibly useful to describe required data formats, or why the information is required. For example, "we need an e-mail address to send your confirmation to" or "passwords must be at least six characters." Consider including reassurances such as "we'll never pass this information on to third parties."

   When an input requires more information, for example, to describe where to find a reference number, use inline help links to provide explanations.

7. **Use sensible defaults:** Reduce the load on the users by using sensible defaults for radio buttons, selection boxes, and other closed inputs. In some cases, this allows the users to see what the standard option is, and view any upgrades. For example, Standard Delivery may be the default selection, but Next Day Delivery is also a clear option.

   You may know that most of your users are in the USA, so default a country selector to this. Consider listing a few common answers at the top of a long selection list, and repeat them in the correct place (usually alphabetically) within the long list. Continuing the country selection example, if you know that the majority of your customers come from the Western, English-speaking world, you may choose to repeat the USA, Canada, Australia, and the UK at the top of your list of all countries.

   The exception here is when you need to be certain that the users have made an active choice. The only way to be certain of this is to ensure that the input has no default, forcing user action.

8. **Show progress:** For long, multi-part forms, show users how they are progressing. Label the steps and show where they are in the process. Keeping the number of steps down to a minimum is preferable, but dishonesty here will erode trust.

Figure 28-2 illustrates some more forms using UX best practices.

1. **Date fields:** In most cases of date entry, use selection boxes instead of free text fields. This helps to avoid errors. Indicate required inputs with Day, Month, and Year as the default options. Using the names of months is sensible as it prevents users wondering whether to put the day or month first. As always, there are exceptions. For example, payment card expiry dates are better expressed with numbers only, as that is how they are presented on the card.

2. **Calendar pickers:** A calendar picker is helpful for many date inputs. It helps prevent error and provides supporting information, such as unavailable options and days of the week. However, consider likely inputs before choosing to use a calendar picker—they are inappropriate for date of birth entries, for example.

3. **Flexible data entry:** Where possible, allow spaces in credit card numbers, commas as thousands separators, brackets for area codes in phone numbers, and other differences in input style. Check any existing form submissions to see the different formats your users employ.

   It's not programmatically difficult to strip out spaces and other formatting before adding it to your database. If data simply must be entered in a specific format, provide an example.

4. **Field size:** Make sure that the size of free-text fields implies the length of the input required. In this example, the 3-digit security number field is much shorter than the others on the form.

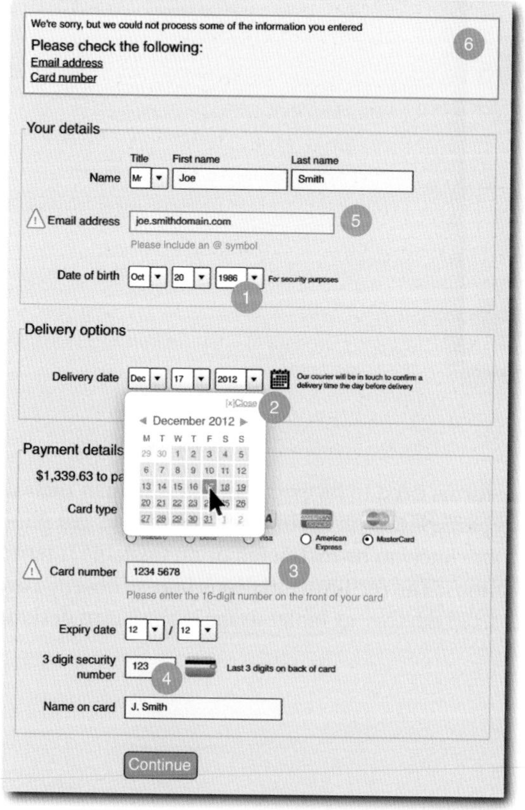

Figure 28-2: Forms best practice wireframe 2

5. **Inline validation:** Where possible, validate all fields following cursor focus moving on. Politely and helpfully indicate the problem with the field entry. Suggest correct answers and don't just repeat the question. Stay away from words like "Error" and "Problem"—be constructive.

6. **Page-level error handling:** There will be situations where form validation can only happen once the form has been submitted. List the errors at the top of the page with links anchored to the field itself. Mark the fields that require attention so that the users can easily scan the page and find them all. Again, be polite and helpful, not belligerent.

Figure 28-3 illustrates some mobile forms using UX best practices.

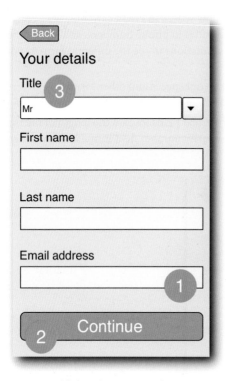

Figure 28-3: Mobile forms best practice wireframe

Efficiency is crucial for mobile forms.

Mobile forms need to be even easier to use than their desktop counterparts. Users on mobile devices such as cell phones are even more likely to be distracted or on unstable Internet connections. The recommendations here primarily cover cell phone sized devices, as tablet usage is similar to desktop usage.

1. **Simplify the form:** Whenever possible, remove all non-mandatory fields. (In the example here, we've removed the Phone Number field.) Consider removing or hiding inessential information such as supporting text and links. This will make the form feel much simpler and cleaner.

   With mobile forms, efficiency becomes crucial. Where appropriate, use the device's location information. For example, when entering an address or finding nearby businesses.

   Consider the best interaction widgets for mobile users. For example, long selection lists do not work as well as on desktop forms. Again, usability testing is the best way of making sure that your form is usable on mobile devices.

2. **Break the form into smaller chunks:** As the users may be distracted or on a poor Internet connection, break long forms into smaller, logical chunks. The users will need to click Continue more often, but is less likely to lose their work.

   Don't forget that the user's view of the page may be further reduced by the device's on-screen keyboard.

3. **Vertical alignment**: Use a vertical alignment, with the form labels above the fields, as this is the easiest to scan at small resolutions.

TOP TIPS FOR DESIGNING FORMS

Consider the following issues when designing your forms.

A FORM IS A CONVERSATION WITH YOUR USERS

A form is a conversation with your customers; be nice to them. Use friendly, simple language, in a tone that's appropriate to your business. This is how you write the rest of your content, why stop at your forms? Forms that are terse or that employ too much developer-speak will be off-putting to users.

> *A form is a conversation with your customers; be nice to them.*

A pleasant form will help users trust you and become happy to part with their precious information. Don't make them feel that you're likely to spam them, or that you're trying to trick them into agreeing to something you don't want. Double negatives and baffling legalese are a big problem here. Adverts can be unsuitable.

To be really sure that your forms are initiating a friendly conversation, you need to run some usability testing (see Chapter 5). Watching real users interact with your form will tell you if they understand the questions and can easily recover from any errors. It will tell you if you are asking for the right amount of information and if you have laid it out correctly.

ALLOW SAVING IF NECESSARY

If your form requires information that a user may not have immediately to hand (such as passport numbers, license details, other people's personal information, and more), list this at the beginning of your form. If possible, allow users to save their progress and come back later with additional information.

COMMON MISTAKES WHEN DESIGNING FORMS

What should you avoid when designing forms?

HARSH ERROR MESSAGING

From a system point of view, there may have been an error. The contents of a form field may be empty when it should be full, or it may not match the required format. However, all the user has done is misunderstood something, mistyped something, not seen a form element, or used a different format to the one required by the system. In short, they have likely made an understandable mistake. If someone you're talking to you in real life makes a small slip-up, how do you react? Do you start shouting "Error! Does not compute!" or do you gently point out what you need to know and perhaps suggest alternative answers? A form on a website constitutes part of a conversation between an organization and its users. Do you really want to be shouting at your customers?

Of course, it is necessary to let users know that their form input does not match the system's needs, but there are plenty of ways of doing this without being scary and aggressive. Here are a few top tips:

- Be flexible with data formats. Why throw an error message if a user puts spaces in their credit card number?
- There's no need to describe anything as an "error." How about a nice polite "please check the following form fields"?
- If possible, provide clear inline validation as the user progresses, rather than saving it all to the end
- Use helpful messaging. There's no point simply repeating the field label. It is much more useful to suggest acceptable alternatives, such as "please include an @ symbol in the e-mail address" or "the date you have chosen, 23 January 2001, is in the past; please choose a delivery date in the future."

TOO MANY QUESTIONS

Every question has a cost—the more questions there are, the lower the form completion rate. It's that simple. The more questions there are, the more complex your form looks. The more compulsory questions there are, the more your users will question why you need the data. We always recommend reducing the number of required questions to a minimum. This recommendation may not sit too well with a business's marketing department—they want to collect all the user data they can. However, you may well find that removal of required questions increases the overall level of form submissions and hence the overall amount of accurate data available to the marketing people. Additionally, users are more likely to lie if they don't like the questions they are being asked.

One manifestation of question overload is enforced account creation. A business wants to gather and store user data as part of their online checkout process, so they ask all users to create an account in order to make a purchase. This strategy is highly likely to backfire, as it is asking users to enter a permanent relationship with the business far too early. This issue is discussed more fully in Chapter 24 on checkout UX.

TOO MUCH LEGALESE

This one comes under the heading "forms are a conversation with your users" again: would you start spouting jargon in the middle of an actual conversation with someone? No. You would explain what they needed to know in their own language, alongside giving them any contracts or other legal agreements to read. There is no reason why websites and apps can't do this too.

Smashing UX Tools and Techniques for Creating the Best Forms

The best way to be certain that your digital forms are understandable and usable is to run usability testing on them. You can do this on live products, wireframes, or even paper prototypes. Try to mimic actual usage scenarios, be that on a desktop, mobile, or tablet device. Look for whether the form's language mimics that of users. There's more on usability testing in Chapter 5.

If there is an existing product, look at any analytics for the form you are redesigning. Are there any pages with a high dropout? Are there any pages with high levels of errors? What are the most common mistakes in fields with high error rates? For more on analytics, see Chapter 8.

If you cannot run usability testing on an existing form, do a quick expert review (see Chapter 10). One good method is to actually treat the form as a conversation—work with a colleague and role-play the form. One of you takes the part of the system and the other the part of the user. This may sound silly, but it's a brilliant way of understanding the tone of the conversation embodied by the form:

> System: "Name?"
>
> User: "Do I need to include 'Mr' I wonder?"
>
> System: "Name?"
>
> User: "OK, Joe Bloggs"
>
> System: "Error!! No title"
>
> User: …

If your product is likely to be used outside your home country, you should make sure that the form is localized correctly. We recently encountered a Contact Us form that had been translated from English to Chinese. The name input fields were translated but not localized: users were asked for Title, First Name, and Surname, which is meaningless for Chinese users. There's more on this in Chapter 32 on designing for internationalization.

If your product is likely to be used on mobile devices (and this is increasingly a hygiene factor for web projects), take a look at Chapter 33 on designing for mobile.

RESOURCES

Forms that Work: Designing Web Forms for Usability (2008) by Caroline Jarrett and Gerry Gaffney

Web Form Design: Filling in the Blanks (2008) by Luke Wroblewski; plus lots more on Luke's website at www.lukew.com

Form design guidelines crib sheet from Joe Leech at cxpartners: www.cxpartners.co.uk/cxblog/form_design_guidelines_crib_sheet_free

Mobile form design strategies from cxpartners' Chui Chui Tan on UX Booth: www.uxbooth.com/blog/mobile-form-design-strategies/

Jessica Enders' articles on form design: formulate.com.au/articles/

An Extensive Guide To Web Form Usability by Justin Mifsud on *Smashing Magazine:* uxdesign.smashingmagazine.com/2011/11/08/extensive-guide-web-form-usability/

29

TABLES, CHARTS, AND DATA UX DECONSTRUCTED

DISPLAYING DATA ONLINE can be tricky. It's a fine balancing act to provide enough detail without causing information overload.

KEY USER TASKS AND QUESTIONS

What do your users want from tables, charts, and other data? If a user is viewing data online, they generally have a question they want to answer. The key is to understand your users' questions before designing your data layout. With data, your users will likely want to:

- Find the answer to a specific question
- Understand complex information
- Compare like items

Once you have decided on a layout for your data, be that a table, a chart, or other design, ensure it is easy to read and interpret. Use plenty of whitespace and, in the interest of simplicity, include no more data than you actually need.

TYPICAL BUSINESS GOALS

Businesses put complex data online for reasons as many and varied as there are websites. Key reasons include:

- Reduce the load on customer services by making information accessible online
- Allow users to compare products or select the right product from a range
- Influence user's decisions to make a choice that is beneficial to the business
- Promote themselves as experts in their field
- Increase time spent on their site or ad impressions

It is important to balance the need to reduce potentially expensive customer contact against the simplicity of the data. It can be tempting to throw everything online, but if that causes the information to be over-complicated it may backfire. For more on how to influence users to make the decision the business would like, see Chapter 31 on designing for behavioral change.

EXAMPLE TABLE WIREFRAME

Figure 29-1 illustrates some key issues with data tables.

1. **Clear labeling:** Clearly label rows and columns with user-centered headings. What terms does your audience use to refer to the information? Try to avoid jargon.
2. **Group related information:** Group related cells with key lines or background shading (but make sure you keep good contrast for legibility). Assist the users in reading the data, for example, by highlighting the rolled-over row or column, or by zebra-striping the row backgrounds and by giving each row and column enough whitespace.
3. **Keep the data simple:** Provide the minimum amount of data to meet your user's needs. This is to keep the layout as simple as possible. If your data is available in multiple units (for example, in centimeters and inches), show only one unit at a time and allow users to

change to the other. It may be possible to only mention the unit in the column or row title—this will reduce visual “noise” within the data. Consider providing a link to more complex data if you think a significant minority of your users will find it useful.

4. **HTML markup:** If you're working on a website, when it comes to writing your markup, this is the place where you still get to use the HTML <table> tag. It's imperative for accessibility purposes and should help mobile devices and printers display your design correctly.

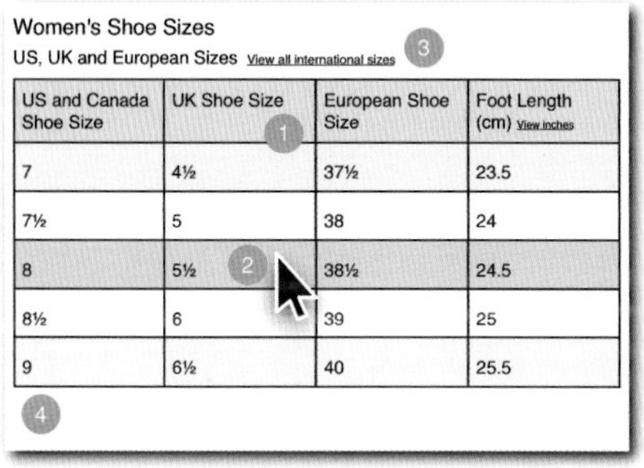
Women's Shoe Sizes
US, UK and European Sizes View all international sizes

US and Canada Shoe Size	UK Shoe Size	European Shoe Size	Foot Length (cm) View inches
7	4½	37½	23.5
7½	5	38	24
8	5½	38½	24.5
8½	6	39	25
9	6½	40	25.5

Figure 29-1: Example table wireframe

TOP TIPS FOR DESIGNING CHARTS AND TABLES

Consider the following issues when designing your data display.

THINK ABOUT THE FORMAT

Consider the best format in which to display the information—is it a table, a line graph, a bar chart, or other diagram? Try to envisage how your users think about the information when making your decision. Which format will allow the information to be understood at a glance?

BEWARE EXPERT KNOWLEDGE

The owner of the data knows it forward and backward, whereas your users are likely to be novices. The data expert is often your client. However, experts can rarely envisage what it's like to be a newbie. Watch out for this potential conflict—it can lead to highly complex data reaching baffled users who just want some simple information.

PRIORITIZE

Prioritize the information that's most useful to your users. It's better to assist the majority of your users in completing their tasks than it is to be completist about the data. Try taking away everything that isn't required for a key user task. Is what remains enough? If not, add items back in one at a time and ask the question again.

Also, consider the business reason for presenting the information to your users. If it is in order to reduce calls to the call center, try to find out about the most common queries to call center staff. If it is to help users select between products, make sure you know which product the business would prefer to be selected.

TEST IT

Try to user test your new layout. Even if it's just asking your other half to spend two minutes to complete a key task, such tests will tell you if you're on the right track.

COMMON MISTAKES WHEN DESIGING TABLES AND CHARTS

What should you avoid when designing data into tabular or chart formats?

SHOWING IT ALL

Don't make users wade through more data than is required to answer their questions. Prioritize the information. It may be that users with unusual questions are better off finding the answer via another means, such as phone or e-mail contact.

CRAMPED DESIGN

Poor use of available space can lead to low readability. If you cannot fit your information into a realistic screen size, don't cram it closer together to fit—consider splitting into two tables or diagrams.

Smashing UX Tools and Techniques for Creating the Best Data Layouts

Usability testing (see Chapter 5) and task models (see Chapter 12) will help you to understand the information your users need from your product. Stakeholder interviews (see Chapter 3) allow you to understand the business reasons behind making the data available to users.

RESOURCES

The Visual Display of Quantitative Information by Edward R. Tufte (2001)

Envisioning Information by Edward R. Tufte (1990)

Visual Explanations: Images and Quantities, Evidence, and Narrative by Edward R. Tufte (1997)

Information is Beautiful by David McCandless (2010)

Simple and Usable: Web, Mobile, and Interaction Design (2010) by Giles Colborne

A Practical Guide to Designing with Data (2010) by Brian Suda, Owen Gregory

30

GREAT CLIENT UX DECONSTRUCTED

WE ARE GREAT at thinking about the experiences that we design for our end users, but what about the experience that our clients and colleagues have when they work with us? We use the term clients but this holds true for anyone you work with from designers and developers to project sponsors and stakeholders. This is vital to successful projects but is rarely discussed so we thought it was worthy of its very own chapter.

Use this chapter to focus your thoughts on who you are working for, why they have employed your services, and how you can provide them with the best possible service. This chapter helps you to evaluate what the experience of working with you is like and how you can change the way you work to avoid common pitfalls.

Many thanks to David Jarvis, online director at Specialist Holidays Group, for his unique perspective as both a client and a UX veteran, which has helped to shape this chapter. Interviewing David made me realize how healthy it can be to simply ask your client "What can we do to make working with us the best possible experience?"

WHY DOES A CLIENT HIRE YOU?

There may be many reasons why a client is seeking to procure UX services. Consider the project you are currently working on now and why you were brought in. Which of the following describe the reasons why your services were procured?

CLIENTS KNOW WHAT THEY WANT BUT DON'T KNOW HOW TO GET THERE

It's common for a client to be very clear on what they want but they may not know the most appropriate process to follow to get them there. It's your job to suggest a process that gives them the outcome they need but also fits the constraints of the project.

THEY DON'T HAVE THE BUDGET TO HIRE A PERM

The practicalities of a budget may mean a client cannot afford full-time staff. Often they may not want to use full-time staff as they are looking to procure a specific skill set or sector expertise that you may be able to offer to them. They also may not want a new hire as they may just need some UX skills for a short-term tactical project.

THEY HAVEN'T DONE THIS BEFORE AND DON'T UNDERSTAND IT

UX as an approach and methodology may be new to your client so they may be hiring you to offer a low risk introduction to how it works and what it brings to a project. Projects will almost always present learning opportunities to everyone that is involved.

THEY HAVE HEARD YOU ARE GREAT!

You may be hired based on your reputation and this may bring kudos to the project for your client. As a supplier make sure you understand why your client was keen to employ you and what specifically they expect you to bring to the project based on your profile.

THEY WANT NEW, FRESH, AND INNOVATIVE IDEAS

We are often asked by clients to show examples of great user experiences from different sectors to their own. This is all about bringing new, fresh ideas into an internal environment that may have become bogged down by political and operational constraints. You will be expected to be a breath of fresh air, brimming with new ideas and great examples from across the web!

TOP TIPS TO PROVIDE BETTER UX SERVICES

UX designers are expected to be able to provide all manner of specific UX services and a rapidly growing pool of designers are getting better at this all the time. You can differentiate yourself as a supplier of UX by taking time to provide a better service to your clients and these tips show you how.

SPEND TIME UNDERSTANDING THE BUSINESS PROPERLY

Too little time is spent on UX projects getting to properly know the intricacies of the business. You must properly understand the business model before you start suggesting how it should be changed. Make sure you ask those "stupid" questions and unpick those acronyms. This understanding of context will make your recommendations more useful.

UNDERSTAND WHAT YOUR CLIENT IS REALLY TRYING TO ACHIEVE

There are likely to be some secondary objectives to a "UX" objective, such as improving conversion or reducing customer churn. What will a successful project mean to your client? Who will they be trying to impress? Consider how you can make your client look good and what else your project could deliver for them.

UNDERSTAND THE RELATIONSHIP

When we work for UX clients, the relationship is often peer-to-peer and we learn from one another. When our clients do a different role to us we are often the teacher and they are the pupil. By identifying the nature of the relationship early in the project you can tailor everything that you subsequently do to suit.

BE PREPARED TO OWN THE RELATIONSHIP WITH THE CLIENT

Despite working with project managers and account managers, as the UX designer you will be working very closely with the client. It is the quality of your work that will determine whether the project is a success. You might not feel that this is your role but in reality this is exactly the case. You will need to develop both account and project management skills regardless of whether you see yourself as having those responsibilities.

GET TO THE HEART OF THE BUSINESS

To understand a business properly, you need to see the business in action. Go to the stores where the deals are being done. Go to the call center and listen to customer calls. This experience will give you a true feel for the nature of the business and what is and isn't working. These are the experiences you remember and learn from, so get out there and get your feet wet!

AGREE ON WHAT YOU ARE GOING TO DO AND DO IT

At the beginning of the project, check whether there are any preferred ways of working with suppliers. If they do use them, don't reinvent them. Agree on what deliverables your client needs and when they need them. Then just deliver what you said you would when your client wants it; simple!

TAKE TIME TO SIT BACK AND REVIEW YOUR PROGRESS

As a UX designer you will be up to your eyeballs in the detail. This makes stepping back and reviewing the bigger picture, such as project progress, really difficult unless you make time to do it. This also offers up a great opportunity to have an open and frank chat with your clients to ask whether you are delivering what they need or whether you need to change tack.

WHAT CLIENTS NEED FROM UX DELIVERABLES

It is critical to understand that UX deliverables need to not only communicate their intended purpose but to also meet a set of more subtle requirements. Let's explore a few of these requirements here.

QUALITY

First and foremost you will have been commissioned to provide a specific set of services and you must deliver quality and value for your client. Your client will expect a certain level of quality, service, and finish that is commensurate to what they have paid for your services.

VISUALLY ATTRACTIVE AND ATTENTION TO DETAIL

You will be expected to produce work that is well designed in its own right, whether it is a well-formatted e-mail or a functional specification document. Attention to detail within your deliverables is vital. Why should a client pay you any attention to your recommendations if you cannot present them in a professional manner? What credibility can you have as a UX professional if your deliverables are not easy to use?

APPROPRIATENESS

Every deliverable has an intended audience. The audience will determine the nature of the deliverable, how it is delivered, and the level of detail that is included. As UXers, we are great at thinking about end users but not so good at thinking about stakeholders within our projects and what their needs might be from our deliverables.

We can also be guilty of getting carried away with the deliverables we produce. A deliverable such as a report or set of personas should meet its intended purpose and allow you to move on within a project and nothing else.

SIGNS OF PROJECT PROGRESS

Deliverables are often the only clear sign that the project is happening and that you are doing what you said you would. Consider how your client's stakeholders perceive your deliverables. What will your client want these deliverables to communicate to their peers? What will these more distant stakeholders require from your deliverables and what will they want to use them for?

DELIVERABLES MUST BE ABLE TO STAND BY THEMSELVES

Every time you produce a deliverable, consider whether it would make any sense if it were to be viewed in isolation by someone who hasn't worked on your project. Would it make sense? Does it rely on an understanding of other documents in order to make sense? Design your deliverables so that they could be picked up and understood by anyone and you will see them improve.

CLASSIC SUPPLIER MISTAKES THAT ANNOY CLIENTS

No one is perfect but clearly some are less perfect than others! Have a read through these common mistakes and make sure you don't repeat them yourself!

THINKING OF YOURSELF AS SUPERIOR TO YOUR CLIENT

Regardless of the context of a supplier/client relationship, pompous people who proclaim to know everything annoy everyone! You may have been employed to be an expert but this doesn't mean that you should treat your client as an idiot. It sounds obvious but we often hear of stories where suppliers have been sacked because clients have been left to feel stupid.

LACK OF PROFESSIONALISM

Acting professionally is not just about delivering what you were asked to deliver. You will differentiate yourself as a supplier by doing the simple things well. You may have delivered a great set of wireframes but you will drive your client mad if you don't return their calls or e-mails when they ask you questions.

NOT ANSWERING DIRECT QUESTIONS WITH DIRECT ANSWERS

Often as a UX supplier, you may feel that you are expected to know the answers to every question. It can feel tempting to try not to lose face and attempt to fluff an answer to a question you really know nothing about. Your client will respect you more if you tell them you will take that question away with you and respond when you have had time to think. This buys you time and results in your client getting a useful response and you'll probably learn something too.

NOT GETTING TO KNOW YOUR CLIENT

A simple question to a client such as "show me what websites/apps/software/companies. you love and tell me why" can uncover a lot about what makes them tick. This knowledge can be put to good use throughout the project and your client will enjoy telling you about what they love. This relationship building is critical and the knowledge it uncovers will make getting sign off a great deal easier.

LACK OF RESPONSIVENESS

Your client doesn't know (or often care) how busy you are. You may justify not getting back to a client straight away because of your bulging inbox or deadlines you may have for other clients. Make sure you acknowledge a client request and let them know when you will get back to them if you can't respond immediately.

FAILURE TO DELIVER

If you don't deliver what you said you would, when you said you would, be prepared for a hiding. If you run into trouble and think you can't deliver, speak to your client and agree what you will do instead. When things start to go wrong, a failure to communicate will quickly make a relationship go from bad to worse. Take the initiative; be honest and deal with the issue before it becomes a monster!

Tools and Techniques for Creating the Best Client UX

A solid plan that both you and your client fully understand is the basis to every great project. Check out Chapter 2 on how to plan your UX projects.

Understanding your client and their objectives is critical to gaining a good understanding of the business and its specific needs. You can learn more about how to gather business requirements in Chapter 4.

RESOURCES

It's Not How Good You Are But How Good You Want To Be by Paul Arden

31

DESIGNING FOR BEHAVIORAL CHANGE

THE KEY TO DESIGNING to influence behavior is a good understanding of actual user behavior. If you have this knowledge you are much more likely to be able to influence behavior to whatever outcome you are designing to achieve.

If you want to influence the behavior of people with the things you design first you must understand what they are trying to do. Once you understand their core tasks and why they need to complete them, you can better design something that addresses these tasks and answers their anxieties. Consider which stage they are in the customer/buying/usage lifecycle. Have you designed something that is robust enough to cater to them at every stage? Will your design

meet the needs of users who are just looking as well as those that are ready to buy?

Persuasive design is often cited when considering how one can design to influence behavior and encourage a certain outcome. By understanding your users and what they are trying to achieve, you stand a chance of designing something that lets them do what they want to do. You are not persuading them to do anything. You are simply not giving them a reason to do what they are trying to do elsewhere. When considering designing for online, it is better to focus not on selling but helping people to buy. The online environment gives people plenty of alternatives to buy elsewhere and to be vocal about their experiences, both good and bad.

USING DESIGN PATTERNS AGAINST THE USERS

The huge rise in the popularity of UX is mainly due to fact that things that work well and are easy to use make more money than things that don't. But like all things, there is a darker side! Where we used to reference well established design patterns, we can now turn to understanding so-called "dark patterns," which are focused entirely on influencing user behavior for (principally) commercial gain.

Sometimes user goals are far from aligned with business goals, such as within certain e-commerce websites where deliberate design decisions are made to maximize financial return from a customer's visit or transaction.

It is of no surprise that UX designers can find themselves somewhat conflicted. Your role is to champion the users and to meet their needs but you are being paid by your client to design something that maximizes the financial return from each user visit.

The art to great UX design is to meet the needs of your client while also meeting the needs of the users. One can appreciate how these requirements can often conflict and it is the job of the UX designer to solve these often-complex problems.

As a UX designer you will typically be given key commercial objectives by the client such as to increase the sales of accessories, to up-sell customers to more expensive products, or to reduce the amount of paying customers who leave a subscription service. Typically it is for these key commercial reasons that clients will approach you in the first place, regardless of usability or potential improvement to the user experience.

By designing the "experience," the UX designer is placed in a privileged position of determining the likely behavior of potentially millions of people who use the product they are designing. Given this power and responsibility the issue of ethics is pertinent and it is down to the individual to determine which techniques they are suitable and ethical for the job.

PERSUASION PRINCIPLES TO USE WHEN FOR DESIGNING FOR BEHAVIORAL CHANGE

There are a variety of different principles that are commonly used to influence user behavior. This section identifies the commercial reasons they may be used and also typical user responses to them that we have observed in usability testing.

SOCIAL PROOF

Social proof is the phenomenon where our behavior is influenced by the behavior of others. Figure 31-1 shows a classic example of this principle in use online where the opinions of others are linked to products and services to encourage others to purchase.

Liking in Facebook (and on the wider web) is a modern manifestation of social proof that represents a specific piece of functionality that came from Facebook. This feature can be added to any website and allows people to add a like thus endorsing that particular content object. Figure 31-2 shows an example of how this is often used, note how the total number of people who have also liked an object is shown to reinforce its popularity (or unpopularity).

Figure 31-1: Customer reviews are a classic example of social proof

Figure 31-2: When users notice the amount of Likes, they might feel more inclined to take notice of something

The following list summarizes the commercial motive behind applying the principle of social proof to your designs and how users are likely to respond to it.

- **Commercial motive:** Remove barriers to purchase.
- **Ideal behavioral response:** "Other people have bought it, so it must be good."
- **Typical user response:** In the form of reviews within domains such as hotel and travel booking, user reviews from websites such as Tripadvisor form a hugely influential part of the planning and purchase of these products.

The future of social proof is when a digital product shows people you know from your social networks who have bought a product you are interested in. This is so effective because this acts as an endorsement from someone you know, as opposed to one from a stranger. This is already beginning to happen and represents one of the most effective methods for encouraging purchases online.

RECIPROCITY

If you give someone something they feel obliged to give you something in return. This is the principle of reciprocity. Figure 31-3 shows how this principle can be applied online.

To download the **free** 150 page report that contains full league tables and case studies please enter your contact details:

Email

Phone

We will never share your contact details with any third parties.

(Download FREE report)

Figure 31-3: Users are often happy to share their personal data
in return for free material

The following list summarizes the commercial motive behind applying the principle of reciprocity to your designs and how users are likely to respond to it.

- **Commercial motive:** Offer something to the customer to initiate a reciprocal offer of something in return.
- **Ideal behavioral response:** "They are giving me a free download so I'm more than happy to give them my e-mail address."
- **Typical user response:** This varies depending on how valuable the users think the item is.

SCARCITY/ LIMITED AVAILABILITY

When supplies are scarce we feel compelled to act fast and gather what we can before they run out. Scarcity has been always been used in retail to help to sell stock and is commonly used online as Figure 31-4 shows.

Ticket King

Paul Simon World Tour

Madison Square Garden - July 23rd, 2011
Front row $250 - Only 3 tickets left!
Middle tier $175 - Buy now

Figure 31-4: Scarcity encourages people to buy before they
miss out

The following list summarizes the commercial motive behind applying the principle of scarcity to your designs and how users are likely to respond to it.

- **Commercial motive:** Encourage customer to buy before it runs out.
- **Ideal behavioral response:** "I was going to shop around but they only have a few of these left and I would kick myself if I procrastinated and missed out on this great price!"
- **Typical user response:** This is typically quite effective if it is accompanied by a price that the customer feels is competitive. Some web customers have become skeptical of scarcity

when they have visited websites subsequently to find time limited offers unchanged from their last visit. The ease of access to competitor's products can also reduce the effectiveness of scarcity-based persuasion approaches.

AUTHORITY, ENDORSEMENT, AND AFFILIATION

People will generally follow the actions of figures of authority or those who have been decorated with endorsements that represent expertise and experience. Figure 31-5 shows an example of how this principle is often used online where a supplier uses endorsement and affiliation to reassure the customer that they are a safe bet to buy from.

Figure 31-5: Customers will look for reassurance when buying online

The following list summarizes the commercial motive behind applying the principle of authority, endorsement and affiliation to your designs and how users are likely to respond to it.

- **Commercial motive:** Customers are more likely to take advice from someone who they see as a figure of authority.
- **Ideal behavioral response:** "Ah, these guys are the experts; I'll do what they suggest."
- **Typical user response:** Users like to get advice from figures of authority and look out for indicators of authority, such as memberships of affiliated groups or official marks of quality such as Kite marks and Chartered status. These help users to trust websites and products.

TRUST

People take advice from people and companies that they trust. When people purchase goods online they look for reasons to trust that supplier to alleviate any concerns they may have about sharing their personal details. Figure 31-6 shows how this anxiety is often addressed on transactional websites.

Figure 31-6: Once customers trust a supplier they are more likely to repeatedly use them

The following list summarizes the commercial motive behind applying the principle of trust to your designs and how users are likely to respond to it.

- **Commercial motive:** Customers are more likely to buy from suppliers that they trust.
- **Ideal behavioral response:** "I trust this website to provide a secure checkout and to ensure that my purchases will get to me on time."
- **Typical user response:** Users will often determine whether they trust a website from their first impressions of it, particularly when they haven't heard of the brand before. Photos can also influence trust, particularly if people who are shown do not appear genuine—stock photography often suffers from this response. Users will also look for messages around security and return policies on e-commerce websites to help them to determine whether they trust the provider.

PROBLEM MITIGATION

When users complete complex tasks online they will often have a series of questions or concerns they need to get answers to before they can proceed. In a bricks and mortar shop these will simply be asked but online we need to second guess theses key user questions and ensure they are answered within the interface. Figure 31-7 shows an example of how a simple worry that the recipient of a gift will see the receipt can be addressed within website copy.

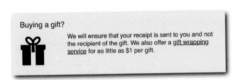

Buying a gift?

We will ensure that your receipt is sent to you and not the recipient of the gift. We also offer a gift wrapping service for as little as $1 per gift.

Figure 31-7: Answer common user questions to remove potential barriers to purchase

The following list summarizes the commercial motive behind applying the principle of problem mitigation to your designs and how users are likely to respond to it.

- **Commercial motive:** Remove all reasons why the customer shouldn't purchase from this site.
- **Ideal behavioral response:** "I was worried that the recipient of the gift would see the receipt; but it looks like they still send it to me."
- **Typical user response:** There will always be typical barriers to purchase for every product. The trick is to understand what these are and mitigate them through well-placed messaging or site features and/or functionality. In this example, if you can reassure a customer of where receipts are sent, you are removing a potential barrier to purchase.

UP-SELL/CROSS-SELL OF RELATED PRODUCTS

Up-selling is the attempt to try and get a customer to purchase a higher priced product to the one they are considering. Cross-selling attempts to sell an additional product to the one a user is considering with a goal of increasing basket sizes and thus revenue. Figure 31-8 shows how this often manifests itself online and works well, particularly when a discount is offered for buying those two products together.

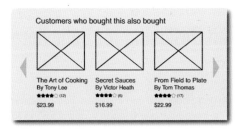

Figure 31-8: Make customers aware of products that they could buy to accompany their intended purchase

The following list summarizes the commercial motive behind applying the principle of up-selling and cross-selling to your designs and how users are likely to respond to it.

- **Commercial motive:** Increase basket size via the suggestion of similar products and higher value products.
- **Ideal behavioral response:** "It looks like I need one of those to go with this."
- **Typical user response:** The effectiveness of this approach depends wholly on the item that is recommended. Is the recommended item an optional accessory, an alternative, a vital accessory, or an unrelated item that others just happen to have bought?

PERSONALIZATION

A personalized experience is likely to influence behavior because people will be more likely to be influenced by products, services and products that are tailored to their preferences. Figure 31-9 shows how personalized recommendations are often displayed to users online.

Figure 31-9: Accurate personalization can significantly increase online purchases

The following list summarizes the commercial motive behind applying the principle of personalization to your designs and how users are likely to respond to it.

- **Commercial motive:** Based on this person's previous behavior, you can give them related items that they will be more likely to purchase.
- **Ideal behavioral response:** "Wow, this is just what I wanted; how did they know that!"
- **Typical user response:** User responses are mixed depending on the accuracy of the algorithm that drives the recommendations. Some users get frustrated by websites that try to tell them what they will like and deliberately ignore these suggestions.

Tools and Techniques to Use When Designing for Behavioral Change

A detailed understanding of users is vital to best understand how you can influence their behavior within the products you design. Check out Chapter 5 to learn how you can use usability testing to learn more about people's behavior and requirements.

Task models (Chapter 12) and customer experience maps (Chapter 13) give you a really detailed understanding of user requirements. Once you understand these requirements you can then decide which of these techniques will be the most suitable to result in the behavioral changes you are wanting to influence.

RESOURCES

Influence: The Psychology of Persuasion by Robert Cialdini

Submit Now–Designing Persuasive Web Sites by Andrew Chak

32

DESIGNING FOR INTERNATION- ALIZATION

INTERNATIONALIZATION AND LOCALIZATION are horribly long words for simple concepts—some products need to be launched in countries they were not designed in. The obvious issue here is translation into different languages, but it is more complex than that.

Just so the terminology's correct, here's how Wikipedia defines the terms:

> *Internationalization is the process of designing a software application so that it can be adapted to various languages and regions without engineering changes. Localization is the process of adapting international-ized software for a specific region or language by adding locale-specific components and translating text.* Wikipedia.org article on "Interna-tionalization and Localization" (15 September 2011)

How does this impact UX design and research? It is easy to consider internationalization as an issue that other people have to deal with—"oh, they just need to get a translator in." However, knowing whether or not a project will be internationalized is important from the outset. Aside from design considerations, it will make a difference to the technical implementation of the project (as content and menu text is likely to be stored differently in a single-language product than in a multi-language one). Timescales and the manner in which copy is generated and stored will also differ. If your job is to gather requirements for the project, internationalization is something you need to capture and communicate early.

Often the most important aspect of localization is the most difficult to predict: cultural differences between territories. If you have not considered the culture of the country you are launching in, and the ways that it differs from the country you designed for, there is a high chance that your project will fail.

What else do you need to worry about as a UXer? If you are being asked to produce designs that can be internationalized, you need to consider word length and allow space for longer copy. You also need to understand that payment methods and form inputs (such as dates and currency) may need to change. If you are being asked to produce localized designs for specific countries, you need a much deeper understanding of legal and cultural differences (such as distance selling regulations, tone of voice, or attitudes to imagery and color).

TOP TIPS FOR INTERNATIONALIZATION

Consider the following issues when designing international products.

LANGUAGE

Make sure you know which languages and which countries you need to localize your product to. The two overlap, but are not necessarily co-incident. For example, a product due to be released in Switzerland may need to be translated into French, German, Italian, and Romansh. Latin-American Portuguese has differences to the language spoken in Portugal. Even American English and British English have differences in spelling, vocabulary, and tone of voice.

All of these examples are languages of European descent. The issue becomes even more complex when you consider that some languages, including Arabic and Hebrew, are read from right to left and generally require design elements to be reflected along the vertical axis.

Do your developers know that your system must accept inputs in all the character sets required?

Different languages also require a different amount of space to display the same information. This matters greatly when you are designing navigation systems where there is no option for the text to wrap. Squeezing something into your navigation in English is not an option if you know that the menu must be translated into German. Typically, the German language requires about 50% more space than English to write the same thing. Dutch is even longer. To compound the issue, the fewer characters you are translating, the larger the likely expansion required. This may be as much as 300% more space needed to translate short menu items from English into other European languages. (Source: http://www.w3.org/International/articles/article-text-size). In some languages, such as German, individual words can be much longer than English. This affects minimum line length. Figures 32-1, 32-2, and 32-3 show a menu from the Charles Tyrwhitt men's apparel website in US English, British English, and German.

Figure 32-1: Main navigation from the Charles Tyrwhitt US website, showing the Shirts menu in US English

SOURCE: Reproduced with permission of Charles Tyrwhitt © 2011 Charles Tyrwhitt LLP

Figure 32-2: Main navigation from the Charles Tyrwhitt UK website, showing the Shirts menu in British English. Note the use of Formal Shirts instead of Dress Shirts

SOURCE: Reproduced with permission of Charles Tyrwhitt © 2011 Charles Tyrwhitt LLP

Figure 32-3: Main navigation from the Charles Tyrwhitt German website, showing the Shirts menu in German. Note that the German for Dress Shirts is the single longer word Businesshemden and that Manschettenknöpfe is nearly twice as long as Cufflinks

SOURCE: Reproduced with permission of Charles Tyrwhitt © 2011 Charles Tyrwhitt LLP

PAYMENT PROCESSES AND LEGAL ISSUES

Understand any legal and functional differences that come with releasing your product in different territories.

The key potential issue is with payment processes. For example, in Germany, some users are accustomed to paying online by invoice rather than credit card. Thus, a translation of your design into German is not enough—the entire payment process must be redesigned for the German market. In Holland, they also use bank transfers, but the process is different than that in Germany. In Brazil, users expect to be able to pay by installments. In Japan and Germany, cash on delivery is common. Make sure you understand any differences you will need to design for, so you can scope your work accurately. It doesn't matter how elegant your design is or how wonderful your product—if the payment process is wrong, no one will buy anything.

Other areas of legal difference may include general terms and conditions and returns laws. For example, the EU has distance-selling laws that require that customers have 30 days to return unwanted items. Consumers in different territories have embraced this with different levels of enthusiasm. For example, anecdotally, UK consumers are more reluctant than others to return items, but the proportion is increasing.

TIME, DATE, CURRENCY, AND MORE

The display of numbers differs from country to country. Your localized site must not only display them correctly, but must also be able to accept form inputs in the local format. Standards to look out are covered in the following sections.

Time

12- or 24-hour clock? Which time zone?

Date

Are dates typically written MM/DD/YYYY, DD/MM/YY or in another way? Is 11/12 the 12th of November (as in the US system) or the 11th of December (UK)?

Number and Currency

One thousand two hundred and thirty-four point five six can be written as 1,234.56 (in the US, UK, and elsewhere), as 1.234,56 (in Germany and elsewhere), or as 1 234,56 (in France and elsewhere).

Does your audience use US dollars, euros, pounds sterling, or something else? Can they pay in their preferred currency? Is it clear which currency the prices are displayed in?

Names and Contact Details

Standard titles and their abbreviations vary from country to country (Mister, Monsieur, Señor, Herr, and so on). Some cultures write the family name followed by the given name, others the opposite. Some would expect a three-name input or to provide a middle initial. Make sure you know all the variations your design must accommodate.

Address formats also vary. Does the postal or ZIP code go on the same line as the State, on the same line as the town, or on its own line? Is it compulsory to form a valid address? How many address lines will users expect to input? Are you planning on using an address lookup system? Are similar systems available for the countries you will localize to?

Phone numbers have different lengths and display conventions. For instance, French phone numbers are written in pairs—01 23 45 67 89—whereas UK numbers tend to be broken into three groups—01234 567 890. You may need to display or accept country codes (for example +1 for the US and +44 for the UK), which your users might not understand. For international or cross-continent dialing, information on time differences is also useful.

Units

Do your users think in metric or imperial units? Do you need to provide information in more than one unit per territory? For example, most European countries use metric units (such as centimeters) to measure length, but in the UK there is a mixture of understanding between imperial units (such as feet and inches for human height or miles for distance) and metric (such as ISO paper sizes). Even where imperial units are used consistently, there may be confusion. For example, the United States tends to discuss weight in pounds, whereas the British use stones and pounds; an American Cup is a different volume than a UK Cup.

If you are selling clothing, are you sure that all your users understand whether the size they are ordering will fit them?

GET LOCAL INPUT

Shared language does not mean that a successful localization to one territory will work in a different country with the same language. There are cultural differences that can be very difficult to predict. For example, the color orange may not have strong connotations to most Westerners, but in Ireland its association with Protestantism is still widely recognized. In user testing, we have seen South American users complain that images on a large international website were "US-biased."

Tip: Getting local help is really important when designing for internationalization— don't expect to know it all at the outset. If possible, utilize local knowledge within your client's team. They can help with translation, etiquette, imagery, and cultural insights. Share your designs with them early on, so they get a chance to comment before you've gone too far down any design path.

COMMON MISTAKES WHEN DESIGNING FOR INTERNATIONALIZATION

We've seen the following issues crop up regularly.

POOR TRANSLATION

Poor translation is often the result of two different issues:

■ First, the need to fit words into a space that is too small. This is generally the result of a navigation structure that is too narrow to accommodate one or more of the local languages. This can lead to abbreviations that users struggle to decode, or to navigational links that are not as clear as they should be.

■ Second, poor translation can occur if the translator does not understand the context of the copy. For example, if all they see is a text file and not a wireframe or website, they may not understand the need for consistency of language throughout a particular user journey.

PREDICTABILITY OF DIFFERENCES FOR LOCALIZATION

Figure 32-4 shows Giles Colborne's hierarchy of predictability in territorial differences. This is a useful guide when considering how much time and effort to devote to UX activities. How much do you know at the outset about the territories you are localizing to? Are they similar or different than the one the product was designed for? How much research will you need to do to be sure you have an appropriate design?

TASK

Booking a hotel, buying a shirt, finding a phone number—users' tasks and how they go about them are fairly consistent from country to country. If you know the task structure in the US, you'll have a good idea of how people will do it in, for example, the UK or Brazil.

INFRASTRUCTURE

Infrastructure can affect how technology is used. When broadband speeds are high, users are accepting of video and Flash. When most Internet access is mobile-based or pay-per-megabyte, this is less acceptable. If Internet access is on a shared computer in a public space, users will have a different attitude to sharing private information. Understand your users' likely access to technology before starting design work. This information can often be found online from industry sources and economic monitoring organizations.

LEGAL

Differences in legislation can profoundly affect the steps your users need to go through to complete their tasks. For example, payment methods differ from country to country and distance-selling regulations mean that users in some territories expect free returns when others do not. Other legal issues to consider include tax and privacy laws. If your client has a local office, they should be able to apprise you of these differences. Show them the non-localized designs and ask what does and doesn't work.

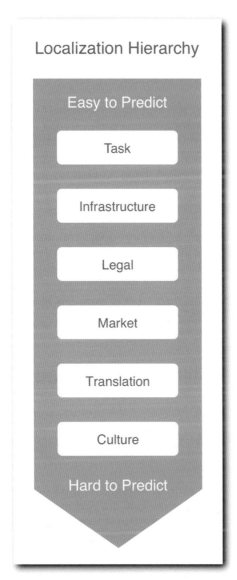

Figure 32-4: Localization hierarchy, showing the predictability of UX differences for localized products

SOURCE: Reproduced with permission of Giles Colborne
© 2012 cxpartners Ltd

MARKET

Market norms can change users' expectations of their task. For instance, in one market it may be normal for cars to come packaged with lots of features; in another, users may expect cars to be basic and to pay extra for all the bells-and-whistles. In some countries, business travelers may not be allowed to expense meals, so a hotel room with breakfast included is preferable to one without. Again, if your client has a local office, they should be able to help out here. Alternatively, user testing with a local audience will expose these issues.

TRANSLATION

Although translation of copy may seem simple, subtleties in meaning can have a profound influence. For example, on a car website, German users would expect a section called Technical Specifications to have a more engineering slant than UK users, who would expect to find out about performance and dimensions. Make sure your translator sees the copy in context— this will allow them to translate the meaning rather than simply translate the word.

CULTURE

Everything else! For example, meanings of imagery and colors, social status, acceptability of betting, public holidays, morality, good manners, tone of voice, cultural icons, and lots, lots more.

Your client's local office will be able to comment on these types of issues, but testing with real users is invaluable here.

Smashing UX Tools and Techniques for Creating the Best International UX

User testing (see Chapter 5) in the local territory is a sure-fire way of validating your designs. It's a great way of uncovering subtle cultural issues. There are usability agencies all over the world that will happily conduct user tests and report back to you.

If commissioning user tests in foreign climes is beyond your budget, another option is to conduct user tests in your country, with test participants who grew up in the territory you are localizing to. You need to be careful to recruit participants with a good cultural understanding of your destination territory—people who left the country as children will be unlikely to provide the insights you need. Students who are studying away from their home country for a few years may be a good option.

If you have the opportunity to involve your client's local teams in your project, their input will prove invaluable. Talk to them early on, perhaps during stakeholder interviews (see Chapter 3) or requirements workshops (see Chapter 4), and keep talking to them throughout the design process. If they can come to ideation workshops (see Chapter 11), all the better. Localized personas (see Chapter 14) will help keep many and varied users alive for the whole team. Share and take local feedback on any information architectures (see Chapter 15) and wireframes (see Chapter 17).

RESOURCES

Global UX: Design and Research in a Connected World (2011) by Whitney Quesenbery and Daniel Szuc

W3C article on relative text sizes in translation: http://www.w3.org/International/articles/article-text-size

Wikipedia article on Internationalization: http://en.wikipedia.org/wiki/Internationalization_and_localization

A staggeringly comprehensive list of international address formats: http://www.bitboost.com/ref/international-address-formats.html#Formats

A list of international number formats: http://www.codeproject.com/KB/locale/Number Formats.aspx

CHAPTER

33

DESIGNING
FOR MOBILE

MOBILE UX IS a hot topic. Internet access from mobile devices is growing explosively, providing a huge business opportunity. Not only does this represent new Internet users, but also new contexts of use. There's lots of talk of mobile strategies and the relative merits of apps, dedicated mobile websites, or responsive websites.

It can be argued that mobile UX matters even more than desktop UX: distracted people on a small screen don't have the option to work around your interface problems. Technologies are often in a state of flux, but we have found that if you understand the business needs, the product's end users, and the context they are in, you can make the right decisions for your product. In short, the principles behind good mobile UX are the same as for any other UX.

UNDERSTAND YOUR USERS AND THEIR CONTEXT

Who are your users? Where are they when they are using your product? What else are they doing when they are using your product? What are the primary tasks that your product should support in different contexts? If you can answer these questions, you can make design decisions to support genuine mobile usage.

There are a number of UX tools you can use to gain answers to these questions:

- Task models (see Chapter 12) help you prioritize features to support user needs.
- Adding a mobile slant to your personas (see Chapter 14) will paint vibrant pictures of the people you are designing for.
- Usability testing (see Chapter 5) an existing or competitor product on mobile devices is guaranteed to reveal insights. If you can't arrange usability testing, an expert review (see Chapter 10) on mobile devices is the next best thing.
- Use analytics (see Chapter 8) to understand mobile usage of an existing product. Look to future users by examining smartphone sales trends.

USERS MAY BE OUT AND ABOUT

There are a number of patterns emerging in mobile Internet usage. For smartphones, which are used out and about, this can be summed up as:

- To kill time. For example, when commuting, queuing, or waiting for an appointment.
- To find items of interest locally. For example, the nearest vendor of a particular product, the nearest Italian restaurant with good reviews, or the best local tourist attractions.
- When stressed or in an emergency. For example, "my flight's been canceled; I need to find a hotel in a hurry," or "my car has broken down, I want to call the nearest mechanic," or "I need the notes for my presentation now!"

There are specific activities that are particularly common to mobile use on the move:

- Mobile use with a camera. For example, shortlisting products via saving a photo and barcode scanning, or sharing products with other decision makers.
- Saving items of interest for later. For example, sending links to interesting articles to a desktop computer for easier perusal.
- Checking and updating status: social networking. Whether it be Twitter, Facebook, or another favorite social network, keeping track of others and updating your status is a key smartphone activity.

USERS MAY BE AT HOME OR WORK

Of course, not all mobile device usage is on the move. People use their smartphones and tablets in a huge number of situations, including at mealtimes, holding the baby, watching TV, in bed, or for doing personal stuff at work.

DESIGN FOR DISTRACTION

A clear commonality here is that mobile usage is often in short bursts and with distracted users. Luke Wroblewski uses a brilliant phrase to describe mobile users: "one eyeball, one thumb." Support distracted users, who want a quick fix, not a long engagement, by:

Mobile usage is often in short bursts and mobile users are frequently distracted.

- Providing quick and easy ways to complete key tasks.
- Allowing easy sharing and saving for later.
- Reducing the need for filling in forms. If forms are really necessary, use sensible defaults to minimize data entry.
- Using contextual information when you have it. For example, use geolocation information to skew search results locally.

MULTI-CHANNEL USER JOURNEYS

The abundance of Internet-enabled devices means designing for many different screen sizes and resolutions. Although far from mobile, wide-screen TVs are more and more likely to be browsing devices, thanks to Internet connected TVs and games consoles. This adds up to a potential website canvas ranging from wall-sized to palm-sized (see Figure 33-1).

Figure 33-1: Websites are viewed on a wide range of canvas sizes

SOURCE: Reproduced with permission of cxpartners © 2012 cxpartners Ltd.

Importantly, users are probably accessing your organization's products and services on many different devices, and in some cases via offline channels (such as shops and catalogues). There is a balance to be struck between designing interfaces optimized for each screen size and context of use versus providing a consistent multi-channel offering. An organization's brand encompasses its multi-channel presence. A poor experience on mobile will mar a good one on the desktop or offline.

> *Tip: Think twice before restricting functionality on a mobile website. What's the user journey? Is it wholly mobile or a multi-channel mix? If users have learned to use your desktop website, do you really want to force them to learn an entirely different interface simply because they are visiting your site on their iPhone? How many times have you found yourself frantically scrolling to the bottom of a website on your smartphone, hoping to find a link to the "standard" version?*

SUPPORT MULTI-CHANNEL USE

Are there changes in primary tasks across devices? There are certainly changes in screen size. Consider TVs, desktop computers, laptop computers, tablets, and a plethora of mobile devices. Perhaps there are core tasks that must be supported via all channels.

There are often user journeys that begin on one channel and continue on others. Consider the purchase of a pair of shoes for a special occasion:

- The user journey may begin with an unsuccessful trawl of local bricks-and-mortar stores.
- The journey continues with the user's favorite online shoe stores, where a preferred purchase is identified.
- The journey ends with a purchase made in a physical store in a nearby city, having used a smartphone to identify and locate the nearest stocklist.

Support multi-channel use by:

- Allowing registered users to quickly and easily complete the same transactions they do on desktop.
- Prioritizing content and calls to action for specific screen sizes. De-prioritizing content less important to the context of use, but thinking twice before removing it entirely.
- Advertising apps, but not forcing (or expecting) their use.
- Allowing easy sharing and saving for later.
- Providing easy access to information about the organization in the real world. For example, location of stores, stock levels, opening hours, and available facilities. Where catalogs and other printed materials exist, ensure a good correlation between the printed, digital, and in-store versions.

DIFFERENT APPROACHES TO MOBILE PRODUCTS

At the time of writing, the best practices for mobile products are in flux. The first big wave was for dedicated apps, but the market is saturated, and there are depressing figures about how many times any individual app gets used. Then it was dedicated mobile sites, and now more and more people are producing full websites with responsive layouts. As such, it makes sense to write about the theories underpinning the UX, not the underlying technologies.

As everywhere else in this book, good UX is about designing for real users in context. Technology-wise, it's starting to feel like the old days: "best viewed in Netscape Navigator" or "download Flash to view this." Just as we're finally moving away from restrictive technologies in the desktop world, we're into it on mobile. It's useful to remember that users don't have a choice as to what device to use—they own one phone. They might not want to install an app for a single interaction, especially if they're off WiFi.

Mobile does not mean less content, less functionality. If you've ever howled at a dumbed down mobile site and looked for the full site on your mobile, you know this is true. Mobile devices are often more capable than PCs (unless your PC has GPS) so people often want more.

Prioritize designs for the most important tasks, but don't assume people don't want to complete transactions or perform detailed research on mobile devices. If you're making a mobile-only website, make sure users have access to the standard version. If you're designing an app, don't assume your users aren't also using your websites on mobile.

PRIORITIZE, PRIORITIZE, PRIORITIZE

Most of the wireframes and examples in this book pertain to desktop sized design. But the design principles and methodologies are device agnostic. It's all about the research. We have found that design for smaller screens is all about the priorities. With a desktop screen you put the important things front and center and you often use large images to tell a rich, compelling story. This doesn't work so well on mobile, where you might have a much smaller viewport and slow download times. You can't show primary content supported by secondary content in (for example) a right column. You need to get your message across in just a few pixels.

Priority becomes particularly important when you consider patchy 3G coverage and expensive data plans. Consider what the user most needs to do, and design for that. Search? Prioritize the search box. See the latest headlines? Place them at the top of the page. Find a suitable location? Your clickable world map may no longer be the best interaction method.

Task models (see Chapter 12) become ever more important as you prioritize. If you know what users need in their particular context, you can design for it.

Figure 33-2 shows a mobile and desktop wireframe for our fictional shoe retail website, ShoeUX.com. The same content is present (or linked to) on each design, but that content has been reprioritized for the different screen sizes. On mobile, search has been given plenty of prominence. The hero area is still present to provide branding and visual interest, but the image size has been greatly reduced to improve download times. The store finder was in the footer on the desktop site, but is the next link on mobile. A good deal of space is given over to navigation on the mobile site, in order to drive users to products as efficiently as possible. Other sites will be better off prioritizing content over navigation items. Link areas are sized to be large and finger friendly. Editorial content is still present for those who want it, but it does not have the visual priority of the desktop. The footer area contains a link to view the (perhaps more familiar) full website.

Chapter 11 discusses prioritization techniques on ideation, and Chapter 17 covers wireframes. These methods can be easily adapted to prioritize content for mobile and tablet design.

TOP TIPS WHEN DESIGNING FOR MOBILE

Getting mobile UX right means beginning with a clear task model and a content hierarchy. Then designing layout. No different from desktop, of course, but the consequences for not doing so are far greater. Here are some of our top tips when working on your mobile design.

USE YOUR DESIGN TIME CREATIVELY

Producing wireframe templates for a desktop, mobile, and tablet website may be too many to be practical. One solution to this is to produce wireframes for one size and then produce one or two templates for the other sizes—it is likely that the developers can extrapolate the additional templates. Alternatively, work straight into responsive HTML (yourself or sitting with a developer) once you have your prioritized content lists.

DESIGN FOR TOUCH

Mobile devices generally use different interaction styles. They often inhabit the world of direct manipulation via touch, rather than older WIMP (windows, icon, menus, pointer) interactions used by desktop computers. Although tablet computers have a tendency to be used in a much more desktop like manner, their screen is still significantly smaller than desktop machines and their users will have different interaction styles such as swiping and pinching.

Allow for touch gestures. Provide large hit areas for fat fingers. Don't rely on hover states.

Content you can touch is enticing, but make sure you allow for the fact that human fingers are larger and more imprecise than a mouse pointer. Buttons and other hit targets should be large and not too close together. For any mobile devices, hover states like drop-down menus can be problematic.

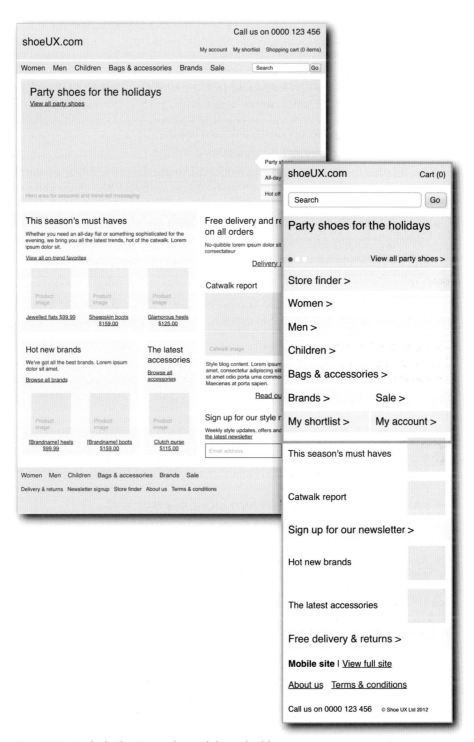

Figure 33-2: Designs for the ShoeUX.com website on desktop and mobile

EFFICIENCY IS CRUCIAL

When designing for distracted users on small screens, with expensive and unreliable data connections, efficiency becomes crucial. Real estate, bandwidth, and the user's attention may be in short supply, so getting straight to the point is essential. Strategies for improving efficiency include these pointers:

- Where appropriate, remove distractions and images.
- If navigation is curtailed, consider promoting search.
- Use information from the device to reduce data input. Location details are the obvious application here, but camera input is useful too, as are hooks into phone and e-mail functionality.
- For transactional mobile products, stored payment methods become hugely important. Would you happily get your wallet out on the bus on the way home? Probably not. Would you happily click on a Buy Now with 1-Click button on Amazon or enter your PayPal password? Much more likely.

Not only do mobile products need to be more efficient, but they also need to feel simple. Simplicity is subjective and difficult to measure, but testing with users will give you a picture of how your product feels to use.

OPTIMIZE YOUR FORMS

Spend time on optimizing your mobile forms.

- Align form labels vertically, so they don't get lost on narrow screens.
- Data entry is trickier on mobile, especially with software keyboards, so remove unnecessary fields. Use device information to reduce data input, especially for location and addresses.
- Sensible default answers can save users a lot of data entry work.
- Don't forget that the user's view of a page may be further curtailed by the device's on-screen keyboard.
- Appropriate interaction widgets can differ across platforms. For example, long drop-down menus and lists often don't translate well onto small mobile screens.
- Make sure all form validation is friendly and actionable.

TEST YOUR DESIGNS

As with all UX, test your designs with real users and you'll be sure they're right (or understand how to fix them!) Chapter 5 covers usability testing in detail. Figure 33-3 shows usability testing mobile UX.

Figure 33-3: Usability testing mobile UX

With mobile, the question arises as to which devices to test on. Differences in browser chrome and physical buttons will impact how easy or difficult it is to press your buttons and links, as well as expectations of standard interactions.

- You may decide that you need the level of control obtained only by using your own device. For example, you may be testing prototypes that you need to install on the phone. Or you may need to connect the device to a computer for screen recording.
- Alternatively, you may ask test participants to view a live website on their own phone, potentially giving you a much wider range of test devices. If you are going to test users on their own devices, there is an option to ask participants to play with the products you want to test in advance. This could be your website or perhaps competitor apps.
- You may choose to include the device type as one of your participant recruitment criteria. For example, the organization may know that 90% of its mobile traffic comes from iPhone users, but that they want to target the growing Android audience. In this circumstance, you need to recruit a mix of iPhone and Android users to test.

The key with mobile testing is to consider context. If the main use of your mobile product is likely to be in particularly stressed or distracted circumstances, a cozy, quiet test lab may not be the best place to test. Consider guerilla testing in more plausible contexts.

COMMON MISTAKES WHEN DESIGNING FOR MOBILE

We've seen the following issues crop up in mobile UX.

FORCED APP DOWNLOAD

The organization assumes that all iPhone users will download their app. But not all mobile users are using iOS. Those who are may not be on WiFi or not want to download an app for a single transaction. Even if they do download the app, it will often languish on a forgotten screen and never get used again.

RESTRICTIVE MOBILE WEBSITES

How many times have you browsed to a website on your smartphone only to find yourself frantically scrolling to the bottom of the page to look for the Full Site link? Curtailed content and transactions unavailable on mobile-specific sites can prevent users from completing their tasks. It is wrong to assume that, just because users have a small screen, they have small expectations and requirements. Our boss, Richard Caddick, did all the research for the holiday of a lifetime to Nepal on his iPhone.

FORMS OPTIMIZED FOR DESKTOP

Forms that are not mobile optimized can be extremely problematic. On small screens, left-aligned form labels become lost. Long copy becomes difficult to understand. Supporting information provides clutter. Long drop-downs become unusable. Long forms and poor validation are exacerbated by slow download speeds.

TOUCH-UNFRIENDLY WIDGETS

Common desktop design approaches don't always work well on mobile devices with touch interfaces. For example, website navigation via drop-down menus doesn't work when there's no such thing as a hover state. Additionally, touch users will want to use gestures such as swiping and pinching, and desktop websites don't allow for this.

Smashing UX Tools and Techniques for Creating the Best Mobile Products

Competitor benchmarking (see Chapter 6) will paint a great picture of the world your product inhabits. It will establish best practices and features to avoid. Task models (see Chapter 12) help you prioritize features to support user needs. Adding mobile contexts to your personas (see Chapter 14) will paint vibrant pictures of the people you are designing for. Sketching (see Chapter 16) and wireframing (see Chapter 17) will get your ideas into a testable format quickly and easily. Prioritization is particularly important for mobile UX. Usability testing (see Chapter 5) on mobile devices is guaranteed to reveal insights. Usability testing your designs as you work will tell you if you're on the right track.

RESOURCES

Mobile First (2011) by Luke Wroblewski

Responsive Web Design (2011) by Ethan Marcotte

Mobile form design strategies from Chui Chui Tan at cxpartners: www.cxpartners.co.uk/cxblog/mobile_form_design_strategies

Mobile UI patterns: mobile-patterns.com/

Luke Wroblewski's blog: www.lukew.com/ff/

Apple's iOS human interface guidelines: developer.apple.com

User experience design guidelines for Windows phones: msdn.microsoft.com/en-us/library/hh202915%28v=VS.92%29.aspx

Android user interface guidelines: developer.android.com/guide/practices/ui_guidelines/index.html

Smashing Magazine Free Wireframing Kits, UI design kits, PDFs, and resources: www.smashingmagazine.com/2010/08/27/free-wireframing-kits-ui-design-kits-pdfs-and-resources

It's about people, not devices... Slide deck from workshop presented by Bryan Rieger and Stephanie Rieger at UX London 2011: http://www.slideshare.net/yiibu/its-about-people-not-devices

Responsive design and ROI from Chris Berridge on the cxpartners blog: http://www.cxpartners.co.uk/cxblog/responsive-design-roi-observations-from-the-coalface/

INDEX